TOP FEDERAL TAX ISSUES FOR 2011
CPE COURSE

CCH Editorial Staff Publication

Contributors

Technical Reviewer...................................... George G. Jones, J.D., LL.M
Contributing Editors...................................... Torie D. Cole, J.D., MAcc
Hilary Goehausen, J.D.
Brant Goldwyn, J.D.
Deborah M. Petro, J.D., LL.M
James Solheim, J.D., LL.M
George L. Yaksick, Jr., J.D.
Production Coordinator.. Gabriel E. Santana
Design/Layout..Laila Gaidulis
Production ....Lynn J. Brown

This publication is designed to provide accurate and authoritative information in regard to the subject matter covered. It is sold with the understanding that the publisher is not engaged in rendering legal, accounting, or other professional service. If legal advice or other expert assistance is required, the services of a competent professional person should be sought.

ISBN 978-0-8080-2423-1

© 2010, CCH INCORPORATED
4025 W. Peterson Ave.
Chicago, IL 60646-6085
1 800 248 3248
www.CCHGroup.com

No claim is made to original government works; however, within this Product or Publication, the following are subject to CCH's copyright: (1) the gathering, compilation, and arrangement of such government materials; (2) the magnetic translation and digital conversion of data, if applicable; (3) the historical, statutory and other notes and references; and (4) the commentary and other materials.

Introduction

Each year, a handful of tax issues typically require special attention by tax practitioners. The reasons vary, from a particularly complicated new provision in the Internal Revenue Code, to a planning technique opened up by a new regulation or ruling, or the availability of a significant tax benefit with a short window of opportunity. Sometimes a developing business need creates a new set of tax problems, or pressure exerted by Congress or the Administration puts more heat on some taxpayers while giving others more slack. All these share in creating a unique mix that in turn creates special opportunities and pitfalls in the coming year. The past year has seen more than its share of these developments.

CCH's *Top Federal Tax Issues for 2011 CPE Course* identifies the events of the past year that have developed into "hot" issues. These tax issues have been selected as particularly relevant to tax practice in 2011. They have been selected not only because of their impact on return preparation during the 2010 tax season but also because of the important role they play in developing effective tax strategies for 2011. Some issues are outgrowths of several years of developments; others have burst onto the tax scene unexpectedly. Among the latter are issues directly related to the recent economic downturn. Some have been emphasized in IRS publications and notices; others are too new or too controversial to be noted by the IRS either in depth or at all.

This course is designed to help reassure the tax practitioner that he or she is not missing out on advising clients about a hot, new tax opportunity or is not susceptible to being blindsided by a brewing controversy. In short, it is designed to give the tax practitioner a closer look into the opportunities and pitfalls presented by the changes. Among the topics examined in the *Top Federal Tax Issues for 2011 CPE Course* are:

- Health Care Incentives and Responsibilities for Small Businesses
- Worker Classification: Employment Taxes Issues
- Trends in Business Structures/Entity Formation
- Wealth Building Under Changing Tax Laws
- Individuals: Handling Losses and Debts
- Business Disclosure Rules in Transition
- New Challenges for Nonprofits
- Retirement Plan Compliance Rules

Throughout the course you will find Study Questions to help you test your knowledge, and comments that are vital to understanding a particular strategy or idea. Answers to the Study Questions with feedback on both correct and incorrect responses are provided in a special section beginning on page 9.1.

To assist you in your later reference and research, a detailed topical index has been included for this course beginning on page 10.1.

This course is divided into three Modules. Take your time and review all course Modules. When you feel confident that you thoroughly understand the material, turn to the CPE Quizzer. Complete one, or all, Module Quizzers for continuing professional education credit. Further information is provided in the CPE Quizzer instructions on page 11.1.

October 2010

COURSE OBJECTIVES

This course was prepared to provide the participant with an overview of specific tax issues that impact 2010 tax return preparation and tax planning in 2011. These are the issues that "everyone is talking about;" each impacts a significant number of taxpayers in significant ways.

Upon course completion, you will be able to:

- Identify what small businesses should do to respond to the tax benefits and requirements enacted in sweeping 2010 health reform legislation;
- Apply developing rules on worker classification to determine business's entitlement to new hiring tax incentives, or exposure to costly employment tax audits;
- Advise a business whether to operate as a traditional corporation or partnership or whether to follow certain recent trends toward operating as limited liability companies (LLC), limited liability partnerships (LLC) or a combination of hybrid forms of doing business;
- Determine best practices for facing an upcoming shift in individual income tax rates, including a new 3.8 percent Medicare tax;
- Implement strategies for turning losses and debt relief during the current economic downturn into valuable tax deductions and exclusions;
- Help a business comply with the flood of new tax disclosure and information reporting requirements imposed by several new laws and regulations;
- Advise a non-profit organization, based on its size and function, how to comply with a new set of reporting rules being vigorously enforced by the IRS; and
- Determine what strategies and relief are available to a retirement plan that remains underfunded because of market declines.

CCH'S PLEDGE TO QUALITY

Thank you for choosing this CCH Continuing Education product. We will continue to produce high quality products that challenge your intellect and give you the best option for your Continuing Education requirements. Should you have a concern about this or any other CCH CPE product, please call our Customer Service Department at 1-800-248-3248.

NEW ONLINE GRADING gives you immediate 24/7 grading with instant results and no Express Grading Fee.

The **CCH Testing Center** website gives you and others in your firm easy, free access to CCH print courses and allows you to complete your CPE exams online for immediate results. Plus, the **My Courses** feature provides convenient storage for your CPE course certificates and completed exams.

Go to **www.cchtestingcenter.com** to complete your exam online.

One **complimentary copy** of this course is provided with certain CCH Federal Taxation publications. Additional copies of this course may be ordered for $37.00 each by calling 1-800-248-3248 (ask for product 0-0971-200).

TOP FEDERAL TAX ISSUES FOR 2011 CPE COURSE

Contents

MODULE 1: SMALL BUSINESS:
NEW OPPORTUNITIES AND STRATEGIES

1 Health Care Incentives and Responsibilities for Small Businesses

Learning Objectives 1.1
Introduction 1.1
Various Meanings For *Employee* In The Health Care
  Reform Package 1.2
Code Sec. 45R Small Employer Health Insurance Tax Credit 1.2
New Employer Responsibilities........................... 1.15
State Insurance Exchanges. 1.21
Simple Cafeteria Plans 1.22
New Form W-2 Disclosure Requirements................... 1.24
Employer-Provided Coverage and Adult Children. 1.25
Small Employers and COBRA Premium Assistance 1.27
Conclusion 1.29

2 Worker Classification: Employment Taxes Issues

Learning Objectives 2.1
Introduction 2.1
NRP Employment Tax Project 2.2
New Tax Law Incentives for Hiring Employees............... 2.4
Employees... 2.5
Independent Contractors 2.9
Determining Worker Status: Control 2.10
Section 530 Safe Harbor................................ 2.15
Proposed Reforms of Worker Classification Rules............. 2.19
Conclusion 2.22

3 Trends in Business Structures/Entity Formation

Learning Objectives 3.1
Introduction 3.1
Overview of Entity Types 3.1
Key Factors in Comparing Types of Business Entities 3.9
Choosing a Business Entity.............................. 3.10
Liability Issues 3.11
Organizational Issues 3.13
Formation Tax Issues.................................. 3.15

Operating Tax Issues 3.27
Disposing of a Business 3.38
Conclusion 3.43

MODULE 2: INDIVIDUALS: WEALTH BUILDING AND LOSS PROTECTION

4 Wealth Building Under Changing Tax Laws

Learning Objectives 4.1
Introduction 4.1
Individual Marginal Income Tax Rates 4.2
Impact on Personal Tax Planning 4.4
Alternative Minimum Tax 4.8
Coming Changes for Capital Dividends and Capital Gains 4.15
Medicare Tax Changes 4.19
Roth IRAs 4.24
Designated Roth Accounts 4.27
Health Savings Accounts 4.28
Federal Estate Tax 4.32
Conclusion 4.35

5 Individuals: Handling Losses and Debts

Learning Objectives 5.1
Introduction 5.1
Tax Losses 5.2
Limitations on Deducting Business Losses 5.13
Forgiveness of Debt 5.22
Conclusion 5.25

MODULE 3: COMPLIANCE AND DISCLOSURE

6 Business Disclosure Rules in Transition

Learning Objectives 6.1
Introduction 6.1
Tiered Issue Process 6.1
Economic Substance 6.9
Uncertain Tax Positions 6.12
Foreign Asset/Account Reporting 6.17
Stopgap Reporting 6.23
Conclusion 6.27

7 New Challenges for Nonprofits

Learning Objectives 7.1
Introduction 7.1
Significant Changes to Form 990 .... 7.2
Small Exempt Organizations............................. 7.7
Effects of New Return Requirements 7.8
Supporting Organizations............................... 7.10
Hospitals.. 7.12
Medical Resident FICA Claims........................... 7.17
Colleges and Universities 7.19
Governance... 7.23
Conclusion 7.27

8 Retirement Plan Compliance Rules

Learning Objectives 8.1
Introduction 8.2
Form 5500 Compliance 8.2
Pension Plan Funding Relief............................. 8.11
The IRS 401(K) Questionnaire........................... 8.21
Restrictions on Plan Terminations....................... 8.24
Conclusion 8.36

Answer to Study Questions 9.1
Index.. 10.1
CPE Quizzer Instructions 11.1
Quizzer Questions: Module 1 .... 11.3
Quizzer Questions: Module 2 .... 11.9
Quizzer Questions: Module 3 .... 11.13
Module 1: Answer Sheet 11.21
Module 2: Answer Sheet 11.25
Module 3: Answer Sheet 11.29
Evaluation Form 11.33

MODULE 1: SMALL BUSINESS: NEW OPPORTUNITIES
AND STRATEGIES — CHAPTER 1

Health Care Incentives and Responsibilities for Small Businesses

This chapter explores one of the most far-reaching tax developments in a generation: comprehensive health care reform and its impact on small employers. In early 2010, after months of negotiations among the White House leaders, lawmakers, and stakeholders, Congress passed a nearly $1 trillion health care reform package. Included in the health care reform package are new responsibilities and incentives for small employers.

LEARNING OBJECTIVES

Upon completion of this chapter, you will be able to:

- Understand major features of the Code Sec. 45R small employer health insurance tax credit;
- Identify employer responsibilities under the health care reform package;
- Explain premium assistance, cost-sharing, and free choice vouchers for qualified employees;
- Understand the role of state insurance exchanges in delivering health insurance coverage;
- Describe simple cafeteria plans for qualified small employers;
- Identify new reporting requirements for employer-sponsored health insurance coverage;
- Describe new requirements for employer-sponsored coverage of adult dependents; and
- List the COBRA premium assistance requirements of small employers.

INTRODUCTION

The *Patient Protection Act of 2010* (P.L. 111-148) and the *Health Care and Reconciliation Act of 2010* (P.L. 111-152) (together known in this course as the *health care reform package*) initiate many fundamental and far-reaching reforms for the delivery of health care by employer-sponsored health insurance plans. Although the health care reform package does not mandate employer-provided coverage, employers that do not offer minimum essential coverage to their employees or offer coverage that is deemed unaffordable will pay a penalty after 2013. Very small employers are exempt from the "play or pay" rules but may obtain coverage for their employees in soon to be established state insurance exchanges. Some new health care incentives and responsibilities take effect immediately, such as the Code Sec. 45R small employer health insurance tax credit. Other provisions take effect over the next 5 to 10 years. This chapter explores some of the health care reform package's major initiatives and requirements for *small employers* (generally, those with fewer than 100 employees).

VARIOUS MEANINGS FOR *EMPLOYEE* IN THE HEALTH CARE REFORM PACKAGE

The health care reform package defines *employee* differently for various provisions. In some cases, it does not define *employee*, leaving it to the IRS and other federal agencies to craft that definition in rules and regulations.

Code Sec. 45R Credit

An *employee* for purposes of the new Code Sec. 45R small employer health insurance tax credit is a *full-time equivalent employee,* which equals the total number of hours for which wages were paid to employees during the tax year divided by 2,080 but if an employee worked more than 2,080 hours of service, then only 2,080 hours are taken into account. Additionally, some employees, such as self-employed individuals, are excluded from the definition of employee for purposes of the Code Sec. 45R credit.

Employer Play or Pay Shared Responsibility Penalty

An *employee* for purposes of the new employer shared responsibility requirements applied after 2013 is an employee who works for that employer on average for at least 30 hours each week.

Simple Cafeteria Plans

The health care reform package does not define *employee* for purposes of the new simple cafeteria plan rules.

CODE SEC. 45R SMALL EMPLOYER HEALTH INSURANCE TAX CREDIT

Congress created the new Code Sec. 45R small employer health insurance tax credit for two reasons:
- To help offset the *cost* to small business that offer health insurance coverage to their employees.
- To encourage small businesses that do not offer health insurance coverage to *start* offering coverage.

The Code Sec. 45R small employer health insurance tax credit is available immediately for 2010.

> **PLANNING POINTER**
>
> According to the U.S. Department of Health and Human Services (HHS), a qualified small business can choose to start offering health insurance coverage to employees in 2010 and be eligible for the credit. HHS has also indicated that the credit is retroactive to January 1, 2010.

Maximum Credit

For tax years beginning in 2010 through 2013, the maximum Code Sec. 45R credit reaches:

- 35 percent of qualified premium costs paid by for-profit employers; and
- 25 percent of qualified premium costs paid by tax-exempt employers.

The maximum credit for tax years beginning in 2010 through 2013 is available to qualified employers having no more than 10 full-time equivalent (FTE) employees and paying average annual wages per FTE of $25,000 or less. Additionally, the employer must pay the premiums under a qualifying arrangement. The credit phases out as the number of FTEs increases to 25 and as average annual wages increase to $50,000.

> **EXAMPLE**
>
> Belt Co is a small manufacturer. Belt employs nine FTEs with average annual wages of $23,000 for each FTE in 2010. Because the company employs no more than 10 individuals and pays average annual wages per FTE of less than $25,000, Belt is eligible for the maximum 35 percent Code Sec. 45R credit (assuming it meets all of the other requirements for the credit). In 2010, the company pays $72,000 in health care premiums for its employees. Belt's credit is 35 percent × $72,000, which equals $25,200.

Phaseout

The Code Sec. 45R credit is subject to phaseout. If the number of FTEs exceeds 10 or if average annual wages exceed $25,000, the amount of the credit is reduced (but not below zero) using a formula:

1. If the number of FTEs exceeds 10, the reduction is determined by multiplying the otherwise-applicable credit amount by a fraction. The numerator (the top number) is the number of FTEs in excess of 10 and the denominator (the lower number) is 15.
2. If average annual wages exceed $25,000, the reduction is determined by multiplying the otherwise-applicable credit amount by a fraction.

The numerator is the amount by which average annual wages exceed $25,000 and the denominator is $25,000.

3. In (1) and (2) above, the result of the calculation is subtracted from the otherwise-applicable credit to determine the credit to which the employer is entitled. For an employer with both more than 10 FTEs and average annual wages exceeding $25,000, the reduction is the sum of the amount of the two reductions.

EXAMPLE

Strapping Co. has 12 FTEs and pays average annual wages per employee of $30,000 in 2010. The company pays $96,000 in health care premiums for those employees. Assuming that Strapping meets all of the requirements for the Code Sec. 45R credit, the credit is calculated as follows:

1. Initial amount of credit determined before any reduction: (35% × $96,000) = $33,600;
2. Credit reduction for FTEs in excess of 10: ($33,600 × 2/15) = $4,480;
3. Credit reduction for average annual wages in excess of $25,000: ($33,600 × $5,000/$25,000) = $6,720;
4. Total credit reduction: ($4,480 + $6,720) = $11,200.

Total 2010 tax credit: ($33,600 – $11,200) = $22,400.

COMMENT

Expressed another way, the Code Sec. 45R is reduced by 6.667 percent for each FTE in excess of 10 employees and is reduced by 4 percent for each $1,000 that average annual compensation paid to the employees exceeds $25,000.

Table 1. Code Sec. 45R Credit in For-Profit Firms 2010–2013

FTEs	Average Wage Up to $25,000	$30,000	$35,000	$40,000	$45,000	$50,000
Up to 10	35%	28%	21%	14%	7%	0%
11	33%	26%	19%	12%	5%	0%
12	30%	23%	16%	9%	2%	0%
13	28%	21%	14%	7%	0%	0%
14	26%	19%	12%	5%	0%	0%
15	23%	16%	9%	2%	0%	0%
16	21%	14%	7%	0%	0%	0%
17	19%	12%	5%	0%	0%	0%
18	16%	9%	2%	0%	0%	0%

FTEs	Average Wage					
	Up to $25,000	$30,000	$35,000	$40,000	$45,000	$50,000
19	14%	7%	0%	0%	0%	0%
20	12%	5%	0%	0%	0%	0%
21	9%	2%	0%	0%	0%	0%
22	7%	0%	0%	0%	0%	0%
23	5%	0%	0%	0%	0%	0%
24	2%	0%	0%	0%	0%	0%
25	0%	0%	0%	0%	0%	0%

Source: Congressional Research Service, 2010.

Increase in Credit in Subsequent Years

The maximum credit for for-profit employers climbs to 50 percent for tax years beginning in 2014 through 2015 (35 percent for tax-exempt employers). However, the employer must participate in a state insurance exchange to obtain the credit and other restrictions apply. The health care reform package requires states to create insurance exchanges by January 1, 2014. Specifically, each state must establish an American Health Benefit Exchange and Small Business Health Options Program (SHOP) Exchange.

STUDY QUESTION

1. The maximum Code Sec. 45R credit for tax years beginning in 2010 through 2013 available to a qualified for-profit small employer is:

   a. 25 percent
   b. 35 percent
   c. 50 percent

Full-Time Equivalent Employees

To determine eligibility for the credit, employers have to calculate their number of FTEs. The number of an employer's FTEs is determined by dividing the total hours of service (but not more than 2,080 hours for any employee) by 2,080. The result, if not a whole number, is rounded to the next lowest whole number.

EXAMPLE

For the 2010 tax year, Signoff Co. pays wages to:

> Alex: 2,080 hours
> Barry: 2,080 hours
> Connie: 2,080 hours
> David: 2,080 hours
> Ernesto: 2,080 hours
> Francine: 1,040 hours
> Gary: 1,040 hours
> Henri: 1,040 hours
> Joan: 2,300 hours

Signoff's FTEs are calculated as follows:

1. Total hours not exceeding 2,080 per employee is the sum of:
   - 10,400 hours for the 5 employees paid for 2,080 hours each ($5 \times 2,080$);
   - 3,120 hours for the 3 employees paid for 1,040 hours each ($3 \times 1,040$);
   - 2,080 hours for the 1 employee paid for 2,300 hours (lesser of 2,300 and 2,080);
2. These amounts add up to 15,600 hours;
3. The number of FTEs is $15,600 \div 2,080 = 7.5$, which rounded to the next *lowest* whole number is 7.

COMMENT

Certain owners and partners, as well as their family members and dependents, are excluded in calculating FTEs. This exclusion is discussed later in this chapter.

COMMENT

Lawmakers selected 2,080 hours because 2,080 hours comprise the number of hours in a 52-week year assuming a 40-hour work week. Paid vacation time is counted in the FTE calculation.

COMMENT

Any hours beyond 2,080, such as overtime hours, are not taken into account in calculating FTEs.

PLANNING POINTER

An employer determines its status as an eligible small employer each tax year. Consequently, if an employer adds to its payroll in one year, it may not be a qualified employer in the succeeding year.

Part-Time and Other Employees

Because the Code Sec. 45R credit is based on FTEs, an employer with 25 or more employees may qualify for the credit if some or all of its employees work part-time. Seasonal workers are disregarded in determining FTEs and average annual wages unless the seasonal worker works for the employer on more than 120 days during the tax year. However, an employer may include the amount of premiums paid on behalf of a seasonal worker in determining the Code Sec. 45R credit. Finally, leased employees are considered employees for purposes of the Code Sec. 45R credit.

STUDY QUESTION

2. Hours worked by a seasonal worker are not counted in determining the number of FTEs for the Code. Sec. 45R credit unless the seasonal employee works for the employer on more than _____ days during the tax year.

  a. 100
  b. 110
  c. 120

Average Annual Wages

Employers need to calculate average annual wages for the Code Sec. 45R credit. The amount of average annual wages is determined by first dividing the total wages paid by the employer to employees (subject to limitations discussed below) during the employer's tax year by the number of the employer's FTEs for the year. The result is then rounded down to the nearest $1,000 (if not otherwise a multiple of $1,000).

EXAMPLE

Glosk Co. employer pays $224,000 in wages and has 10 FTEs for 2010. Glosk's average annual wages would be $224,000 ÷ 10 = $22,400, which rounded down to the nearest $1,000, is $22,000.

Excluded Employees for FTEs and Average Annual Wages

Congress expressly excluded some employees from the calculation of FTEs and from the calculation of average annual wages. These excluded employees fall into three major categories.

Owners. In the first category are owners. The following owners are excluded from the calculation of FTEs:

- Sole proprietors;
- Partners in a partnership;
- Shareholders owning more than 2 percent of an S corporation; and
- Any owner of more than 5 percent of other business entities (non-S corporation entities).

Family. In the second category are certain family members of the owners and partners. For purposes of Code Sec. 45R, a family member is defined as a:

- Child (or descendant of a child);
- Sibling or step-sibling;
- Parent (or ancestor of a parent);
- Step-parent;
- Niece or nephew;
- Aunt or uncle;
- Current son-in-law, daughter- in-law, father-in-law, mother-in-law, brother-in-law, or sister-in-law.

Dependents. Additionally, any other member of the household of these owners and partners who qualifies as a dependent under Code Sec. 152(d)(2)(H) is not taken into account as an employee for purposes of Code Sec. 45R.

Hours of Service

Employers also must determine the number of hours of service performed by employees. The IRS has provided three methods that employers may use to calculate the total number of hours of service that must be taken into account for an employee for the year:

- Actual hours of service;
- Days-worked equivalency; or
- Weeks-worked equivalency.

The actual hours of service method is based on each hour of service performed by the employee for the employer, including vacations, holidays, and other paid time off. The days-worked equivalency is based on an 8-hour work day, and the weeks-worked equivalency is based on a 40-hour work week.

> **EXAMPLE**
>
> In 2010 Adam Gerston worked 2,000 hours and was paid for an additional 80 hours of vacation and holidays. Adam's employer counts hours actually worked. Under this method, Adam would be credited with 2,080 hours of service (2,000 hours worked and 80 hours for which payment was made or due).

> **EXAMPLE**
>
> Priscilla worked 48 weeks, took 3 weeks of vacation, and took 1 week of unpaid leave in 2010. Priscilla's employer uses the weeks-worked equivalency method to calculate the total number of hours of service. Using this method, Priscilla would be credited with 2,040 hours of service (51 weeks × 40 hours per week).

STUDY QUESTIONS

3. Among the individuals excluded from the calculation of FTEs for purposes of the Code Sec. 45R credit are:

   a. Cousins
   b. Sole proprietors
   c. Former in-laws

4. All of the following are methods for determining employees' hours of service for the Code Sec. 45R credit *except:*

   a. Months-worked equivalency
   b. Actual hours of service
   c. Weeks-worked equivalency

Premiums

Only premiums paid by the employer under a qualifying arrangement are counted in calculating the Code Sec. 45R credit. In calculating the credit for a tax year beginning in 2010, an employer may count all premiums paid in the 2010 tax year, including premiums that were paid in the 2010 tax year before the health care reform package was enacted on March 23, 2010. Under a qualifying arrangement, the employer pays premiums for each employee enrolled in health care coverage offered by the employer in an amount equal to a uniform percentage (not less than 50 percent) of the premium cost of the coverage. If an employer pays only a portion of the premiums for the coverage provided to employees under the arrangement (with employees paying the rest), the amount of premiums counted in calculating the credit is only the portion paid by the employer.

EXAMPLE

Dulcetone Co. pays 80 percent of the premiums for employees' coverage (with employees paying the other 20 percent). For purposes of the Code Sec. 45R credit, the 80 percent premium amount paid by Dulcetone is included in calculating the credit.

For years prior to 2014, health insurance coverage for purposes of the Code Sec. 45R credit means benefits consisting of medical care (provided directly, through insurance or reimbursement, or other arrangement) under:

- Any hospital or medical service policy;
- A plan contract; or
- A health maintenance organization offered by a health insurance issuer.

Health insurance coverage for purposes of the Code Sec. 45R credit also includes the following types of coverage:

- Dental;
- Vision;
- Long-term care;
- Nursing home care;
- Home health care;
- Community-based; and
- Any combination of the above.

Included coverage. Additionally, health insurance coverage for purposes of Code Sec. 45R includes coverage for only:

- A specified disease or illness;
- Hospital indemnity or other fixed indemnity coverage; and
- Medicare supplemental health insurance.

Excluded coverage. Certain coverage is excluded for purposes of the Code Sec. 45R credit, such as:

- Coverage only for accident, disability income insurance, or any combination thereof;
- Workers' compensation; and
- Automobile medical payment insurance.

> **COMMENT**
>
> Only nonelective contributions by the employer are taken into account in calculating the credit. Therefore, any amount contributed under a salary reduction arrangement under a cafeteria (Code Sec. 125) plan is not treated as an employer contribution for purposes of the credit.

The amount of an employer's premium payments that counts for purposes of the Code Sec. 45R credit is capped by the premium payments the employer would have made under the same arrangement if the average premium for the small group market in the state (or an area within the state) in which the employer offers coverage were substituted for the actual premium. The average premium for the small group market in a state (or an area within the state) is determined by the Department of Health and Human Services (HHS). In Rev. Rul. 2010-13, the IRS released the average premium for the small group market in each state for the 2010 tax year.

> **COMMENT**
>
> Family coverage under Rev. Rul. 2010-13 includes any coverage other than employee-only (or single) coverage.

Table 2. Average Premium for the Small Group Market in Each State for the 2010 Tax Year

State	Employee-only Coverage	Family Coverage
Alaska	$ 6,204	$ 13,723
Alabama	4,441	11,275
Arkansas	4,329	9,677
Arizona	4,495	10,239
California	4,628	10,957
Colorado	4,972	11,437
Connecticut	5,419	13,484
District of Columbia	5,355	12,823
Delaware	5,602	12,513
Florida	5,161	12,453
Georgia	4,612	10,598
Hawaii	4,228	10,508
Iowa	4,652	10,503
Idaho	4,215	9,365
Illinois	5,198	12,309
Indiana	4,775	11,222
Kansas	4,603	11,462
Kentucky	4,287	10,434
Louisiana	4,829	11,074
Massachusetts	5,700	14,138
Maryland	4,837	11,939
Maine	5,215	11,887

State	Employee-only Coverage	Family Coverage
Michigan	5,098	12,364
Minnesota	4,704	11,938
Missouri	4,663	10,681
Mississippi	4,533	10,501
Montana	4,772	10,212
North Carolina	4,920	11,583
North Dakota	4,469	10,506
Nebraska	4,715	11,169
New Hampshire	5,519	13,624
New Jersey	5,607	13,521
New Mexico	4,754	11,404
Nevada	4,553	10,297
New York	5,442	12,867
Ohio	4,667	11,293
Oklahoma	4,838	11,002
Oregon	4,681	10,890
Pennsylvania	5,039	12,471
Rhode Island	5,887	13,786
South Carolina	4,899	11,780
South Dakota	4,497	11,483
Tennessee	4,611	10,369
Texas	5,140	11,972
Utah	4,238	10,935
Virginia	4,890	11,338
Vermont	5,244	11,748
Washington	4,543	10,725
Wisconsin	5,222	12,819
West Virginia	4,986	11,611
Wyoming	5,266	12,163

Source: IRS Rev. Rul. 2010-13.

EXAMPLE

Gorstin Co. offers a health insurance plan with single and family coverage. Gorstin has nine FTEs with average annual wages of $23,000 per FTE. Alan, Brenda, Carey, and Dustin are enrolled in single coverage. Eve, Freddie, Geoff, Hilda, and Jenny are enrolled in family coverage. Annual premiums for single coverage are $4,000 and annual premiums for family coverage are $10,000. The company pays 50 percent of the premiums for all employees enrolled in single and family coverage. The average premium for the small group market in Gorstin's state is $5,000 for single coverage and $12,000 for family coverage. ABC's premium payments for each FTE ($2,000 for single coverage and $5,000 for family coverage) do not exceed 50 percent of the average premium for the small group market in its state. The amount of premiums paid by the company for purposes of calculating the Code Sec. 45R credit is 4 FTEs × $2,000 plus 5 FTEs × $5,000, for a total of $33,000.

State credits. Some states offer health insurance tax credits and premium subsidy payments to small employers. Qualified employers can claim the Code Sec. 45R credit even if they receive state tax credits for their insurance premiums. Although state tax credits and payments do not reduce an employer's otherwise-applicable Code Sec. 45R credit, the amount of the Code Sec. 45R credit cannot exceed the amount of the employer's net premium payments.

Transition Relief

Because the Code Sec. 45R credit is effective for tax years beginning in 2010 but was not enacted until March 23, some small businesses providing health insurance in 2010 may not meet all the specific requirements for a qualifying health insurance arrangement. To ensure that these businesses benefit from the credit, special transition relief for tax years beginning in 2010 is being granted. Specifically, for tax years beginning in 2010, an employer that pays an amount equal to at least 50 percent of the premium for single (employee-only) coverage for each employee enrolled in coverage offered to employees by the employer will be deemed to satisfy the uniformity requirement for a qualifying arrangement even if the employer does not pay the same percentage of the premium for each employee. The uniformity requirement generally means that an employer pays a uniform percentage (not less than 50 percent) of the health insurance coverage provided to employees.

EXAMPLE

For the 2010 tax year, Claxo Co. has nine FTEs with average annual wages of $23,000 per FTE. Six employees are enrolled in single coverage and three employees are enrolled in family coverage. The premiums are $8,000 for single coverage for the year and $14,000 for family coverage for the year (which do not exceed the average premiums for the small group market in the employer's state). The employer pays 50 percent of the premium for single coverage for each employee enrolled in single or family coverage (50 percent × $8,000 = $4,000 for each employee). Thus, the employer pays $4,000 of the premium for each of the six employees enrolled in single coverage and $4,000 of the premium for each of the three employees enrolled in family coverage. Under the transition relief for 2010, the employer is treated as satisfying the uniformity requirement for a qualifying arrangement.

EXAMPLE

For the 2010 tax year, Waxo Co. has nine FTEs with average annual wages of $23,000 per FTE. Six employees are enrolled in single coverage and three employees are enrolled in family coverage. The premiums are $8,000 for single coverage for the year and $14,000 for family coverage for the year (which do not exceed the average premiums for the small group market in the employer's state). The employer pays 50 percent of the premium for single coverage for each employee enrolled in single coverage; that is, the employer pays $4,000 of the premium for each of the six employees enrolled in single coverage. However, the employer pays none of the premium for the three employees enrolled in family coverage. In this case, the employer is not treated as satisfying the uniformity requirement for purposes of the transition relief for 2010.

Carry Back and Carry Forward

As a general business credit, an unused Code Sec. 45R credit amount can generally be carried back 1 year and carried forward 20 years.

CAUTION

The Code Sec. 45R credit is effective for tax years beginning in 2010. Consequently, the credit cannot be carried back to a year before the effective date of the credit. Additionally, any portion of the Code Sec. 45R credit not claimed by the expiration of the 20-year carryforward period may be claimed as a deduction in the first tax year after expiration of the carryforward period.

PLANNING POINTER

Qualified employers may reflect the Code Sec. 45R credit in determining estimated tax payments for the year to which the credit applies in accordance with regular estimated tax rules. However, qualified employers may not reduce federal employment taxes (withheld income tax, Social Security tax, and Medicare tax) during the year because the credit applies against income tax and not employment tax.

Health insurance deduction. Under Code Sec. 162, employers may generally deduct, as an ordinary and necessary business expense, the cost of providing health coverage for employees. The IRS has explained that in determining the employer's deduction for health insurance premiums, the amount of qualified premiums that can be deducted by the employer is reduced by the amount of the Code Sec. 45R credit.

Credit for exempt organizations. For tax-exempt organizations, instead of being a general business credit, the small business tax credit is a refundable tax credit limited to the amount of the payroll taxes of the employer during the calendar year in which the taxable year begins. For this purpose, payroll taxes of an employer encompass the:

- Amount of income tax required to be withheld from its employees' wages;
- Amount of hospital insurance tax under Code Sec. 3101(b) required to be withheld from its employees' wages; and
- Amount of the hospital insurance tax under Code Sec. 3111(b) imposed on the employer.

EXAMPLE

Advocations, an entity exempt from tax under Code Sec. 501(c), employs nine FTEs with average annual wages of $21,000 per FTE in 2010. Advocations pays $80,000 in health insurance premiums for its nine FTEs. The total amount of income tax and Medicare tax withholding plus the employer's share of Medicare tax equals $30,000 in 2010.

Assuming Advocations meets all of the requirements for the Code Sec. 45R credit, the initial amount of the credit is determined before any reduction. As a tax-exempt organization with nine FTEs and average annual wages per FTE of $21,000, the organization qualifies for the 25 percent credit (25% × $80,000 in health insurance premiums = $20,000). Advocations' withholding and Medicare taxes are $30,000. Advocations' credit is the lesser of $20,000 or $30,000. In this case, the organization's credit is $20,000.

STUDY QUESTIONS

5. State tax credits and payments reduce an employer's otherwise-applicable Code Sec. 45R credit dollar-for-dollar. *True or False?*

6. As a general business credit, an unused Code Sec. 45R credit amount can generally be carried back ____ year(s) and carried forward ____ years.
   a. 1; 20
   b. 10; 20
   c. 20; 20

NEW EMPLOYER RESPONSIBILITIES

The health care reform package does not mandate that employers offer health insurance coverage to their employees, but the package does include *play or pay rules* applicable after 2013. These provisions are intended to encourage employers to offer coverage rather than having to pay a *shared responsibility penalty*. The play or pay provisions apply to *large employers,* which the new law generally treats as employers with 50 or more full-time employees. Employers with 49 or fewer full-time employees are exempt from the shared responsibility penalty. Additionally, employers that offer free choice vouchers to qualified employees will be free from the penalty.

> **CAUTION**
>
> The definition of FTE for purposes of the new employer responsibilities after 2013 is not the same as the definition of FTE for purposes of the Code Sec. 45R small employer health insurance credit.

Minimum Essential Coverage

The health care reform package defines *minimum essential coverage* as coverage under any of the following:

- Government-sponsored insurance, including Medicare and Medicaid;
- Qualified employer-sponsored health insurance plans;
- Qualified individual market health insurance plans; and
- Grandfathered health insurance plans.

> **COMMENT**
>
> Workers' compensation, coverage only for a specified disease or illness, hospital indemnity or other fixed indemnity insurance, and automobile medical payment insurance do not qualify as minimum essential coverage.

Grandfathered Health Insurance Plans

Employer-provided health insurance coverage in effect on March 23, 2010—the date of enactment of the *Patient Protection and Affordable Care Act* (PPACA)—is generally exempt from certain provisions in the PPACA. These plans are known as *grandfathered plans*. In June 2010 the IRS issued temporary and proposed regs (TD 9589) on which health insurance plans will be treated as grandfathered under the PPACA. Plans that are not grandfathered or that lose their grandfathered status will be subject to the health care reform package's shared responsibility requirements for employers after 2013.

The regs explain when changes to the terms of a plan or health insurance coverage cause the plan to cease to be a grandfathered health plan. Generally, changes in benefits, cost-sharing, and employer-paid premiums may trigger a loss of grandfathered status.

> **COMMENT**
>
> A plan's grandfathered status may be revoked if it is bought by or merges with another plan to circumvent compliance with the health care reform package.

To retain its grandfathered status, a plan generally must not:

- Eliminate all or substantially all benefits to treat a particular condition;
- Raise coinsurance charges;
- Raise fixed-cost-sharing requirements other than a copayment by more than the rate of medical inflation plus 15 percentage points;
- Raise copayments by more than the greater of an amount equal to $5 increased by medical inflation or medical inflation plus 15 percentage points;
- Lower employer contributions by more than 5 percent; and
- Add or tighten an annual limit on what the insurer pays.

> **EXAMPLE**
>
> On March 23, 2010, Redux's employer-sponsored health plan provides benefits for a particular mental health condition, the treatment of which is counseling and prescription medications. Redux's plan eliminates benefits for counseling after March 23, 2010. The plan loses its grandfathered status because counseling is an element necessary to treat the condition. Redux's plan is deemed under the IRS regs to have eliminated substantially all benefits for treatment of the condition.

Shared Responsibility Penalty

The PPACA imposes a *shared responsibility penalty* on two groups of employers after 2013:

- Large employers that do not offer qualified health insurance coverage; and
- Large employers that offer coverage but have one or more employees receiving premium assistance tax credits or cost-sharing because the coverage is deemed unaffordable.

> **NOTE**
>
> Keep in mind that the health care reform package defines a *large employer* as an employer with 50 or more full-time employees for purposes of the shared responsibility penalty.

PLANNING POINTER

To ease the burden on employers, the health care reform package allows employers to subtract the first 30 workers from the calculation of the shared responsibility penalty.

Penalty amount. The amount of the shared responsibility penalty paid by an affected employer is calculated under a complex formula. Generally, employers with 50 or more full-time workers that do not offer coverage will pay an assessment of $2,000 per full-time worker (not including the first 30 workers) if any of their employees obtains premium assistance tax credits through a state insurance exchange. Employers that offer unaffordable coverage will pay $3,000 for any employee who receives a tax credit in the exchange up to a cap of $2,000 for every full-time employee.

Unaffordable coverage. If an employee is offered minimum essential coverage by his or her employer that is deemed unaffordable, the employee is eligible for a premium assistance tax credit and cost-sharing reductions, but only if the employee declines to enroll in the coverage and purchases coverage through a state insurance exchange instead. The health care reform package defines *unaffordable coverage* as coverage with a premium required to be paid by the employee that is more than 9.5 percent of the employee's household income.

CAUTION

Some large employers may be tempted to break into smaller companies to avoid the new shared responsibility requirements. However, the health care reform package generally treats individual employers within the same controlled group of companies as one employer.

Large employers. A *large employer* for purposes of the shared responsibility penalty is an employer that employed an average of at least 50 full-time employees on business days during the preceding calendar year. However, the definition has some exceptions. An employer will not be treated as a large employer if:

- Its workforce exceeds 50 full-time employees for 120 or fewer days during the calendar year; and
- The employees in excess of 50 employed during the 120-day period are seasonal workers.

EXAMPLE

Except Sales Co. employs 30 full-time employees. For six weeks during the holiday season (late November and through December), Except hires an additional 40 full-time employees to help with retail sales. The 40 additional full-time employees are disregarded for purposes of treating Except as a large employer.

Full-time employees. For purposes of the shared responsibility penalty, a *full-time employee* is an individual employed on average at least 30 hours of service per week. The IRS is expected to issue guidance on the definition of full-time employee with respect to employees who are not compensated on an hourly basis and guidance on part-time employees.

Free Choice Vouchers

The health care reform package requires employers that offer minimum essential coverage to their employees and that pay any portion of the plan's costs to provide free choice vouchers to qualified employees. The health care reform package defines a *qualified employee* for purposes of the free choice vouchers as an employee:

- Whose required contribution for minimum essential coverage through an eligible employer-sponsored plan exceeds 8 percent of the employee's household income for the tax year that ends with or within the plan year and does not exceed 9.8 percent of the employee's household income for the tax year;
- Whose household income for the tax year is not greater than 400 percent of the poverty line for a family of the size involved; and
- Who does not participate in a health plan available from the offering employer.

The amount of a free choice voucher is generally equal to the monthly portion of the cost of the eligible employer-sponsored plan that would have been paid by the employer if the employee was covered under the plan. Employers providing free choice vouchers to qualified employees will not be liable for a shared responsibility penalty on behalf of that employee.

Free choice vouchers are deducted by employers and excluded from the employee's gross income. If the amount of the free choice voucher is more than the cost of the monthly premium, the health care reform package directs that the excess be paid to the employee. The excess, in this case, would be included in the employee's gross income. The amount of the free choice voucher is for self-only coverage unless the individual purchases family coverage in a state insurance exchange.

> **COMMENT**
>
> After 2014, the 8 percent and the 9.8 percent amounts are indexed to the excess of premium growth over income growth for the preceding calendar year.

If an employer offers multiple plans, the amount of the free choice voucher is the dollar amount that would be paid if the employee selected the plan for which the employer would pay the largest percentage of the premium cost.

> **EXAMPLE**
>
> Andersonville Co. offers two health insurance plans to its employees that satisfy the requirements of minimum essential coverage. The monthly premiums for the two plans are $400 and $600, respectively. Andersonville provides a payment of 60 percent of premiums for any plan purchased. In this case, the amount of the free choice voucher will be 60 percent the higher-premium plan, which is 60 percent of $600, or $360.

Premium Assistance Tax Credit

The health care reform package provides qualified individuals with a premium assistance tax credit to help offset the cost of health insurance premiums. A *qualified individual* is an individual with household income between 100 percent and 400 percent of the federal poverty level.

The health care reform package defines *household income* as the sum of the:
- Taxpayer's modified adjusted gross income; plus
- Aggregate modified adjusted gross incomes of all other individuals taken into account in determining the taxpayer's family size (but only if the individuals are required to file a tax return for the tax year).

Modified adjusted gross income is defined as adjusted gross income increased by:
- The amount (if any) normally excluded by Code Sec. 911 (the exclusion from gross income for citizens or residents living abroad); plus
- Any tax-exempt interest received or accrued during the tax year.

> **EXAMPLE**
>
> Barry Wetherston is employed by Questor Co., which does not offer minimum essential coverage to its employees. Barry enrolls in a health insurance plan offered through a state insurance exchange and reports his income to the exchange. Based on the information provided to the exchange, Barry receives a premium assistance credit based on income. The U.S. Treasury Department pays the premium assistance credit amount directly to the insurance plan in which Barry is enrolled. The premium payments are made through payroll deductions.

PLANNING POINTER

Married couples must file a joint return to qualify for a premium assistance credit. Individuals who are listed as dependents on a tax return are ineligible for the premium assistance credit.

For purposes of the premium assistance tax credit, an employee is not considered eligible for minimum essential coverage under an employer-sponsored plan, including a grandfathered health plan, if the employee's required contribution would exceed 9.5 percent of the employee's household income. In addition, an employer-sponsored plan that provides less than 60 percent coverage for total allowed costs does not provide minimum essential coverage. After 2014, the employee's contribution limit of 9.5 percent is subject to adjustment to reflect the excess of premium growth over income growth for the preceding calendar year. After 2018, an additional adjustment involving the Consumer Price Index rate of growth for the preceding calendar year may be required.

Cost-sharing

The health care reform package provides for cost-sharing to help qualified individuals pay for health insurance after 2013. Generally, a qualified individual is one whose household income does not exceed 400 percent of the federal poverty guidelines.

STATE INSURANCE EXCHANGES

By January 1, 2014, each state must establish an American Health Benefit Exchange from which qualified individuals may obtain health insurance coverage. Also by January 1, 2014, each state must establish a Small Business Health Options Program (SHOP) Exchange to help qualified small employers enroll their employees in health plans in the state's small group market.

COMMENT

The health care reform package allows states to create one exchange to provide services to qualified individuals and qualified businesses.

Levels of Coverage

The state insurance exchanges will have four levels of minimum essential benefits coverage.

Table 3. Minimum Essential Benefits Coverage for State Insurance Exchanges

Plan Type	Percentage of Actuarial Value of Benefits
Bronze	60%
Silver	70%
Gold	80%
Platinum	90%

Small Employers

Starting in 2014, qualified small employers may access their state insurance exchange. A *qualified small employer* is an employer with up to 100 employees. Starting in 2017, the health care reform package allows states to open their state insurance exchanges to employers with more than 100 employees.

SIMPLE CAFETERIA PLANS

The health care reform package allows a cafeteria (Code Sec. 125) plan of certain small employers to qualify as a *Simple Cafeteria Plan* after 2010. The change in treatment permits these plans to avoid the more administratively difficult nondiscrimination requirements of a classic cafeteria plan under Code Sec. 125(b).

A *cafeteria plan* is an employer-sponsored plan that provides participants an opportunity to receive certain benefits on a pretax basis. Participants in a cafeteria plan must be permitted to choose among at least one taxable benefit (such as cash) and one qualified benefit. Qualified benefits in a cafeteria plan include:

- Accident and health benefits (but not Archer medical savings accounts or long-term care insurance);
- Adoption assistance;
- Dependent care assistance; and
- Group-term life insurance coverage.

Employer contributions to the cafeteria plan are usually made under salary reduction agreements between the employer and the employee in which the employee agrees to contribute a portion of his or her salary on a pretax basis to pay for the qualified benefits. The contributions are not considered wages for federal income tax purposes and generally are not subject to FICA and FUTA.

Highly Compensated Participants and Key Employees

A cafeteria plan must be a written plan and may not discriminate in favor of highly compensated participants. A cafeteria plan discriminates in favor of highly compensated participants if the plan provides greater benefits to those employees in comparison to nonhighly compensated employees. Additionally, a cafeteria plan may not favor key employees. A cafeteria plan favors key employees if more than 25 percent of the nontaxable qualified benefits provided under the plan are provided to key employees. If a plan discriminates in favor of highly compensated participants or key employees, the highly compensated participants or key employees will be subject to tax on the benefits they receive under the plan. Such discrimination is often determined under relatively complex rules.

COMMENT

A *highly compensated participant* is:

- An officer or spouse, or dependent of an officer, of the employer;
- A stockholder or spouse or dependent of a stockholder owning more than 5 percent (determined by voting power or value) of all classes of the stock of the employer; or
- A highly compensated employee or spouse or dependent of a highly compensated employee (Code Sec. 125(e)).

An individual is highly compensated for purposes of these nondiscrimination rules if he or she had compensation in excess of an annually adjusted amount ($110,000 in 2010).

A *key employee* is:

- An officer with compensation in excess of an inflation-adjusted amount ($160,000 for 2010);
- A 5-percent owner; or
- A 1-percent owner with compensation in excess of $150,000 (not adjusted for inflation).

Small Employers

Many small employers have a higher percentage of highly compensated participants or key employees compared to larger employers. Consequently, small employers may be discouraged from offering cafeteria plans for fear of discriminating in favor of highly compensated participants or key employees. The health care reform package allows qualified small employers to establish simple cafeteria plans that provide a safe harbor from the nondiscrimination rules.

To be eligible to establish a simple cafeteria plan, the employer must have employed an average of 100 or fewer employees on business days during either of the two preceding tax years. A year may only be taken into account if the employer was in existence throughout the year. If an employer was not in existence throughout the preceding year, the employer may nonetheless be considered as an eligible employer if it reasonably expects to average 100 or fewer employees on business days during the current year.

> **COMMENT**
>
> The heath care reform package recognizes that an eligible small employer may grow. If an employer has 100 or fewer employees for any year and establishes a simple cafeteria plan for that year, it can be treated as meeting the requirement for any subsequent year even if the employer employs more than 100 employees in the subsequent year. However, this exception does not apply if the employer employs an average of 200 or more employees during the subsequent year.

Eligibility and Participation

A simple cafeteria plan must satisfy minimum eligibility and participation requirements in addition to the employer fitting within the 100 or fewer employee limit. The eligibility and participation requirements are met if:

- All employees who had at least 1,000 hours of service for the preceding plan year are eligible to participate; and
- All employees have the same election rights under the plan.

STUDY QUESTIONS

7. For purposes of the employer's shared responsibility penalty, a full-time employee is an individual employed on average at least ___hours of service per week.

   a. 30
   b. 32
   c. 35

8. A qualified small employer for purposes of accessing a state insurance exchange starting 2014 is an employer with up to ___ employees

   a. 25
   b. 50
   c. 100

NEW FORM W-2 DISCLOSURE REQUIREMENTS

Every employer is required to furnish each employee with a statement of compensation information, including wages, paid by the employer to the employee, and the taxes withheld from such wages during the calendar year.

This statement is made on Form W-2, which must be provided to each employee by January 31 of the succeeding year.

The PPACA requires employers to identify the cost of employer-sponsored health coverage on the employee's Form W-2. Generally, employers must disclose the aggregate cost of applicable employer-sponsored coverage provided to employees annually on the employee's Form W-2. The health coverage reporting requirement under the PPACA is effective for tax years beginning after December 31, 2010 (and therefore is first applicable to Form W-2s due by January 31, 2012).

Aggregate cost. Employers must report the aggregate or total cost of employer-sponsored health insurance coverage provided to the employee. Employers need not provide a specific breakdown of the various types of medical coverage.

EXAMPLE

For the 2011 tax year, Devon Washington is enrolled in his employer-sponsored health insurance program. Devon's coverage includes a medical plan, a dental plan and a vision plan. Devon's employer must report the total cost of all of these health related insurance policies.

COMMENT

On its website, the IRS has reminded employees that health coverage reporting is only for informational purposes.

EMPLOYER-PROVIDED COVERAGE AND ADULT CHILDREN

The health care reform package makes two important changes to insurance coverage for young adults:

- Employer health insurance plans that provide coverage to children of participants are required to make the coverage available to adult children until age 26; and
- The law extends certain favorable tax treatment to coverage for young adults.

Increased Age of Coverage

Traditionally, many plans and insurers would remove adult children from their parents' policies because of age, status as a student, or residence. The health care reform package allows young adults to remain on their parents' health insurance plans until age 26. This requirement applies to all plans in the individual market, all new employer plans, and existing employer plans if the young adult is not eligible for employer coverage on his or her own. This requirement applies even if the young adult:

- No longer lives with his or her parents;
- Is not a dependent on a parent's federal tax return;
- Is no longer a student; or
- Is married.

Exception. The health care reform package includes one exception to the expansion of coverage until age 26. If a young adult is eligible to obtain health insurance from his or her own employer, the parent's plan is not obligated to extend coverage to age 26. This exception is temporary and expires after 2013.

> **COMMENT**
>
> The health care reform package does not require an employer health insurance plan to cover adult children under these rules but if it does, the employer plan must offer coverage to adult children until age 26.

> **EXAMPLE**
>
> Lucy Collins is 22 years old. She is a full-time university student and expects to graduate in 2011. Lucy is covered by her mother's employer-provided health insurance plan. The plan traditionally terminated coverage for adult children after their 23rd birthday or when they graduated from postsecondary school, whichever came first. The health care reform package requires her mother's employer plan to make coverage available until Lucy reaches age 26.

Effective date. The expansion to age 26 is effective for plan years beginning on or after September 23, 2010. Many insurance companies agreed to implement the new requirement before the effective date.

Income Tax Exclusion

Before passage of the health care reform package, employer-provided health insurance coverage was generally excluded from income only if the employee's child was younger than age 19 or age 24 if a student. The health care reform package makes an important change. The health care reform package extends the income tax exclusion to any employee's child who has not attained age 27 as of the end of the tax year. For most individuals, this is the calendar year. This change is effective March 30, 2010.

> **COMMENT**
>
> An employer plan is not required to offer this benefit past age 26 but may do so if the plan is amended.

Under the health care reform package, it is also no longer necessary for the child of the employee to be a tax dependent of the employee for the income tax exclusion to apply. A *child* for purposes of the extended exclusion is an individual who is the son, daughter, stepson, or stepdaughter of the employee. The definition of child also includes adopted children and eligible foster children.

> **EXAMPLE**
>
> Adam Graystone works for Excelsior Co., which provides health care coverage for its employees and their spouses and for any employee's child who has not attained age 27 as of the end of the tax year. For the 2010 tax year, Excelsior provides health care coverage to Adam and his son Matthew, who will not attain age 27 until after the end of the 2010 tax year. The health care coverage for Matthew under the company's plan for the entire 2010 tax year is excluded from Adam's gross income.

> **COMMENT**
>
> Effective September 23, 2010, health insurance companies that cover children cannot deny coverage based on a preexisting condition. This requirement applies to:
>
> ■ All new employer-sponsored health insurance plans;
> ■ New plans in the individual market; and
> ■ Existing employer-sponsored health insurance plans.

SMALL EMPLOYERS AND COBRA PREMIUM ASSISTANCE

Congress passed the *Consolidated Omnibus Budget Reconciliation Act* (CO-BRA) health benefit provisions in 1986. COBRA gives qualified individuals the right to temporary continuation of health coverage at group rates. However, coverage is only available when coverage is lost due to certain events. Employers with 20 or more employees are generally required to offer COBRA coverage and to notify their employees of the availability of such coverage. Additionally, many states have mini-COBRA laws that extend COBRA to employees of firms with fewer than 20 employees.

The health care reform package did not make any changes to COBRA. However, separate legislation, the *American Reinvestment and Recovery Act of 2009* (2009 Recovery Act) and subsequent bills, created a special subsidy to help individuals pay for COBRA coverage. Qualified employers are eligible for a payroll tax credit.

> **COMMENT**
>
> Due to the statutory sunset, the COBRA premium reduction under the 2009 Recovery Act and subsequent legislation is not available for individuals who experience involuntary terminations after May 31, 2010. However, individuals who qualified on or before May 31, 2010, may continue to pay reduced premiums for up to 15 months, as long as they are not eligible for another group health plan or Medicare.

Assistance-Eligible Individuals

Assistance-eligible individuals pay 35 percent of their COBRA premiums and the remaining 65 percent is reimbursed to the employer or other coverage provider through a tax credit. An *assistance-eligible individual* is the employee or a member of his or her family who elects COBRA coverage timely following a qualifying event related to an involuntary termination of employment that occurs at any point on or after September 1, 2008, and on or before May 31, 2010.

Additionally, a reduction in hours followed by an involuntary termination may qualify an individual for COBRA premium assistance. The reduction in hours must have occurred during the period that begins with September 1, 2008, and ends with May 31, 2010, followed by an involuntary termination of employment on or after March 2, 2010, and by May 31, 2010.

Involuntary Termination

An *involuntary termination* for purposes of COBRA premium assistance is generally an involuntary separation from employment. An involuntary termination includes a lay-off, being told to "resign or be fired," and other actions that separate an employee from employment nonvoluntarily.

Payroll Tax Credit

Employers making a 65 payment on behalf of an assistance-eligible individual are entitled to a payroll tax credit. The credit is claimed on Form 941, *Employer's Quarterly Employment Tax Return.*

Table 4. Timeline of Selected Health Reform Changes

Feature	Tax Year of Implementation
Code Sec. 45r small employer health insurance tax credit	2010
Extension of coverage for young adults	2010
Income tax exclusion for young adults	2010
W-2 disclosure requirements	2011
Shared responsibility penalty for individuals	2014
Shared responsibility penalty for businesses	2014
Premium assistance tax credits for individuals	2014
Cost-sharing	2014
Free choice vouchers	2014

STUDY QUESTIONS

9. Although the health care reform package does not require an employer's health insurance plan to cover adult children, if the plan offers coverage to dependents, the plan must offer coverage to adult children until age 26. *True or False?*

10. Under COBRA premium assistance:

    a. Employers will receive a onetime tax credit on their federal income tax return for the 2010 tax year

    b. Assistance-eligible individuals pay 35 percent of COBRA premiums, whereas coverage providers pay 65 percent

    c. Former employees may claim a credit on their 2010 income tax returns even if they separated from employment voluntarily

CONCLUSION

The health care reform package was a massive undertaking by Congress and will require significant resources from all employers to set the provisions in motion. Although some of the package's features, such as the Code Sec. 45R small employer health insurance credit and the expanded coverage for young adults, are effective immediately, many others will not become effective until after 2013. The delay is intended to give employers, states, and the federal government time to implement the new provisions and set in place a new infrastructure to administer the provisions. Small employers, in particular, need to pay attention to the new provisions, carveouts, and new rules and regulations as health care reform gets underway.

MODULE 1: SMALL BUSINESS: NEW OPPORTUNITIES
AND STRATEGIES — CHAPTER 2

Worker Classification: Employment Taxes Issues

This chapter discusses the growing importance of properly classifying workers as employees or independent contractors, and the IRS's increasing efforts to tackle the misclassification of workers as independent contractors. The distinction has significant federal tax consequences for all parties involved.

LEARNING OBJECTIVES

Upon completion of this chapter, you will be able to:

- Identify traditional, common-law factors used to differentiate employees from independent contractors;

- Discuss current IRS activities and initiatives aimed at addressing employment tax compliance and worker classification issues;

- Understand the employment tax obligations of employers regarding employees and independent contractors;

- Describe the tax consequences to employers of misclassifying employees as independent contractors; and

- Discuss key features of pending legislation addressing worker misclassification.

INTRODUCTION

The misclassification of employees as independent contractors is seen as an increasing problem by the IRS and Congress. Although the issue of worker misclassification is not new and has been a growing problem for many years, the current economic downturn has heightened the significance of the issue. Employers may classify workers as independent contractors to avoid federal employment tax obligations, which include withholding federal income tax on an employee's wages, paying unemployment taxes (FUTA taxes), and paying the employer's share of Social Security and Medicare taxes under the *Federal Insurance Contribution Act* (FICA). Misclassifying an employee as an independent contractor also enables the employer to exclude the worker from health and retirement benefits. The IRS and other federal agencies have estimated that the nonpayment and underpayment of employment taxes have contributed approximately $54 billion to the tax gap (the difference between taxpayers' actual tax liability and taxes reported and paid).

According to the Government Accountability Office (GAO), approximately 10 million workers are classified as independent contractors, whereas as many as 20 percent of employers misclassify workers as independent contractors. Although many employers may be misclassifying workers as independent contractors to escape their employment tax responsibilities, many others mistakenly misclassify workers as independent contractors due to a misunderstanding of conflicting rules. Regardless of the reason for erroneous classification, the IRS has become increasingly active in enforcing the collection of employment taxes.

NRP EMPLOYMENT TAX PROJECT

History of the NRP

As part of its effort to close an estimated $455 billion tax gap, the IRS launched a National Research Program (NRP) study of employment tax compliance in 2010. The IRS's employment tax NRP involves the random selection and examination of Forms 941, *Employer's Quarterly Federal Tax Return*, filed during the 2008, 2009, and 2010 tax years. The IRS will randomly select 2,000 from each tax year, for a total of 6,000 returns. The NRP's first wave of random audits began in February 2010 with the examinations of 2008 Forms 941. The second iteration began in November 2010 with examinations of Forms 941 filed for the 2009 tax year. The third, and final, wave of NRP audits examine Forms 941 filed for the 2010 tax year.

The NRP will examine returns filed by taxpayers under the jurisdiction of the IRS Large and Mid-Size Business (LMSB), Small Business/Self Employed (SBSE), and Tax-Exempt and Government Entities (TEGE) divisions. The Exempt Organization (EO) unit's participation is anticipated to result in the examination of 500 charities and other tax-exempt organizations.

The NRP will focus on employment tax issues, with a specific emphasis on worker classification, officer compensation, fringe benefits, and employee expense reimbursement. The NRP will also examine issues related to nonfilers. The IRS and Treasury Department have identified the nonpayment and underpayment of employment taxes as a significant contributor to the tax gap, accounting for approximately $54 billion in lost revenue. By misclassifying employees as independent contractors for federal payroll tax purposes, employers attempt to escape income tax withholding and paying Social Security and Medicare taxes (FICA) and unemployment taxes (FUTA), as well as workers' compensation.

Revenues lost may be broken down as shown here.

Table 1. Tax Gap Components Related to Employment Taxes

Type of Tax Underreported	Estimated Amount Underreported
FICA taxes	$14 billion
Self-employment tax	$39 billion
FUTA taxes	$ 1 billion

COMMENT

The last comprehensive employment tax study conducted by the IRS occurred 25 years ago. However, employment tax reporting and compliance and worker misclassification issues have remained a significant priority of the IRS. In 2007, for example, the IRS announced the Questionable Employment Tax Practices (QETP) initiative, which was intended to deter employers from avoiding employment tax liabilities through illegal employment tax practices, such as by misclassifying employees. A number of agencies have also published reports on the effect of worker misclassification on IRS revenue and the tax gap, including the:

- Treasury Inspector General for Tax Administration (TIGTA);
- Government Accountability Office (GAO); and
- Congressional Research Service (CRS).

Purpose

The IRS intends to use information gained from the NRP examinations to improve its process for selecting employment tax returns for examination. In "fine-tuning" the audit selection formula, the IRS hopes to also decrease the future number of "no change" audits. According to the IRS, the NRP has two goals:

- To secure statistically valid information for computing the employment tax gap; and
- To determine compliance characteristics so the IRS can focus on employment tax areas with the most compliance problems.

A focus of the employment tax NRP is to study the impact of worker classification on the employment tax gap. If a worker is reported as an employee, the employer is obligated to collect and remit all employment taxes (income tax withholding, FICA taxes, and FUTA taxes). The employer is also responsible for workers' compensation and unemployment insurance. On the other hand, if a worker is classified as an independent contractor, the employer does not have to collect and remit employment taxes; it is the worker's responsibility to remit self-employment tax to the IRS. Thus, there is an incentive for employers to classify employees as independent contractors in order to escape these reporting and payment obligations.

The IRS's employment tax NRP will not only examine worker classification issues but also will look closely at the interrelated issues of:

- The application of Section 530 relief under Section 530 of the *Revenue Act of 1978*;
- Fringe benefits, including whether they are provided to workers nonetheless classified as independent contractors by the employer;
- Executive compensation;
- Backup withholding; and
- Form 1099-MISC, *Miscellaneous Income*, filing, including whether Forms 1099-MISC contain correct taxpayer identification numbers (TINs) for payees.

Any employment tax issues that arise during the audits themselves will be examined by the IRS. Even in situations in which it appears that all workers are employees, the IRS is nevertheless instructed to conduct worker classification determinations.

NEW TAX LAW INCENTIVES FOR HIRING EMPLOYEES

Recent tax laws have created several incentives for employers to hire certain new individuals as employees rather than as independent contractors:

- Payroll tax forgiveness and the new hire retention credit under the *Hiring Incentives to Restore Employment Act* (HIRE Act); and
- Small employer health insurance tax credit under the health care reform package (the *Patient Protection and Affordable Care Act* (PPACA) and the *Health Care and Education Reconciliation Act*).

The small employer health insurance tax credit under the PPACA is intended to help qualified small employers (including nonprofit employers) reduce the cost of providing health insurance to their employees in 2010. However, qualified employers may only take into account "employees" for purposes of calculating the tax credit. Independent contractors do not qualify for inclusion in computing the credit.

The HIRE Act, through payroll forgiveness, provides relief from the employer's share of OASDI (Social Security's Old-Age, Survivors, and Disability Insurance) taxes on wages paid by a qualified employer. Although the HIRE Act's payroll forgiveness is geared toward reducing the unemployment rate, it also provides an indirect incentive for employers to classify workers as employees rather than as independent contractors.

The HIRE Act also provides an incentive to encourage employers and businesses to hire and retain unemployed workers. Under the HIRE Act, qualified employers can claim a tax credit, commonly referred to as the *new hire* or *employee retention credit*, which increases the employer's general business credit by the lesser of $1,000 or 6.2 percent of salary for each newly hired worker who:

- Was previously unemployed for a certain period; and
- Satisfies a minimum employment period with the employer.

The credit cannot be claimed for workers hired by the employer to replace another employee, unless the employee voluntarily quits or is fired for cause. Moreover, the credit can only be claimed for qualified employees, as defined for purposes of the payroll tax exemption, who meet a number of other criteria established by the HIRE Act. For example, the credit cannot be claimed for an employee who is related to the employer, such as a spouse. Additionally, the credit also cannot be claimed for independent contractors.

STUDY QUESTIONS

1. The IRS's National Research Program (NRP) employment tax study examines compliance by auditing 6,000:

   a. Forms 941, *Employer's Quarterly Federal Tax Form*
   b. Schedules SE, *Self-Employment Tax*
   c. Forms 1099-MISC, *Miscellaneous Income*

2. Which of the following is *not* a HIRE Act incentive for classifying workers as employees?

   a. Payroll forgiveness
   b. New hire retention credit
   c. Work opportunity tax credit

EMPLOYEES

When a company hires workers, the employer must decide whether they are employees or independent contractors. The distinction is crucial for federal tax purposes. If an employer incorrectly classifies an employee as an independent contractor, the financial penalties imposed by the IRS can be steep. It is looking for employers that misclassify their workers—usually, employees being misclassified as independent contractors.

Withholding Requirements

Employers must withhold income tax, FICA (Social Security and Medicare) tax, and FUTA (unemployment insurance) tax from wages paid to employees. On the other hand, a worker who is an independent contractor is solely responsible for the payment of self-employment and income taxes on his or her earnings (discussed later). Employers have no employment tax withholding or reporting obligations related to independent contractors, other than to furnish the independent contractor with a Form 1099-MISC, *Miscellaneous Income*, reporting the amount that the employer has paid to the independent contractor for that tax year.

FICA Taxes

When an employer hires an individual as an employee, the law imposes many tax requirements on the employer. Employers are responsible for:

- Federal income tax withholding;
- FICA taxes (Social Security and Medicare);
- FUTA taxes (unemployment insurance); and
- Railroad Retirement Tax Act taxes (if applicable).

An *employee* for FICA and FUTA purposes is "any individual who, under the usual common-law rules applicable in determining the employer–employee relationship, has the status of an employee." An employer is liable for the employee's share of FICA taxes for all taxable wages it pays to each of its employees regardless of whether the employer actually collects these taxes from the employee.

When an employer hires an independent contractor, the contracted worker is responsible for calculating and paying self-employment tax. An employer is not required to withhold income tax, or pay FICA taxes or FUTA taxes on amounts paid to independent contractors. Employers provide independent contractors with Form 1099-MISC, *Miscellaneous Income*, if the employer has paid the contractor $600 more during the tax year. The independent contractor reports the amount from Form 1099-MISC on Form 1040 Schedule SE, *Self-Employment Tax*. This includes workers who are classified as independent contractors under the Section 530 safe harbor relief provision of the *Revenue Act of 1978*. Under the Section 530 safe harbor (discussed in further detail later), an employer is relieved from withholding FICA taxes on any worker who would otherwise be considered an employee if the employer has consistently treated the worker as an independent contractor, unless the employer had no reasonable basis for not treating the worker as an employee.

However, this does not change the status, liabilities, or rights of the worker. Therefore, a worker who would be considered an employee but for the employer's consistent tax treatment of him or her as an independent contractor continues to be classified as an employee with regard to tax liabilities and is thus subject only to the employee's share of FICA taxes. The offset is imposed even when a final decision by the Tax Court or the statute of limitations governing liability for FICA taxes would otherwise have barred the tax assessment.

The worker cannot get credit for either income taxes or FICA taxes that the employer should have paid but did not. Incorrectly paid FICA tax can be offset against self-employment tax liability. However, this rule applies only to the employee's share of FICA tax. Therefore, if an employer incorrectly pays the employer's share of FICA tax with respect to a worker later determined to be subject to self-employment tax, the FICA tax paid by the employer cannot be credited against the employee's self-employment tax liability.

Thus, employers may be tempted to classify workers as independent contractors because the employers thereby save payroll overhead costs. Classifying workers as independent contractors can also help employers avoid the additional cost of sharing fringe benefits and retirement plan contributions with these workers.

FUTA Taxes

FUTA taxes pay for unemployment compensation to workers who lose their jobs. Employers do not withhold FUTA taxes from employees' wages, but report and pay the tax from their own funds. FUTA taxes are reported on Form 940, *Employer's Annual Federal Unemployment (FUTA) Tax Return.*

Only common-law employees, agent- or commission-drivers, and traveling and city salespersons are employees for purposes of federal unemployment (FUTA) tax. Other workers who are statutory employees for FICA tax purposes are not employees for FUTA tax purposes. However, statutory nonemployees for FICA tax purposes are nonemployees for FUTA tax purposes as well.

Common-Law Employees

Common-law relationship. A person is an employee for FICA and other employment tax purposes if the person is a *common-law employee.* A common-law relationship between an employer and employee exists when the employer has the right to control and direct the worker's performance of services, not only as to the result to be accomplished but also as to the means of providing those services.

The degree of employer control necessary to indicate that a worker is an employee as opposed to an independent contractor varies with the nature of the worker's job. An employer does not need to actually exercise the control over the workers; it is sufficient that he or she has the right to do so. Moreover, the employer need not set the employee's hours or supervise every detail of the work environment in order to control the employee.

Section 530 safe harbor. A safe harbor rule, commonly referred to as *Section 530 relief,* protects employers who have consistently treated workers as independent contractors (but should in actuality be treated as employees) and can demonstrate a reasonable basis for doing so. For employers that can show, among other justifications, they had a reasonable for not treating workers as employees, Section 530 relief allows an employer to continue treating workers as nonemployees (i.e., independent contractors) for employment tax purposes, regardless of the individual's actual status under the common-law test for determining a worker's status. The Section 530 safe harbor comes from Section 530 of the *Revenue Act of 1978* (discussed in further detail later).

Statutory Employees

Statutory employees are workers who may appear to be independent contractors but under federal law qualify as employees. Employers must therefore withhold and pay FICA taxes on the taxable compensation earned by workers who are statutory employees. Statutory employees include the following workers:

- An agent- or commission-driver (such as one distributing meat, vegetables, bakery products, beverages other than milk, or laundry and dry cleaning services);
- A full-time insurance sales representative;
- A homeworker performing work according to specifications provided by the person for whom services are performed on materials or goods that are furnished by the person that are required to be returned to that person; and
- A traveling or city salesperson, other than an agent-driver or commission-driver.

Statutory Nonemployees

On the other hand, federal tax law treats two types of workers as nonemployees: real estate agents and direct sellers. For federal tax purposes, these *statutory nonemployees* are treated as self-employed. Payments made to such individuals are not subject to employment taxes. Instead, statutory nonemployees must pay self-employment taxes.

> **COMMENT**
>
> For FICA and FUTA tax purposes, full-time traveling or city sales representatives and agent- or commission-drivers are considered statutory employees. However, life insurance sales representatives and homeworkers are considered statutory employees for FICA purposes only. A homeworker who is a statutory employee subject to FICA taxes must have earned at least $100 in cash wages for the year in order to be subject to such taxes.

STUDY QUESTIONS

> **3.** Employers of common-law employees are *not* responsible under the tax law for:
>
>   **a.** *Railroad Retirement Tax Act* taxes
>   **b.** FUTA taxes
>   **c.** Form 1099-MISC filing
>
> **4.** All of the following workers are statutory nonemployees who must pay self-employment taxes *except:*
>
>   **a.** A real estate agent
>   **b.** Traveling salesperson
>   **c.** Direct seller

INDEPENDENT CONTRACTORS

Generally, a worker is an independent contractor for tax purposes if he or she is subject to the direction or control of another merely as to the result to be accomplished by the work, but not as to the means and methods by which to accomplish the result. Workers who make substantial financial investments in tools, equipment, or a place to work, or those who undertake some entrepreneurial risks, are more likely to be deemed by the IRS or Tax Court as independent contractors. Entrepreneurial risks are evidenced if there is a possibility of a profit or loss through the exercise of managerial skill, or a dependence on more than one client.

Typical hallmarks of an independent contractor include the following:

- The worker cannot be "fired" as long as he or she produces a result that meets contract specifications rather than employer standards of performance;
- He or she provides his or her own tools and supplies;
- The individual stands to make a profit (or loss) from the work; and
- The worker is free to contract with other clients.

If the common-law tests do not indicate that an employer–employee relationship exists, and the payee is not a statutory employee, then he or she is an independent contractor.

Reporting Payments to Independent Contractors

Employers use Form W-2 to report wages, tips, and other compensation paid to employees to the IRS. In the case of independent contractors, employers use Form 1099-MISC, *Miscellaneous Income,* to report total taxable payments of $600 or more during the tax year to independent contractors made in the course of a trade or business.

General criteria for reporting a payment as nonemployee compensation include:

- Payments to the worker totaled at least $600 during the year;
- The payment was made to a nonemployee; and
- The payment was made for services provided in the course of business.

> **EXAMPLE**
>
> Lucy Riordan operates a small business. Lucy pays Anne Marie Alvarez $30 each week to help her prepare invoices and do other bookkeeping. Anne Marie is not Lucy's employee. Because Lucy paid a nonemployee more than $600 (30 × 52 = $1560) during the year for services provided in the course of business, Lucy must report this payment to the IRS on Form 1099-MISC.

DETERMINING WORKER STATUS: CONTROL

The IRS considers three aspects of control when determining whether a worker is an employee or an independent contractor:

- Behavioral control;
- Financial control; and
- Relationship of the parties.

Behavioral Control

Behavioral control is shown by facts regarding the right to direct or control how the worker performs the specific tasks for which he or she is hired, such as through instructions, training, or other means.

Financial Control

Financial control is shown by facts regarding a right to direct or control the financial and business aspects of the worker's activities. These include whether:

- There is a significant investment by the worker;
- The worker's success depends on entrepreneurial skill; and
- The worker makes his or her services available to the relevant market in addition to the service recipient.

Relationship of the Parties

The relationship of the parties is generally shown by the parties' agreements and actions with respect to each other, paying close attention to those facts that show not only how the parties perceive their own relationship but also how they represent their relationship to others.

Traditional Factors

Traditionally, the IRS has used a list of judicially developed 20 factors to determine a worker's status as an employee or independent contractor. Today, the IRS looks at all the facts and circumstances surrounding the parties' relationship as well as the 20 factors. The IRS considers these factors to the extent they are relevant in illustrating behavioral controls, financial controls, and the relationship of the parties.

The 20 traditional factors are:

- **Control of when, where, and how the worker performs services.** A person who is required to comply with instructions about when, where, and how to work is ordinarily considered an employee. The control factor is present if the employer has the right to instruct, whether or not the employer does so.

- **Training.** Training by an experienced employee is a factor of control because it is an indication that the employer wants the services performed in a particular method or manner. For example, in addition to training, requiring services to be performed with other workers and requiring a worker to attend meetings are indicative of an employer–employee relationship.

- **Integration into firm operations.** Integration of the worker's services into the operations of the business generally shows that the person is subject to the employer's direction and control and is indicative of an employer–employee relationship.

- **Requirement that services be personally performed.** If the services must be rendered personally, it indicates that the employer is interested in methods as well as results. Independent contractors are often not required to personally perform the services. However, exceptions do apply and this factor is alone not determinative.

- **Control over assistants.** When the employer has the right to hire, supervise, and pay the worker's assistants, an employee-employer relationship is indicated.

- **Length of relationship.** A long-term continuing relationship is a factor tending to indicate an employer–employee relationship. However, this factor by itself is not enough to determine the degree and extent to which the employer exercises control.

- **Work schedule.** The establishment of set hours of work by the employer is a factor indicating control by the employer and of an employer–employee relationship.

- **Number of service hours required.** The amount of time the worker is required to provide services to the employer is indicative of the worker's status. If the worker is required to devote full time to the business of the employer and the employer has control over the time spent working, it is implied that the worker is an employee restricted from doing other gainful work, whereas an independent contractor may choose for whom and when to work. On the other hand, if the worker provides part-time services while performing services for others, a lack of control over the work is indicated, and this situation suggests a client–independent contractor relationship.

- **Location of services.** The requirement that services be provided on the employer's premises suggests an employer–employee relationship. However, certain services or work cannot be performed elsewhere, such as improvements to the employer's facilities. This factor alone, therefore, is not determinative.
- **Control over technique or sequence.** If the person must perform services in the order or sequence set by the employer, it shows that the worker may be subject to the employer's control and thus indicates an employer-employee relationship.
- **Reports to employer.** If regular or periodic oral or written reports must be submitted to the employer, it suggests there is a degree of control indicating an employer–employee relationship. However, the requirement that progress reports be provided may not be enough to establish an employer–employee relationship.
- **Payment method.** The interval of payment may indicate an employer–employee relationship. An employee is usually paid by the hour, week, or month. Payment by the job or based on invoices submitted by the worker is indicative of an independent contractor status.
- **Work-related expenses.** Payment by the employer of the worker's business or traveling expenses is a factor suggesting control and indicating an employer–employee relationship. However, reimbursement of business and travel expenses pursuant to a contract may simply be part of an arrangement made between the employer and an independent contractor.
- **Tools.** The furnishing of tools, materials, etc., by the employer is indicative of control. However, the fact that a worker supplies or is required to supply his or her own tools and equipment is not necessarily determinative.
- **Work facilities.** Investment in and the provision of work facilities by the worker, especially if of a type not generally maintained by employees, indicates a client–independent contractor relationship. On the other hand, the furnishing of all necessary facilities by the employer tends to indicate employee status.
- **Profit and loss.** People who are in a position to realize a profit or suffer a loss as a result of their services are generally independent contractors. Workers paid a fixed rate based on time with the employer, with no possibility of loss, are more likely to be employees.
- **Multiple employers.** If a person works for a number of employers or firms at the same time, it usually indicates an independent status.

- **Restrictions on customers and clients.** Workers who offer their services to the general public on a regular, consistent basis are usually independent contractors. Workers who are significantly restricted as to whom they can work for are typically employees.
- **Termination of worker.** The right to discharge is an important factor indicating that the person possessing the right is an employer.
- **Termination of relationship by worker.** A worker's ability to end the relationship at any time, without penalty, indicates an employer–employee relationship. On the other hand, an independent contractor usually agrees to complete a specific job and is responsible for its satisfactory completion or is legally obligated to make good for failure to complete the job.

CAUTION

These factors have been developed over many years of litigation between employers and the IRS about who should be treated as an independent contractor. As the workplace has undergone radical changes in recent years and continues to do so, all of the factors will not necessarily apply in every situation. For example, many of these cases were decided long before telecommuting became viable, allowing employees to work remotely from the job site. Bottom-up, results-oriented management techniques in which workers are given more control over their workflow further blur the lines on worker classification. In today's economy, many individuals also work multiple jobs.

Facts and Circumstances

Notwithstanding the factors that the IRS and courts use to help determine worker status, every employment situation is different and to a great extent the final determination of whether an individual is an employee or an independent contractor is largely based on the particular facts and circumstances of each case. Certain factors may indicate that the individual is an employee; others suggest that the individual is an independent contractor. No one factor is determinative and, depending on the occupation, factors that are relevant in one employment situation may be not relevant in another. This is also true for independent contractors. The entire worker–employer relationship is considered when a service recipient and worker are determining the extent of the right to direct and control the worker's services.

> **COMMENT**
>
> Individuals who are employed by temporary employment agencies may be employees of the employment agencies themselves or of the agencies' clients. The control factors are used to determine which of the potential multiple employers will be treated as the employer for employment tax purposes.

Occupations

The tests regarding financial control, behavioral control, and the parties' relationship used to determine whether a worker is a common-law employee or independent contractor are applied to workers in many occupations, including:

- Accountants;
- Attorneys and their staff;
- Utility workers;
- Contractors and building trade workers;
- Buildings and ground maintenance service personnel;
- Managers;
- Physicians and other health care providers;
- Teachers, working students, and education workers;
- Sales representatives;
- Barbers and beauticians;
- Performers;
- Drivers;
- Guards;
- Stenographers and transcribers;
- Athletes and sports industry workers;
- Editorial and publishing workers; and
- In-home and residential community care providers.

STUDY QUESTIONS

> **5.** Under the 20 traditional factors for determining worker status, a person is typically considered an employee if he or she:
>
> **a.** Must perform a specific technique or sequence for work as set by the employer
>
> **b.** Sets his or her own work schedule
>
> **c.** Will profit or risk loss depending on success of the business as measured by income and expenses

---

6. The 20 traditional factors resolve worker classification issues. *True or False?*

SECTION 530 SAFE HARBOR

Section 530 relief (after Section 530 of the *Revenue Act of 1978*) protects employers that have consistently treated workers as independent contractors for employment tax purposes. Although the rule covers workers who otherwise should be treated as common-law employees, it does not provide a safe harbor for individuals who are technical service workers. Section 530 relief is for employers, not workers, and as such, it does not convert a worker from the status of employee to that of independent contractor.

A worker who has not been treated as an employee will not be reclassified as an employee if the employer:

- Had a reasonable basis for not treating the individual as an employee;
- Did not treat the worker or any worker in a similar position as an employee for payroll tax purposes; and
- Filed all required federal tax returns, including information returns, in a manner consistent with the worker not being an employee.

If an employer is unable to show that his or her treatment of a worker was based on one of the IRS's 20 factors (discussed earlier) the employer must otherwise show a reasonable basis for treatment the individual as an independent contractor.

Reasonable Basis

Employers are considered to have a reasonable basis for not treating an individual as an employee if their treatment was based on any of the following:

- Judicial precedent or published rulings, regardless of whether such authority relates to the particular industry or business in which the taxpayer is engaged;
- Technical advice, a letter ruling, or a determination letter by the IRS pertaining to the taxpayer;
- A past examination by the IRS (not necessarily for employment tax purposes) of the taxpayer, if the exam entailed no assessment relating to the taxpayer's employment tax treatment of individuals holding positions substantially similar to that held by the individual whose status is at issue; and/or
- Long-standing industry practice in which the employer is engaged. It is not necessary that the practice be uniform throughout the industry.

Consistent Treatment

The IRS provides guidelines for use in determining whether an employer has consistently treated a worker as an employee for any period (Rev. Proc. 85-18). The following are considered evidence of consistent treatment of a worker as an employee:

- The withholding of income tax or FICA tax from the workers' compensation (other than from a statutory employee), whether or not the tax is remitted to the government; and
- The filing of an employment tax return for any period with respect to the worker, whether or not tax was withheld from the individual.

> **CAUTION**
>
> Reliance on any of these factors is insufficient unless the reliance was reasonable. If no reasonable person could have believed that the worker was anything other than an employee, the employer is ineligible for this safe harbor relief.

> **CAUTION**
>
> The safe harbor governs employer status only for employment taxes and not for other purposes. If required information returns are not timely filed, no relief is granted from income tax withholding and FICA and FUTA taxes.

> **EXAMPLE**
>
> Siteworthy Co. has consistently treated Karen Graystone, a computer programmer, as an independent contractor and has a reasonable basis for not treating her as an employee. However, Siteworthy has failed to file all of the required information returns with respect to Karen. The safe harbor does not apply, because Siteworthy failed to satisfy the requirement that all required federal tax returns, including information returns, be filed. However, Karen is not automatically reclassified as an employee. Instead, her status is determined according to the common-law rules for determining whether an individual is an employee or an independent contractor.

An employer does not satisfy the requirements for Section 530 relief if it treats certain workers as employees and others as independent contractors when the two groups hold substantially similar positions. For example, a taxpayer who provided health physics consultants (HPCs) to public utilities to perform services did not meet the safe haven rule when it treated some of its HPCs, who held substantially similar positions as others, as employees.

EXAMPLE

Speedable Trucking Co. treated its drivers as employees from 2000 through 2006. In 2007, the company reclassified its drivers as independent contractors even though their working relationship had not changed. The IRS audited Speedable's 2007 tax return but did not question the employment status of the drivers. The company is not entitled to relief under the Section 530 safe harbor despite the fact that it treated the drivers as independent contractors since 2007. The reasonable basis exception does not apply because the employer treated the drivers as employees in 2006 and improperly reclassified them as independent contractors in 2006 although no change occurred in their employment relationship.

IRS Notification

If the employment status of any worker is going to be a subject of an audit, the IRS must give written notice of the Section 530 safe harbor before or as the audit begins.

Other Reasonable Basis

Courts have noted that, in addition to qualifying for the Section 530 safe harbor, an employer may demonstrate any other reasonable basis for the treatment of an employee for tax purposes. Congress intended that the courts construe this reasonable basis inquiry liberally in favor of the taxpayer.

Notice of Determination of Worker Classification

If the IRS determines that an employer is not entitled to Section 530 relief, the IRS cannot assess the proposed tax until:

- It issues a Notice of Determination of Worker Classification (NDWC) and the employer either exhausts its remedies in the U.S. Tax Court or fails to pursue them; or
- The employer signs the appropriate waiver of restrictions on assessment.

Congress, in 2000, gave the Tax Court jurisdiction to determine the correct amounts of employment taxes relating to determinations of worker classification.

The NDWC:

- Informs employers of the opportunity to seek review;
- Includes a schedule of workers classified as employees; and
- Shows the type of employment tax and its adjustment.

Upon the mailing of the NDWC to an employer, the period for assessment of taxes attributable to the worker classification is suspended for a 90-day period. During this time, the employer can file a petition with the Tax Court and preclude the IRS from assessing the taxes identified as owed in the NDWC prior to the expiration of the 90-day limitation period. If the IRS erroneously assesses taxes attributable to the worker classification issues without first either issuing an NDWC or obtaining a waiver of restrictions on assessment from the employer, the employer is entitled to an automatic abatement of the assessment.

Form 8919, *Uncollected Social Security and Medicare Tax on Wages*

Although Section 530 relief is intended for employers, not workers, employees who have been misclassified as independent contractors should file Form 8919, *Uncollected Social Security and Medicare Tax on Wages*, in order to calculate and report their share of uncollected Social Security and Medicare taxes.

Workers should file Form 8919 if all of the following apply:

- The worker performed services for an employer;
- The employer did not withhold the worker's share of Social Security and Medicare taxes;
- The worker's pay from the employer was not for services as an independent contractor; and
- The worker meets one of several other additional criteria (discussed next).

Form 8919 should be filed if the worker meets one of the following criteria:

- The worker filed Form SS-8, *Determination of Worker Status for Purposes of Federal Employment Taxes and Income Tax Withholding*, and received a determination or other correspondence that he or she is employee of the employer;
- The worker is a Code Sec. 530 designated employee;
- The worker was previously treated as an employee and is doing the same or similar work;
- Co-workers doing the same or similar work are treated as employees or have received a determination letter or other correspondence from the IRS stating the worker is an employee; or
- The worker has filed Form SS-8, *Determination of Worker Status for Purposes of Federal Employment Taxes and Income Tax Withholding*, and has not yet received a reply from the IRS.

Form SS-8

A worker who is unsure whether he or she is an independent contractor or employee may request an official determination by the IRS regarding his or her status by filing Form SS-8, *Determination of Worker Status for Purposes of Federal Employment Taxes and Income Tax Withholding*. An employer that is unable to clearly determine the proper classification of the worker can also request the IRS to determine the worker's status by filing Form SS-8 as well. In order to file the form and receive a determination, the IRS requires the worker to be currently performing services or to have already completed services for the employer. When the worker requests a determination of status, the IRS will also request the employer to complete SS-8. If the employer fails to respond, the IRS will nevertheless issue a determination.

Form SS-8 requires detailed information about the work performed by the individual, including:

- How the worker obtained the job;
- A description of the employer's business; and
- An explanation of why the filer believes the individual is an employee or an independent contractor.

The form also asks the filer to answer questions describing behavioral control, financial control, and the parties' relationship. A determination may take up to six months for the IRS to make after an employer files Form SS-8.

STUDY QUESTIONS

7. An employer shows consistent treatment of a worker as an employee if:

   a. The employer relies on long-standing industry practice in treating the worker as an employee

   b. The employer withholds income tax or FICA from the worker's wages

   c. The employer provides the employee with a Form 1099-MISC

8. If the IRS erroneously assesses taxes related to worker classification but has not issued an NDWC or obtained a waiver of restrictions on assessment:

   a. The employer is entitled to an automatic abatement of the assessment

   b. The period for assessment is extended to grant both the employer and IRS more time to determine worker status

   c. The worker should request an abatement of employment taxes

PROPOSED REFORMS OF WORKER CLASSIFICATION RULES

The Obama Administration has moved, on several fronts, to combat what it sees as worker classification abuses. The administration's fiscal year (FY) 2011 federal budget proposes to:

- Reform the Section 530 safe harbor rules for worker misclassification;
- Allow the IRS to issue generally applicable guidance about the proper classification of workers; and
- Increase funding for the Department of Labor (DOL) to hire additional enforcement personnel to curb abuse and more closely coordinate activities with the IRS.

COMMENT

According to the GAO, approximately 10 million workers are classified as independent contractors.

One of the most far reaching of the Obama Administration's proposals is reform of Section 530 of the *Revenue Act of 1978*. The Obama Administration proposes giving the IRS authority to require prospective reclassification of workers who are currently misclassified. The proposal would be effective on the date of enactment. However, prospective reclassification of currently misclassified workers would not be effective until the first calendar year beginning at least one year after the date of enactment. According to the administration, the transition period could be up to two years for independent contractors with existing contracts establishing their status.

The administration also proposes permitting the IRS to issue guidance about the proper classification of workers. According to the administration, the guidance would interpret the classification of workers under common-law standards in a neutral manner, recognizing that many workers are, in fact, not employees. The IRS would also develop safe harbors and/or rebuttable presumptions, both of which would be narrowly defined. Moreover, the IRS would prioritize delivery of the guidance, taking into account the history of noncompliance in certain occupations.

The administration would retain reduced penalties under current law for misclassification of workers. However, lower penalties would apply only if the employer voluntarily reclassifies its workers before being contacted by the IRS or another enforcement agency and if the employer filed all required information returns reporting payments to the independent contractors. Penalties would be waived for employers with only a small number of employees and a small number of misclassified workers, if the employer had consistently filed all required information returns reporting all payments to all misclassified workers and the employer agrees to prospective reclassification of misclassified workers.

> **COMMENT**
>
> Employers would be required to give notice to independent contractors when they first begin performing services for the employer. The notice must explain how the independent contractor will be classified and, among other things, the tax consequences of that classification.

> **COMMENT**
>
> When President Obama was a member of the U.S. Senate, he cosponsored legislation to reform Section 530. The *Independent Contractor Proper Classification Act of 2007* would have required a change in the treatment of workers when the IRS determines that the workers are employees and would have allowed the IRS to issue generally applicable worker classification guidance.

Enforcement

The Obama Administration's fiscal year 2011 budget for the DOL includes an additional $25 billion to hire more enforcement personnel. The enforcement personnel will work with the Treasury Department to target worker misclassification. The administration predicted that the joint DOL-Treasury activity would collect $7 billion over 10 years.

Proposed Legislation

Four bills were introduced during the 111th Congress as of August 1, 2010, to address the misclassification of workers and thereby assist in reducing the tax gap. The *Taxpayer Responsibility, Accountability, and Consistency Act of 2009* (H.R. 3408, and its companion bill with the same title, S. 2882) would repeal Section 530 of the *Revenue Act of 1978* and replace it with new rules. Such rules would make it more difficult for employers to avoid paying employment taxes if they have misclassified workers as independent contractors. The legislation, more specifically, would modify the three "statutory standards" (reasonable basis, substantive consistency, and reporting consistency) under Section 530 and would generally require an employer to have a "reasonable basis" for classifying a worker as an independent contractor. The "reasonable basis" standard would be met only if an employer:

- Classified a worker as an independent contractor based on:
  - A written determination addressing the employment status of either the worker at issue or another individual holding a substantially similar position in the employer's business; or
  - An employment tax examination of the worker, or other individual holding a substantially similar position in the employer's

business, that did not conclude the worker should be treated as an employee; and
— Has not treated any other individual holding a substantially similar position as an employee for employment tax purposes for any period beginning after December 31, 1977.

The Misclassification Prevention Bill, introduced in the spring of 2010 (H.R. 5107, S. 3254), would amend the *Fair Labor Standards Act of 1938* by requiring every employer to:
■ Maintain records of nonemployees (contractors) who perform labor or services; and
■ Provide certain notice to new employees and new nonemployees of their classifications and information regarding their legal rights.

STUDY QUESTIONS

9. The proposal to reform Section 530 of the *Revenue Act of 1978* would:
    a. Give the IRS authority to require prospective reclassification of workers who are currently misclassified
    b. Increase penalties for misclassification of workers
    c. Separate enforcement activities for misclassifications between the Department of Labor and IRS

10. Employers would meet the "reasonable basis" standard as proposed by the *Taxpayer Responsibility, Accountability, and Consistency Act of 2009* allowing them to classify workers as independent contractors if the employers meet all of the following requirements *except:*
    a. Treating all workers holding similar positions since 1977 as non-employees
    b. Providing notice to new and existing workers of their classification status
    c. Relying on a previous employment tax examination of the worker or a worker in a substantially similar position concluding the worker should not be treated as an employee

CONCLUSION

Worker misclassification continues to be a significant issue for the IRS. Whether workers are misclassified by employers mistakenly or intentionally, the federal government loses out on substantial revenue each year through the underpayment and nonpayment of employment tax liabilities. Consequently, the IRS and other federal agencies continue to take proactive steps to more fully understand the scope of the problem and to increase compliance by employers, employees, and independent contractors alike. As the federal government looks to find ways to increase federal revenues, the misclassification of workers and concomitant employment tax issues will certainly remain at the forefront, and become even more important, of this mission.

MODULE 1: SMALL BUSINESS: NEW OPPORTUNITIES
AND STRATEGIES — CHAPTER 3

Trends in Business Structures/Entity Formation

This chapter explores the various issues to consider when business owners create or purchase a business, including liability, organizational costs, and tax-related issues. The chapter also covers some of the state and federal reporting requirements for the different entity types.

LEARNING OBJECTIVES

Upon completion of this chapter, you will be able to:

- Identify the different types of business entities;
- Explain the different organizational, liability, and tax issues for each business entity;
- Describe the organizational and reporting requirements for each type of business entity;
- Understand the different state and federal reporting requirements for different entities; and
- Discuss factors to consider in choosing a business entity.

INTRODUCTION

This chapter discusses the various business entities that are recognized for federal tax purposes. Within these basic entities, there are variations that differ slightly. These differences and their impact on the business's choice of entity are covered as well as the state law organizational requirements for each entity type and how each type impacts a business owner(s)' personal liability for the business's obligations. The chapter is organized to roughly move from the simplest form of business entity to the most complex.

OVERVIEW OF ENTITY TYPES

There are five basic business entities recognized under the federal tax law:
- Sole proprietorship;
- Partnership;
- Limited liability company;
- C corporation; and
- S corporation.

Within the basic list of business entities, certain variations have recently developed within the partnership form to respond to changing tax and business needs. In addition to the traditional use of general and limited partnerships, current practice has seen the development of limited liability partnerships and limited liability limited partnerships, as well as the use of LLCs, C corporations, S corporations, and other partnerships as partners.

The Sole Proprietorship

A *sole proprietorship* is a business entity owned by a single individual. A sole proprietorship is not an entity separate from its owner. Thus, the sole owner has unlimited personal liability for all of the business's activities, and both the business's assets and the owner's personal assets are at risk.

All of a sole proprietorship's income is taxed to the sole owner, who also deducts any business expenses and claims any business-related tax credits. All of the business's net income, regardless of the time the owner works in the business, is subject to self-employment tax. In addition, a sole proprietorship expires with its owner.

A sole proprietorship may be operated in the owner's name or the owner may choose another name. When using another name, the proprietor must register the business's "trade name" or "fictitious name" with the state or local government where the business is located.

A sole proprietorship usually does not have to file annual business reports or a tax return separate from its owner. Depending on the type of business, however, a sole proprietorship may have to have a business license and/or pay state business taxes.

Generally, converting an existing sole proprietorship into a corporation, partnership, or LLC is a nontaxable event.

A sole proprietorship reports business income and deductions on the owner's Form 1040, Schedule C. A sole proprietor's net business income is subject to self-employment tax, which is reported on Form 1040, Schedule SE.

A sole proprietor's fringe benefits generally are not deductible because a sole proprietor is an owner, not an employee, of the business. However, a sole proprietor may contribute to a SEP or Keogh plan.

A sole proprietorship may employ family members. A sole proprietor's spouse and/or children may participate in a health insurance or medical reimbursement plan provided by the business.

COMMENT

A proprietor may get deductible health insurance coverage simply by providing family coverage to his or her employee spouse.

Salaries paid to a spouse and/or children are *their* earned income for purposes of contributing to their own IRA or participating in a retirement plan. In addition, no FICA tax is due on salaries paid to employee family members under the age of 18 and no FUTA tax is due for employee family members younger than age 21.

Partnerships

A *partnership* is an unincorporated business entity owned by two or more persons. Any "person" may be a partner including:

- Nonresident aliens;
- C corporations;
- S corporations;
- Other partnerships;
- All types of trusts;
- Decedent's estates; and
- Tax-exempt organizations.

A partnership is an entity separate from its owners. Thus, the partnership's income and expenses are determined at the partnership level for tax purposes and the partnership is required to file a separate tax return.

Partnerships use Form 1065 to report the partnership's income and deductions. The partnership's net income is not subject to tax. Once the partnership's income and expenses are determined at the partnership level, they flow through to the partner/owners. Because of this treatment, a partnership is also categorized as a *pass-through entity* (a label that it shares in the tax world with the S corporation). Schedule K-1 is used to report the partners' shares of the business's income and deductions.

Generally, there are two different types of partnerships; general and limited. These partnerships provide different liability protection and generate different tax issues.

The general partnership. A *general partnership* is an unincorporated business entity having two or more owners. In a general partnership all owners have unlimited personal liability for all of the partnership's activities (except for certain nonrecourse liabilities).

Depending on the law of the state where it is organized, a general partnership may be required to register and to file annual business reports. If the owners do not have a written partnership agreement, the state's default laws usually apply. Most states have adopted the Uniform Partnership Act.

> **COMMENT**
>
> Spouses who jointly own a business are technically partners. By default, they constitute a general partnership that is required to file Form 1065 annually. However, if the spouses comply with the qualified joint venture rules, they may be able to report the income and expenses of their business directly on Form 1040, Schedule C, bypassing the Form 1065 filing requirement.

The limited partnership. A *limited partnership* is also an unincorporated business entity with more than one owner. Generally, limited partnerships must register with the state in which they are organized and also may be required to file annual business reports.

A limited partnership must have at least one general partner and the general partner must run the business. The general partner has unlimited liability for the business's activities; the limited partners' liability is restricted to their capital investment in the business.

To retain their limited liability, limited partners may not be involved in managing the business. Therefore, limited partners are considered passive investors subject to the passive activity loss rules.

Limited partners who take an active role in the business may be reclassified as general partners subject to unlimited personal liability for the business's debts and obligations.

> **COMMENT**
>
> The general partner in a limited partnership may be a corporation or LLC. In this case the general partner corporation or LLC must have its own assets. Generally, these assets should equal at least 1 percent of the entire investment in the business.

A limited partnership is an entity separate from its owners. Therefore, income and deductions are determined at the partnership level for tax purposes, and the partnership is required to file its own tax return. However, once income and deductions are determined at the partnership level, they flow through to the owners. Like general partnerships, limited partnerships annually file Form 1065 and report the partners' share of income and deductions on Schedule K-1.

Limited liability partnerships and limited liability limited partnerships. Limited liability partnerships (LLPs) and limited liability limited partnerships (LLLPs) are partnerships without a general partner. In LLPs the partners are insulated from the liabilities generated by other partners, but not from their own negligence or the partnership's general indebtedness. An LLLP allows a business to be organized as a limited partnership without a general partner and without the fees and taxes frequently imposed on LLCs.

> **COMMENT**
>
> Not all states allow LLPs and LLLPs as entity types.

> **COMMENT**
>
> This form of partnership is popular with professional services firms, such as lawyers, physicians, and accountants because it limits each professional's personal liability.

The Limited Liability Company (LLC)

The *LLC* is a hybrid business entity that combines the corporate shareholder's limited liability with the single level of taxation of a partnership. Thus, unlike limited partners, LLC members may actively manage the LLC's business without losing their limited liability.

An LLC is formed under state law by filing a certificate of formation or other registration document. The owner of an LLC interest is a *member*. The person running the LLC's business is the *manager*.

An LLC may be managed by all of its members *(member-managed)* or have one or more managers *(manager-managed)*. The LLC's manager may or may not be a member of the LLC. The LLC is governed by an operating agreement that typically spells out the rights, duties, and obligations of the members and the manager.

A single-member LLC may elect to be taxed as a sole proprietorship or as a corporation. Absent an election, the entity will be disregarded and taxed as a sole proprietorship (Reg. § 301.7701-2).

A multimember LLC may elect to be taxed as a partnership or as a corporation. A multimember LLC that elects to be taxed as a corporation may also elect to be an S corporation if it qualifies. Absent an election, a multimember LLC is taxed as a partnership (Reg. § 301.7701-2).

> **CAUTION**
>
> One disadvantage to operating an LLC in more than one state is that not all states tax LLCs uniformly. States may have minimum capital taxes on LLCs, impose fees per Schedule K-1 issued, and/or impose taxes on asset transfers to LLCs.

Corporations

A *corporation* is a business entity created under state law. To form a corporation, documents must be filed with the business's state of domicile. There is usually a fee for filing formation documents. In addition, corporations usually must file annual business reports with their domiciliary state and pay annual fees. Corporations may also be subject to state income and franchise taxes.

Generally, characteristics of a corporation as a business entity include:

- Constituting an entity separate from its owners;
- Shareholders who are not personally liable for the corporation's activities. The shareholders' liability is limited to their investment in the corporation;
- Corporate management separated from ownership. Corporations are managed by a board of directors (management) who are elected by shareholders (owners);
- Shareholders who can freely transfer their interests in the corporation; and
- An indefinite lifespan.

C corporation. For federal tax purposes there are two types of corporations: C corporations and S corporations. The distinction between C and S corporations is the manner in which they are taxed:

- A *C corporation* is subject to tax at the entity level and the shareholders are also taxed when the corporation's earnings are distributed as dividends; and
- Conversely, an S corporation's earnings are not taxed at the entity level but are passed through and taxed to the shareholders at the regular income tax rates.

S corporation. The *S corporation* is a regular corporation created under state law that elects under federal tax law to be taxed as an S corporation. The election is authorized by Code Sec. 1362.

An S corporation possesses the same characteristics as any corporation:

- Limited liability;
- Continuity of life;
- Interest transferability; and
- Centralized management.

Unlike a regular corporation, however, an S corporation enjoys *flow-through tax treatment* that avoids tax on regular income at the corporate level.

All the corporation's shareholders must agree to the S election when it is made. The election is made on Form 2553, *Election by a Small Business Corporation.*

> **COMMENT**
>
> Shareholders who acquire S corporation stock after the election is made are not required to agree to the election, but they are bound by it.

Once the election is made, the corporation becomes a pass-through entity subject to a single level of taxation at the shareholder level. However, the S corporation may still be subject to the built-in gains tax or the tax on excess passive investment income.

An S corporation may pass through losses to its shareholders, subject to certain limitations. S corporations are not subject to the accumulated earnings tax, the corporate alternative minimum tax, or the personal holding company tax.

> **CAUTION**
>
> Only individuals, S corporations, and certain trusts and estates may be S corporation shareholders. Generally, an S corporation may not have a partnership, a C corporation, or a nonresident alien as a shareholder.

An S corporation may have only 100 shareholders. However, family members may be treated as a single shareholder. The term *family member* includes the common ancestor, lineal descendants of the common ancestor, and the spouses or widow(er) of such lineal descendants or common ancestor.

> **CAUTION**
>
> The S corporation family shareholder election applies only to determine the number of shareholders. Each family member must be otherwise eligible to be an S corporation shareholder. In addition, certain entities, such as the estate or trust of a deceased shareholder, may be treated as a member of the family for purposes of determining the number of shareholders (Prop. Reg. 1.1361-1(e)).

Comparison with partnerships. Although the tax rules for S corporations are similar to those for partnerships there are some differences:

- Active S corporation shareholders are not liable for self-employment tax on the S corporation's net income;
- An S corporation shareholder's basis does not include the S corporation's debt. Only shareholder loans to the S corporation are included in the shareholder's stock basis;
- The passive activity loss rules apply to S corporation shareholders;
- Generally, an S corporation must use a calendar year for tax reporting.
- An S corporation may only have one class of stock with a limited exception allowing for voting and nonvoting shares; and
- Fringe benefits received by 2-percent S corporation shareholders must be included in the shareholder's income.

> **CAUTION**
>
> S corporation shareholders performing services for the corporation are considered employees and, therefore, are subject to income and employment tax withholding on the amounts earned from their services to the corporation.

Table 1. Business Entities—Summary

Sole Proprietorship	Partnership	LLC	C Corporation	S Corporation
Only one owner allowed	At least two owners required	One or more owners	One or more owners	One or more owners
Only one owner, so only one class of ownership	Multiple classes of ownership allowed	Multiple classes of ownership allowed	Multiple classes of ownership allowed	Only one class of ownership allowed
The owner controls the business	General partners control the business; limited partners excluded	Member or manager managed	Board of directors controls the business	Board of directors controls the business
Only voting ownership allowed	Voting and nonvoting ownership allowed	Voting and nonvoting ownership allowed	Voting and nonvoting ownership allowed	Voting and nonvoting ownership allowed
Net income subject to FICA	Net income subject to FICA	Depends on election	Net income not subject to FICA	Net income not subject to FICA

STUDY QUESTIONS

1. Which type of entity is taxed at the entity level?

   a. C corporation

   b. S corporation

   c. Limited liability company

2. A multimember LLC *cannot* elect to be taxed as a(n):

   a. S corporation

   b. Disregarded entity

   c. Partnership

KEY FACTORS IN COMPARING TYPES OF BUSINESS ENTITIES

Owners investigate various factors when starting or purchasing a business. One of the most important is deciding how to structure the business. Major factors to consider are listed here.

Table 2. Considerations and Indications Affecting the Choice of Business Entity

Question Driving the Choice of Entity Type	Weighting Consideration
How many owners will the business have?	If the business will have only one owner, it cannot be a partnership; however, it can be a sole proprietorship, corporation, S corporation, or LLC.
Are the owners starting a new business or purchasing an existing business?	There are tax issues to explore when a new owner changes the form of an existing business.
Will the business be owned by another entity, such as a corporation, partnership, or LLC?	If the business will be owned by another entity, it cannot be a sole proprietorship or an S corporation (except in certain circumstances).
What kind of business are the owners operating?	Corporations, S corporations, limited partnerships, and LLCs protect their owners' personal assets from business debts. General partnerships and sole proprietorships do not.
How long is the business expected to last?	Sole proprietorships expire with their owners. Corporations, partnerships, and LLCs can have unlimited durations.
Is the business expected to generate a profit or a loss in its early years?	Partnerships, LLCs, and S corporations pass through income and losses to owners. C corporations do not.
Where will the business be located?	Some states do not allow professionals to incorporate their professional practices.
Will the owners be passive or active participants?	Passive owners of pass-through entities are subject to the passive activity loss rules.

Question Driving the Choice of Entity Type	Weighting Consideration
Will the business be managed by all of the owners or only a few?	A general partnership or an LLC may be managed by some or all of the owners; a corporation is managed by a board of directors; a limited partnership is managed by the general partner(s).
Do all of the owners want an equal say in the management of the business or will there be restricted management?	Limited partners in a general partnership have no say in management.
Will the business distribute capital in the future because of redemptions, refinancings, or partial liquidations of the business and other transfers to owners?	Corporate transactions may be taxed at higher rates than those for individual owners. Contributions to and distributions from entities such as partnerships affect basis of owners' interests and taxation of revenues. Succession planning using entities such as a family limited partnership enables a general partner to retain control while including members of the next generation as limited (nonvoting) partners.
Will transfers of ownership be restricted?	S corporation ownership can only be transferred to a qualified S corp shareholder.
Will the owners make different types of contributions to the business?	The value of a capital interest in a partnership received by a partner in exchange for services rendered or to be rendered to the partnership is taxable income to the partner. A shareholder who performs services for a C or S corporation receives compensation subject to employment taxes.
How will the owners be compensated: salary, dividends, interest, rent, royalties?	Salary is always subject to employment taxes; dividends, interest, rent, or royalties are not.
Will the owners lend money to the business?	A partner who lends money to a partnership increases his or her inside basis in the partnership; this does not apply to C or S corporations.
What are the relative tax brackets for the owners and the business?	The C corporation's income is taxed between 15 and 39 percent, and the shareholders are taxed again when the C corp distributes dividends, resulting in double taxation. Income from S corps and partnerships is taxed at the owners' individual rates.
What are the owners' estate planning objectives?	Specialized partnership entities such as the family limited partnership have been used in recent years to facilitate transfer of ownership of family farms and businesses.

CHOOSING A BUSINESS ENTITY

Factors contributing to the complexity of choosing what business entity to adopt include:

- Liability issues;
- Organizational issues;

- Formation tax issues;
- Operating tax issues; and
- Disposing of the business when the owner leaves.

The following sections explore these issues in depth.

LIABILITY ISSUES

The various business structures have different levels of liability protection for the business's owners/operators. Sole proprietors and general partners have unlimited personal liability for the business's activities. Generally, corporate shareholders and limited partners' liability is limited to their investment in the business. LLC owners have limited liability regardless of whether they participate in the business's management.

Sole Proprietorships

A sole proprietorship and its owner are the same entity. Therefore, the business's debts and obligations are the owner's responsibility. When the business's activity is likely to generate liability claims or if the business has employees, the owner should consider forming a single-member LLC.

> **CAUTION**
>
> Because a sole proprietor's personal assets may be used to pay the business's debts and obligations, the business owner should think carefully about whether to hold personal assets jointly with a spouse. The spouse's share of the joint assets may also be subject to business creditors' claims.

Partnerships

A general partner, like a sole proprietor, has unlimited personal liability for the business's debts and obligations. All general partners in a partnership are jointly and severally liable for the business's debts. Thus, a creditor can obtain a judgment and collect the whole debt from one or more of the general partners. That general partner may then collect their shares of the debt from the other general partners.

> **COMMENT**
>
> A limited partnership may be organized with an LLC or a corporation as the general partner. Structuring a partnership in this way will restrict a general partner's liability for the partnership's debts to the partner's investment in the LLC or corporation.

General partners are not personally liable when the partnership's debts are *nonrecourse*. A creditor may only look to the partnership's assets to satisfy nonrecourse debts.

Limited partners do not have personal liability for the partnership's debts. A limited partner's liability is restricted to the partner's interest in the partnership.

> **CAUTION**
>
> Limited partners who actively or materially participate in the partnership's business risk losing the limitation on personal liability.

> **CAUTION**
>
> A business owner's personal guarantee of a business loan puts personal assets at risk even if the business is organized as an LLC or corporation.

Limited Liability Companies

LLC members are insulated from personal liability for the business's liabilities. An LLC member's liability is generally limited to his or her investment in the LLC. However, LLC members who actively manage a business with employees may be personally liable if the business fails to withhold and pay-over employment taxes. LLC members may also be personally liable for any personally guaranteed loans or other obligations.

Corporations

Generally, a corporation's shareholders do not have personal liability for the business's debts and obligations. However, a corporate shareholder who actively or materially participates in the business may be liable for unpaid employment taxes, sales and use taxes, and/or unpaid wage claims.

STUDY QUESTIONS

3. Corporate shareholders are generally not personally liable for:
   a. Corporate income taxes
   b. Debts and obligations of the corporation
   c. Tax on stock received for their services to the corporation

4. The general partner in a limited partnership always has unlimited liability for the business's debts and obligations. *True or False?*

ORGANIZATIONAL ISSUES

Sole Proprietorships

Sole proprietorships are not required to file formation documents. However, the business may need to register under its trade name or doing business as (DBA) name with a state or local agency. The business may also need to obtain a business registration number for income and sales and use tax purposes. If a sole proprietor has employees or sets up a retirement plan, it will need a federal employer identification number (FEIN). Otherwise, sole proprietors may use their Social Security number (SSN) for reporting.

> **CAUTION**
>
> Sole proprietors who use their own SSN may expose themselves to an increased risk of identity theft.

General Partnerships

Documentation. Most states do not require general partnerships to file formation documents. However, the partners should execute a partnership agreement addressing such issues as capital contributions, distributions, profit and loss sharing, management responsibilities, dispute resolution, duration and termination of the business, and transferability of the partner's interest. A general partnership must obtain a FEIN.

Co-ownership of real estate. Co-owners of real estate are partners for tax purposes if they actively carry on a trade or business and divide its profits. For example, co-owners of an apartment building leasing space and, directly or through an agent, providing services to the tenants are partners.

Limited Partnerships

Forming a limited partnership requires filing a formation document (certificate of formation or other document) in which the general partner(s) and the limited partners are identified. Usually, there is a fee for filing the original formation document and in some states there may be an annual filing requirement and fee. The partners should execute a partnership agreement that addresses the duties and obligations of general partner(s) and limited partner(s). A limited partnership will need to obtain an FEIN.

CAUTION

Partnerships that fail to execute a partnership agreement may be bound by the default provisions of state law.

Limited Liability Companies

Limited liability companies are organized by filing a formation document (certificate of formation or other document) and paying a fee to the state of organization. Generally, the following information is included in LLC formation documents:

- The name and address of the entity;
- The purpose for which the entity is organized;
- The name and address of its registered agent; and
- Whether the entity will be member- or manager-managed.

An LLC elects its classification by filing Form 8832, *Entity Classification Election*. The multiowner LLC may elect to be classified as a partnership or a corporation for federal income tax purposes. A single-owner LLC may elect to be treated as a disregarded entity or a corporation.

A multiowner LLC that fails to file Form 8832 will automatically be classified as a partnership. A single-owner LLC that fails to file Form 8832 will automatically be classified as a disregarded entity (Reg. § 301.7701-2(a)).

An LLC that elects to be classified as a corporation may also elect to be taxed as an S corporation if it meets all of the requirements and files Form 2553, *Election by a Small Business Corporation*. An LLC electing to be taxed as an S corporation need only file Form 2553 to make both the election to be taxed as a corporation and the S election (Reg. § 301.7701.3(c)(1)(v)(C)).

When there is reasonable cause, the IRS will treat an untimely entity classification election as timely (Rev. Proc. 2007-41, supplementing Rev. Procs. 2003-43 and 2004-48).

Corporations

Formation of a C or S corporation. Corporations are organized by filing a certificate or articles of incorporation with the state where the business is organized. A corporation is an entity separate from its owners, so it is required to obtain a FEIN for federal tax purposes.

Businesses may obtain a FEIN by filing Form SS-4 or by using the IRS's online application process. The IRS's online application can be found at **http://www.irs.gov/businesses/small/article/0,,id=102767,00.html.**

S corporation election. After a corporation is formed under state law, it can elect to be treated as an S corporation. Corporations and LLCs electing to be treated as S corporations must complete and file Form 2553, *Election by a Small Business Corporation.* The election must be filed:

- No more than two months and 15 days after the beginning of the tax year the election is to take effect, or
- At any time during the tax year preceding the tax year it is to take effect.

If the election is filed late, it will generally be effective for the following tax year (Code Sec. 1362(b)(1)), unless the corporation can prove reasonable cause for late filing to the IRS. The election should be filed when a new entity begins operation. A corporation's taxable year begins on the day it first has shareholders, acquires assets, or begins doing business, whichever occurs first (Reg. §1.1362-6(a)(2)(ii)(c)).

By filing Form 2553, the shareholders agree that all of the corporation's income will pass through the corporation to the shareholders and be taxed to them based on their ownership interests.

In order make an effective S election, Form 2553 must be filed by a corporate officer and all shareholders who are actual, deemed, or beneficial owners of the corporation's stock when the election is made. In community property states, both spouses must consent to the S election. When shares are held by joint tenants, tenants in common, or tenants by the entirety, all of the tenants should sign Form 2553 (Reg. §1.1362-6(b)(2)(i)).

COMMENT

Although new shareholders are not required to agree to the S election, they are bound by it.

A majority of the shareholders must agree to terminate an S election. Once the election is terminated, the corporation generally must wait five years before reapplying for S status. The IRS may consent to earlier reinstatement of a terminated S election (Code Sec. 1362(g)). In addition, the IRS has authority to waive an invalid S election, waive the effect of an inadvertent S termination, or treat a late S election as timely (Code Sec. 1362 (b)(5) and (f)).

FORMATION TAX ISSUES

Transfers to the New Entity

Once the entity is formed, property and/or money may be transferred by the owner(s) to the entity in exchange for an interest or shares in the entity. The following examples illustrate questions important to consider when an owner faces determining which business structure to use.

EXAMPLE

Andy Devalt has just obtained his CPA license and wants to start his own accounting business. Andy has some business equipment that he will transfer to his new business, including a cell phone, a computer, and a filing cabinet. Andy used his personal credit card to buy the property he transferred to the business. When he transferred the property, the business took over the payments.

■ Is Andy's transfer of property to the entity taxable or tax-exempt?

- *Sole proprietorship*—Andy's transfer of his personal property to a sole proprietorship is tax-exempt.
- *LLC*—Andy's transfer of his personal property to an LLC is tax-exempt regardless of whether the business chooses to be a disregarded entity or a corporation.
- *Corporation*—Andy's transfer of his personal property to either a C or S corporation is tax-exempt.

■ Does Andy have taxable income if the property is encumbered and the entity assumes his liability when the property is transferred?

- *Sole proprietorship*—Andy does not have taxable income if the property he transfers is encumbered and the business assumes his liability because Andy and the sole proprietorship are the same entity.
- *C or S corporation or an LLC taxed as either a C or S corporation*—Andy has the same result if his business is a C or an S corporation or an LLC taxed as either a C or an S corporation. However, Andy's basis in any of these business entities is decreased by the amount of debt the business assumes.

EXAMPLE

Andy purchased $5,000 of business equipment with a personal credit card and transferred the business equipment to his business. The business assumes the credit card payments. Andy's basis in the business is reduced by the business's credit card payments.

■ Is property received by Andy in addition to an interest in the entity (boot) taxable to the owner?

- *Sole proprietorship*—No.
- *C or S corporation*—Boot can be taxed as either a dividend or as a sale or exchange.

EXAMPLE

Andy holds 10 shares of Class A stock of his incorporated accounting practice with a basis of $30. Andy's incorporated accounting practice is merging into XMPG International, so Andy is exchanging his 10 shares of Class A stock for 10 shares of XPMG stock and $100 of cash. On the date of the exchange, each share of Class A and XMPG stock is worth $10. Thus, Andy receives XMPG stock with a fair market value of $100 and $100 in cash in exchange for his Class A shares. Andy realizes gain of $170 on the exchange, of which $100 is recognized.

■ What is Andy's income tax basis in his ownership interest in the entity?

■ Generally, an owner's tax basis in his ownership interest in a separate business entity equals the amount paid for the interest. If the owner transfers property in exchange for the business interest, the fair market value of the property is adjusted to reflect any of the owner's liabilities assumed by the business.

EXAMPLE

Andy decides to buy into an accounting firm instead of starting his own business. He pays $100,000 for an interest in Tax Accountants, LLC. Andy's basis in his interest in the LLC is $100,000. If Andy transfers property worth $150,000, but subject to a $50,000 mortgage, which the LLC assumes, then Andy's basis in his LLC interest is still $100,000.

■ What is the entity's income tax basis in the property transferred to it by the owners?

■ A separate business entity's basis in the property it receives from the owners is generally equal to the owner's basis or the fair market value on the date of transfer.

EXAMPLE

See above. The LLC's basis in the assets Andy transferred to it is $100,000. The result is the same if Andy's business entity is a C or S corp.

Sole Proprietorships

Forming a sole proprietorship is not a taxable event. Although the owner commits money and/or property to the business, the owner does not receive any shares or interest in exchange. A sole proprietor's basis in the business's assets is the lower of:

■ The asset's cost; or

■ The asset's fair market value on the date of transfer.

Partnerships

Generally, forming a partnership is a nontaxable event under Code Sec. 721. Contributing property to the partnership in exchange for a partnership interest does not trigger gain or loss to the partners or the partnership. This rule applies not only to the partners' original contributions of property to the partnership but also to partners' subsequent contributions of property.

> **COMMENT**
>
> This applies to both general and limited partnerships and to LLCs taxed as partnerships.

> **CAUTION**
>
> When a partner contributes encumbered property to a partnership or the partnership assumes the partner's liabilities encumbering property transferred to the partnership, the partner recognizes taxable income when the assumed liabilities exceed the partner's share of the partnership's liabilities plus the partner's basis in the property contributed. In these circumstances, the partner is treated as having received a cash distribution from the partnership (Code Secs. 722, 723, 731, 741, and 752).

Partner's basis in the partnership (outside basis). The partners' basis in their partnership interest is the *outside basis*. Generally, a partner's outside basis equals the basis of the property the partner transferred to the partnership in exchange for the partnership interest.

> **COMMENT**
>
> A partner's outside basis is important because it determines deductible losses, taxable distributions, the basis of distributions (other than cash), and the gain or loss on the sale of the partner's partnership interest.

Various transactions increase or decrease a partner's outside basis (Code Sec. 752). A partner's outside basis is increased by:

- Gain recognized by the partner on the property's transfer to the partnership;
- The partner's share of the partnership's recourse liabilities;
- Contributions of cash and property to the partnership;
- An increase in the partner's share of the partnership's liabilities; and
- The partner's share of the partnership's income.

A partner's outside basis is decreased by:

- Partner debts assumed by the partnership;
- A decrease in the partner's share of the partnership's liabilities;
- The partner's share of the partnership's losses; and
- The partner's distributions from the partnership.

> **COMMENT**
>
> Limited partners and LLC members' outside basis is only increased by a share of the partnership's debt if they are required to:
>
> - Make contributions to the partnership;
> - Pay the partnership's debts directly;
> - Restore a capital account deficit balance on liquidation; or
> - Reimburse another partner who pays a partnership debt under an indemnity agreement (Reg. § 1.752-2).

> **COMMENT**
>
> A partner's basis is decreased by distributions before it is decreased by the partner's share of the partnership's losses (Code Sec. 705).

The partner's holding period for the acquired partnership interest carries over from the period the partner held the contributed property (Code Sec. 1223).

> **CAUTION**
>
> A partner's outside basis may be different than the partner's capital account. A partner's outside basis is based on the partner's basis in the property contributed to the partnership. A partner's capital account equals the value of the property contributed to the partnership.

A partnership's basis in its assets. The partnership's basis in its assets is the *inside basis*. Generally, the partnership's basis in the property contributed to it equals the contributing partner's basis in the property. The partnership's basis is increased by any gain recognized by the contributing partner when the property is contributed (Code Secs. 722 and 723).

Code Sec. 754 basis adjustments. When it is formed, a partnership's inside basis usually equals the sum of the partners' outside basis. However, many transactions may cause the partnership's basis and the partners' basis to differ. For example, the heirs of a deceased partner may have acquired the decedent's partnership interest with a stepped-up cost basis. Generally, a transferee's cost basis in an acquired partnership interest equals the price paid by the transferee, not the transferee's share of the adjusted basis of the partnership's assets.

In order to cure any distortion between the partnership's basis and the acquiring partner's basis, the partnership may make a Code Sec. 754 election to adjust the inside basis of its assets. This election is generally made upon the sale or exchange of a partnership, a distribution to a partner, or the transfer of a partnership interest upon the death of a partner. The basis adjustment only affects the inside basis of the transferee partner. Thus, the transferee partner acquires a share of the original inside basis, especially adjusted for that partner. This adjustment is then allocated among the partnership's assets.

A partnership makes a Code Sec. 754 election by attaching a statement to its Form 1065 by the due date, including extensions, for the year of the partnership interest's sale or partner's death. Once the election is made, it applies to all sales, deaths, and distributions to partners. The election may only be revoked with the IRS's permission.

EXAMPLE

After Perry Wilkins sold his interest in Atlas Partners in 2008, the partnership made a Code Sec. 754 election by attaching the following statement to its 2008 Form 1065: "Pursuant to Internal Revenue Code Sec. 754 and Regulation § 1.754-1(b), Atlas Partners hereby elects to adjust the basis of its property under Code Secs. 734(b) and 743(b)."

COMMENT

The tax benefits provided by Code Sec. 754 have a downside: the additional costs and administrative burdens of computing and tracking the basis adjustments applicable to every item of partnership property. This burden is especially cumbersome when there are many partnership assets.

Interest in partnership received for services. Exceptions to the Code Sec. 721 nonrecognition rule apply when a partner receives a partnership interest in exchange for performing services to the partnership. The value of a capital interest in a partnership received by a partner in exchange for services rendered or to be rendered to the partnership is taxable income to the partner (Code Sec. 61; Reg. § 1.721-1(b)(1)).

Interest in partnership's profits for services. A partner's receipt of a profits interest in a partnership in exchange for services to the partnership may be taxable to the partner if the interest has a clearly ascertainable value when received. However, a partnership's transfer of a profits interest to a partner in exchange for services to or for the benefit of the partnership is not a taxable event either to the partner or the partnership unless:

- The profits interest relates to a substantially certain predictable stream of income from the partnership assets, such as income from high-quality debt securities or a high-quality net lease;
- The partner disposes of the profits interest within two years of receipt; or
- The profits interest is a limited partnership interest in a Code Sec. 7704(b) publicly traded partnership (Rev. Proc. 93-27, 1993-2 C.B. 343; Rev. Proc. 2001-43, 2001-2 CB 191).

COMMENT

Notice 2005-43 proposed a new procedure that would require the immediate recognition of income when a partner received an interest in the partnership's profits in return for services. The notice also provided a safe harbor if the partnership interest's value is equal to the liquidation value of the partnership property.

Corporations

Generally, transfers of money and property to a corporation in exchange for stock may be made on a tax-free basis. However, the transaction must follow the Code Sec. 351 rules to qualify for tax-free treatment.

Code Sec. 351 rules. In order for property transfers to form a corporation to be tax-free, the property must be transferred to the corporation solely in exchange for the corporation's stock. In addition, immediately after the property contributions, the transferors must own at least 80 percent of the corporation's voting stock (Code Sec. 351(a)).

The term *stock* includes common and preferred stock, voting and nonvoting stock. It does not include items such as warrants, treasury shares, options, and authorized shares that have not been issued.

The term *property* is broadly defined. It includes cash, real property, furniture and fixtures, leasehold improvements, inventories, stocks and bonds, installment obligations, accounts receivable, patents, know-how, trade secrets, and copyrights.

COMMENT

For purposes of the 80-percent test, the attribution/constructive ownership rules of Code Sec. 318 are not applied. Only stock that is actually owned by the transferor is counted (Rev. Rul. 56-613).

Generally, transferring an asset subject to liabilities to a corporation does not result in boot to the transferor unless the corporation assumes liabilities that exceed the transferor's adjusted basis in the transferred assets (Code Sec. 357(c)).

An individual who receives stock in exchange for performing services for a corporation must recognize income unless the stock is subject to a substantial risk of forfeiture (Code Sec. 83). When both property and services are transferred to the corporation, and the property's fair market value equals or exceeds the value of the services provided, all of the stock is counted as received in exchange for property for applying the 80-percent control test.

A shareholder may not recognize a loss in a transfer of property to a corporation for stock in a Code Sec. 351 transaction. In addition, the corporation does not recognize gain or loss from the receipt of property or money in exchange for stock (Code Sec. 1032).

Corporation and stockholder's basis in stock. Generally, the corporation's basis in the property transferred equals the transferor's basis plus any gain recognized by the transferor. The stockholder's basis in the stock received equals the transferred property's adjusted basis (Code Sec. 358(a)).

> **COMMENT**
>
> A corporation is not required to adjust its basis in encumbered assets when it assumes shareholder liabilities.

Special rules for S corporations. Like C corporations, transfers to an S corporation upon incorporation are tax-free and the basis rules are the same for both entity types (Code Secs. 351 and 1371(a)). A corporation must elect to be taxed as an S corporation (Code Sec. 1362(a)) by filing Form 2553. All persons who are shareholders on the day the election is made must consent to the election (Code Sec. 1362(a)(2)).

For the S election to be valid, the corporation must meet all of the eligibility requirements, as described here.

The corporation must be a U.S. domestic corporation. Insurance companies and certain financial institutions are not eligible to elect S status (Code Sec. 1361(b)(1)).

In order to elect S status, a corporation must have eligible shareholders. The eligibility rules include:

- All S corporation shareholders must be U.S. citizens or residents. Nonresident alien individuals are not eligible S corporation shareholders;
- Decedents' estates and bankruptcy estates are eligible shareholders during the period of administration (Code Sec. 1361(b)(1)(B) and (d)(3));

- 501(c)(3) charitable organizations are eligible to be S corporation share-holders. However, charitable remainder annuity trusts (CRATs) and charitable remainder unitrusts (CRUTs) are not eligible S corporation shareholders (Code Sec. 1361(e)(1)(b));
- A variety of trusts may also qualify to be S corporation shareholders, although some for only a limited time, including
  - Grantor trusts—The grantors of these trusts are treated as the owners of the trust property because they retain certain rights, such as the right to revoke the trust, the right to exercise certain administrative powers, and the right to use the trust income,
  - Qualified Subchapter S trusts (QSSTs)—The current income beneficiary of a QSST must make the QSST election before the QSST can be an S corporation shareholder (Code Sec. 1361(d)(1)-(3)). Once the QSST election is made, any distributions of trust principal current during the income beneficiary's lifetime must be made exclusively to that person. The current income beneficiary's interest in the trust must terminate upon the earlier of the beneficiary's death or the termination of the trust. If the trust terminates during the lifetime of the current income beneficiary, all of the trust assets must be distributed to that person (Code Sec. 1361(d)(1)),
  - Electing small business trusts (ESBTs)—An ESBT may accumulate or distribute income for multiple beneficiaries. The ESBT's beneficiaries must be either individuals or estates eligible to be S corporation shareholders. An ESBT beneficial interest cannot be purchased; it must be acquired by gift, inheritance, bequest, or transfer in trust. Any person who may receive a distribution of trust principal or income is a potential current beneficiary and each potential current beneficiary is counted as a separate shareholder,
  - Voting trusts,
  - Qualified revocable trusts and estate trusts—But only for the reasonable period of estate administration (Code Sec. 645) or two years,
  - Foreign trusts and custodial arrangements—Foreign trusts are not eligible S corporation shareholders but custodial arrangements under the Uniform Gifts to Minors Act, or Uniform Transfers to Minors Act are eligible shareholders (Rev. Rul. 71-287), and
  - Qualified retirement plan trusts—Qualified retirement plan trusts such as qualified pension plans, profit-sharing plans, and ESOPs are eligible S corporation shareholders (Code Sec. 1361(c)(6)), and
  - Retirement plans such as regular and Roth IRAs, SIMPLEs, and SEPs are not eligible S corporation shareholders.

> **COMMENT**
>
> An unexercised power of appointment is disregarded when determining an ESBT's potential current income beneficiaries.

An ESBT becomes an S corporation shareholder when its trustee makes the election. For income tax purposes, an ESBT is subject to the maximum noncorporate tax rate on its S corporation items, without the benefit of a distribution deduction for items distributed to its beneficiaries. An ESBT's non-S corporation income is treated under general trust income tax rules, which allow for slightly graduated income tax rates and an income distribution deduction for payments made to the trust beneficiaries.

> **COMMENT**
>
> Although the ESBT is a more flexible planning vehicle than the QSST because it allows for multiple beneficiaries and accumulating income, the "price" paid for such flexibility is less favorable rules of income taxation.

> **COMMENT**
>
> Generally, partnerships, LLCs, and C corporations are not eligible S corporation shareholders. However, a single-member LLC may be an eligible S corporation shareholder if the single-member LLC is a disregarded entity (PLR 200008015, November 18, 1999).

An S corporation is an eligible shareholder of another S corporation. However, the parent S corporation must elect under Form 8869 to treat the subsidiary S corporation as a qualified S subsidiary (QSub).

For income tax purposes, the subsidiary S corporation is effectively merged with the parent when the QSub election is made. Thus, the QSub ceases to file a separate tax return and its assets, liabilities, revenue, and expenses are added to the parent S corporation's tax return (Code Sec. 1361(b)(3)).

> **COMMENT**
>
> By filing Form 8869, the QSub essentially adopts a plan of liquidation; thus, it is treated as making a tax-free liquidation under Code Secs. 332 and 337. However, the QSub retains its independent legal corporate existence, but is not required to have a separate FEIN.

The following two major eligibility requirements also apply to structures of S corporations.

An S corporation may only have 100 shareholders. Spouses and other family members may be treated as a single shareholder (Code Sec. 1361(b)(1)(A) and (c)(1)). An estate or trust is generally treated as a single shareholder; all of the beneficiaries are not counted separately. However, each *potential current income beneficiary* of an ESBT is a separate shareholder as is each beneficiary or member of a voting trust (Code Sec. 1361(c)(2)(B)).

Also, an S corporation may only have one class of stock (Code Sec. 1361(b)(1)(D)). When shareholders have different dividend or liquidation rights, two classes of stock exist. However, in the following cases, a second class of stock is not created:

Creating voting and nonvoting shares (Code Sec. 1361(c)(4));

■ Borrowing from a lender regularly engaged in the business of lending money or a person eligible to be an S corporation shareholder, as long as the debt is not convertible into stock and the interest rate is not contingent on profits (Code Sec. 1361(c)(5)); and

■ Existence of:
— Buy-sell agreements,
— Employment agreements with stock appreciation rights, and
— Redemption agreements to purchase stock when a shareholder dies, becomes disabled, or retires—even when the price may depend on voluntary or involuntary termination (PLR 200029050).

Formation Expenses

Start-up expenses generally are amounts paid or incurred for investigating the creation or acquisition of an active trade or business, creating the business and income-producing activities prior to beginning the business. *Start-up expenses* are expenses that would qualify as deductible trade or business expenses if they had been paid or incurred after the business began. Start-up expenses may include salaries, wages, and fees paid employees.

Organizational expenses incident to the creation of a proprietorship (Code Sec. 195) a corporation (Code Sec. 248) or a partnership (Code Sec. 709) generally must be amortized. Organizational expenses include legal and accounting services necessary to the organization of the entity, filing fees paid to register the entity, and fees paid to draft the organizational documents, such as partnership and shareholder agreements.

Taxpayers may deduct up to $5,000 of start-up expenses and up to $5,000 of organizational expenses in the tax year the trade or business begins operating. However, each $5,000 deduction is reduced, but not below zero, by the amount by which the cumulative start-up or organizational expenses exceed $50,000, respectively. The start-up and organizational expenses that are not deductible must be amortized over a 15-year period beginning in the month in which the entity begins to do business (Code Secs. 195(b)(1), 248(a), 709(b)).

Choice of Accounting Period

Generally, partnerships must use the same tax year as the partner(s) owning the majority interest in the partnership. A majority interest is over 50 percent of the partnership's profits and capital (Code Sec. 706(b)). If there is no majority interest, then the partnership must adopt the same tax year as its principal partners with at least a 5 percent interest in the partnership's profits and capital. The final default is the calendar year.

S corporations and personal service corporations usually must use the calendar year for income tax reporting. However, in certain circumstances these entities may elect to use a tax year other than the calendar year.

> **COMMENT**
>
> A *personal service corporation* (PSC) is a C corporation whose principal activity is the performance of professional services in health, engineering, law, architecture, accounting, actuarial science, performing arts, or consulting and whose stock is owned by the employee-owners who perform the services.

An entity with a substantial business purpose may adopt a *natural business year*—a period that ends immediately after the expiration of its peak business period. A *peak business period* is one in which the entity receives 25 percent of its gross receipts in the last two months of the natural business year (Rev. Procs. 2002-37 and 38).

Three-Month Deferral Election (Code Sec. 444)

A partnership, personal service corporation, or S corporation may elect to defer its tax year for three months as an *alternate tax year*. The IRS does not approve this election automatically. The IRS will disallow an election when an existing entity requests a deferral period longer than the deferral period being changed (Reg. § 1.444-1T(b)(1)). The *deferral period* is the number of months between the last day of the elected tax year and the last day of the required tax year.

> **EXAMPLE**
>
> Sam's Inc., an S corporation, has a required calendar tax year. Sam's elects a tax year ending on September 30 under Code Sec. 444. Sam's deferral period is three months, the number of months between September 30 and December 31.

For income tax reporting purposes, a C corporation may use a:
- Calendar year;
- Fiscal year; or
- 52-53 week year.

STUDY QUESTIONS

5. When an owner purchases equipment, transfers ownership of the purchases to his or her business, and receives boot in the exchange, which entity type is *not* taxed on the boot?

   a. C corporation
   b. Sole proprietorship
   c. S corporation

6. Which type of trust is *not* eligible to be an S corporation shareholder?

   a. Electing small business trust
   b. Foreign trust
   c. IRA, SIMPLE plan, or SEP

OPERATING TAX ISSUES

Different tax issues arise from operating a business as a sole proprietorship than as a corporation or a partnership. The taxation of compensation and fringe benefits, tax reporting requirements, accounting method, and tax period options generally depend on the type of entity operating the business. Weighing the value of each of these factors to the business in its operations should form part of the decision surrounding an initial choice of business entity or the later decision over whether to change forms as the business develops.

Sole Proprietorships

A sole proprietorship is not an entity separate from its owner. A sole proprietor reports all business income and expenses on Schedule C of Form 1040. The proprietor is taxed at ordinary income tax rates on the total net income from the business. A sole proprietor may deduct all ordinary and necessary business expenses, including reasonable compensation to employees.

When the business sustains a loss that is not limited by the at-risk rules or the passive activity loss limitations, it may be used to offset other income of the owner (Code Secs. 465 and 469). An excess loss may be carried back or forward according to the net operating loss carryback and carryforward rules.

> **COMMENT**
>
> When one spouse materially participates in the business activity, the other spouse is also considered to materially participate for tax purposes (Code Sec. 469(h)(6)).

A sole proprietor is an owner, not an employee, of the business. Thus, the owner's compensation is not a business expense and is not reported on Form W-2. Also, because the sole proprietor is not an employee, the proprietor's fringe benefits may not be deductible.

A sole proprietor may set up a retirement benefit plan such as a SEP, SIMPLE, or defined benefit Keogh plan to which the owner makes deductible contributions. A sole proprietorship may also set up a defined benefit plan that provides an annual retirement benefit. However, such plans generally must cover all the business's full-time employees.

A sole proprietor pays self-employment tax on the business's net income. A sole proprietor must make quarterly estimated payments that include income, self-employment, and Medicare taxes on Form 1040-ES.

> **COMMENT**
>
> The Medicare tax is imposed at a 2.9 percent rate on net business income without any limitation. Self-employment tax is imposed at 12.4 percent on net business income exceeding $400 up to the yearly wage base. The sole proprietor takes an above-the-line credit for one-half of the self-employment tax on page 1 of Form 1040.

> **COMMENT**
>
> Self-employment tax is calculated and reported using Schedule SE of Form 1040.

The basis of property converted from personal to business use is the lesser of its fair market value or its adjusted basis when converted (Reg. §1.167(a)(5)).

The sale of a sole proprietorship is an asset sale, not a sale of the business entity. Thus, the tax consequences of the sale depend on whether the assets are capital assets, depreciable assets, real property used in a trade or business, or ordinary income property. The sale price must be allocated among all of the assets sold, including goodwill.

Partnerships

As an entity separate from its owners, the partnership is a conduit or pass-through entity. The partnership's income, gain, deductions, losses, and credits are taken into account by the partners separately, and each partner is taxed on that partner's share of the partnership's tax items (Code Sec. 702).

Any income, gain, loss, deduction, or credit is allocated to the partners based on the terms of the partnership agreement. If the agreement is silent as to allocations, each partner's share is based on the percentage of partnership interest (Reg. §1.704-1(b)(2)). However, a partnership may allocate items of income, gain, loss, deduction, or credit proportionately or disproportionately as long as the allocation has substantial economic effect, and if family members are involved, the allocation satisfies the family partnership rules.

> **COMMENT**
>
> The opportunity to make special allocations may enable a partnership to return cash to a partner who contributed cash before sharing profits with a service partner or to allocate income to partners in the lowest income tax brackets. Alternatively, losses may be allocated to provide tax benefits to certain partners.

A partnership must report its income and deductions using the required tax year, usually the calendar year, unless the IRS has approved an alternative tax year (Code Secs. 444 and 706).

Generally, a partnership may use either the cash or accrual method of accounting. However, partnerships with gross receipts exceeding $5 million and a C corporation partner must use the accrual method (Code Sec. 448).

> **COMMENT**
>
> A partnership must file an entity-level tax return on Form 1065.

Each partner's share of the partnership's tax items is reported on Schedule K-1. Individual partners annually report the items from Schedule K-1 on Schedule E of Form 1040.

Partners may deduct partnership losses to the extent of their basis in the partnership. Partners' loss deductions are also limited by the at-risk and passive activity loss rules (Code Secs. 465 and 469). Generally, a partner's at-risk amount equals the partner's contributions to the partnership plus a share of the partnership's recourse debt.

Employment taxes. A general partner's share of income and loss from a partnership engaged in a trade or business is net income from self-employment

(Code Sec. 1402(a)). Generally, partnership income generated by dividends, interest, capital gains, and rent is not self-employment income unless the partner in a real estate partnership provides 500 or more hours of services to the partnership. Then, the rent is considered self-employment income.

Limited partnerships. Distributions to limited partners or LLC members are not self-employment income when at least a portion of the partner's distribution is attributable to return of capital. However, guaranteed payments for services rendered to or on behalf of a partnership or LLC engaged in a trade or business are included in a limited partner's net earnings from self-employment (Reg. § 1.1402(a)-2(g)).

Limited partners are not subject to self-employment tax unless:

- The partner has personal liability for the debts of or claims against the partnership by reason of being a partner;
- The partner has authority under state law to enter into contracts on behalf of the partnership; or
- The partner participated in the trade or business for more than 500 hours during the partnerships tax year (Reg. § 1.1402(a)-2(h)).

Even if none of the above applies, a limited partner may be subject to self-employment tax if he or she:

- Receives guaranteed payments for services rendered; or
- Is a service partner in a service partnership.

A *service partnership* is a partnership in which substantially all of the activities involve performing services in the fields of health, law, engineering, architecture, accounting, actuarial science, or consulting (Prop. Reg. §§ 1.1402(a)-2(h)(5) and (6)).

Limited Liability Companies (LLCs)

Because LLCs may choose to be tax as sole proprietorships, partnerships, or corporations, the rules that apply to LLCs depend on the entity's classification election or its default classification. For example, when the LLC defaults or elects to be taxed as a partnership, the rules that apply to partnerships apply to the LLC.

Management. In a manager-managed LLC, the manager is the "general partner" who is subject to self-employment tax. In a member-managed LLC arguably all the members are "general partners" subject to self-employment tax because all of the members have authority under state law to enter into contracts on behalf of the entity.

Like service partners in a service partnership, service members of a service LLC are subject to self-employment tax (Prop. Reg. §1.1402(a)-2(h)(5)).

LLC passive activity losses. The IRS's position is that the activities of an LLC or LLP member are presumed to be passive activities subject to the rules for limited partners because the members enjoy limited liability. However, several courts have rejected the IRS's position, finding that LLC and LLP members are more analogous to general partners whose activities require a facts and circumstances analysis under Code Sec. 469(h)(2) to determine the extent of each member's material participation (*Garnett*, 132 TC No. 19 (2009) and *Thomson*, FedCl, 2009-2 USTC ¶50,501).

> **COMMENT**
>
> Under these rulings, LLC and LLP members may enjoy limited liability and not be restricted by the passive activity loss rules like limited partners.

C Corporations

A C corporation is a separate taxpayer. A C corporation's net taxable income is taxed at the entity level, subject to a graduated rate that ranges from 15 percent to 35 percent. C corporations with taxable income of between $75,000 and $10 million have an effective tax rate of 34 percent. C corporations with taxable income exceeding $10 million have an effective tax rate of 35 percent.

Any C corporation distributions are taxed to shareholders as dividends. Thus, C corporations are "double-tax" entities; the income is taxed at both the entity and owner level.

Alternative minimum tax. C corporations may also be liable for the corporate alternative minimum tax (AMT). The corporate AMT rate is 20 percent of the corporation's alternative minimum taxable income (AMTI) and there is a $40,000 exemption. The exemption phases out for corporations with AMTI of between $150,000 and $300,000 (Code Secs. 53-59).

Corporate AMT does not apply to small business C corporations that have gross receipts less than $5 million in its first tax year after December 31, 1996, and continue to have average gross receipts less than $7.5 million.

Capital gains. A C corporation's capital gains that exceed capital losses are taxed at regular corporate tax rates. A C corporation may not deduct capital losses; however, excess capital losses may be carried back three years and forward five years to offset capital gains in those years (Code Sec. 1211(a)(1)).

Losses. A C corporation's shareholders may not deduct the corporation's operating losses. Instead, the corporation deducts the losses to offset the entity's income. A C corporation's excess net operating losses (NOLs) generally may be carried back 2 years and carried forward 20 years (Code Sec. 172).

> **COMMENT**
>
> Special rules allow 2008 NOLs sustained by certain small business corporations, partnerships, or sole proprietorships to be carried back up to five years if the business has average gross receipts for the last three years of less than $15 million. For the 2009 tax year, NOLs may be carried back up to five years regardless of the business's gross receipts.

A C corporation's NOL deduction may be limited if there is a more than 50 percent change of ownership over a three-year period (Code Sec. 182).

C corporations that are not personal service or closely held corporations may deduct passive activity losses against their income without limitation (Code Sec. 469(a)(2)).

Fringe benefits. Shareholder-employees of a C corporation are eligible for certain employee fringe benefits. A C corporation may deduct payments for these benefits and they are not included in the employee's income. C corporation shareholders are not subject to self-employment tax on dividends received; however, employee-shareholders' wages are subject to income and employment tax withholding. A C corporation employer must pay the employer's portion of employment taxes. The employer's portion of the employment taxes is deductible as an ordinary and necessary business expense.

Qualified personal service corporations. A *qualified personal service corporation* (PSC) is a corporation whose:
- Principal activity is the performance of personal services by employee-shareholders (Code Sec. 269A);
- Employee-shareholders spend at least 95 percent of their time performing services in the fields of health, law, engineering, accounting, architecture, actuarial science, performing arts, or consulting; and
- Stock is held by employees, or retired employees or their estates (Code Sec. 448).

An employee-shareholder is any employee who owns more than 10 percent of the outstanding stock of the PSC on any day during the tax year.

The taxable income of a qualified personal service corporation is subject to a flat tax rate of 35 percent (Code Sec. 11(b)(2)).

Avoiding double taxation. There are several ways for employee-shareholders of C corporations or PSCs to avoid double taxation. The most common tactic is to pay all of the corporation's income to the employees as compensation.

Employee compensation is deductible as an ordinary and necessary business expense and ordinary income to the employee-shareholders.

However, the compensation paid to employee-shareholders must be "reasonable" or the corporation may not claim the compensation deduction. In this case, the excess "compensation" is a nondeductible dividend to the employee-shareholder.

EXAMPLE

Morris Wetherby and his partner Larry Halverston's law practice is a PSC. In 2009, Adam and Larry's business netted $300,000 before compensating the two partners. If Morris and Larry each received compensation of $100,000, the PSC would have a $35,000 tax liability (taxable income of $100,000 × 35% flat tax). However, if Morris and Larry each receive compensation of $150,000, the PSC has no taxable income.

COMMENT

Minimizing the overall tax liability requires calculating not only the PSC's taxes but also Adam and Larry's tax liability. Depending on the individual's ordinary income tax rates, the dividend rate and employment tax rates, it may or may not be cheaper to pay the tax at the corporate level.

Another way to avoid double taxation is to lease real estate owned by an employee-shareholder that the corporation needs to use or to license employee-shareholder patents or copyrights. The lease or licensing payments must be reasonable and the transactions should be structured as bona fide, arm's-length transactions. When the rules are followed, the corporation may deduct the lease or licensing payments as ordinary and necessary business expenses and the employee-shareholder includes the payments as ordinary income.

CAUTION

A shareholder who rents property to a controlled corporation has nonpassive income but passive losses (Code Sec. 469).

Accumulated earnings tax. One way *not* to avoid double taxation of C corporation income is to accumulate the income in the C corporation. Excess accumulated C corporation income is subject to the accumulated earnings tax (AET), which is imposed at a flat 15 percent rate on the corporation's accumulated taxable income. The AET is imposed in addition to the regular corporate income tax.

Personal holding company tax. A C corporation's undistributed personal holding company income is subject to the 15 percent personal holding company tax.

A C corporation is a personal holding company when:

- Five or fewer individuals own, directly or constructively, more than 50 percent of the corporation's outstanding stock at any time during the last one-half of the tax year; and
- At least 60 percent of the corporation's adjusted gross income is personal holding company income.

Personal holding company income is passive investment income, such as:

- Dividends;
- Interest;
- Royalties;
- Annuities;
- Personal service contracts when the contract specifies the person to perform the services;
- Certain rents; and
- Trust and estate income.

Tax-exempt interest and certain royalties from minerals, oil, gas, or copyrights are not included (Code Secs. 542(a), 543(a)(7)).

The personal holding company tax can be avoided by keeping the C corporation's passive income below the 60 percent threshold or by reducing the C corporation's adjusted gross income by increasing compensation payments or dividends (Code Sec. 574).

S Corporations

Like a partnership, an S corporation is a pass-through entity. An S corporation may use any permissible method of accounting, including the cash method. An S corporation's default tax year is a calendar year. However, an S corporation may choose a fiscal year if doing so has a valid business purpose and the corporation can demonstrate a different natural tax year. An S corporation may also choose a fiscal year ending on September 30, October 31, or November 30 if it makes a Code Sec. 444 election and the required payments.

The S corporation's income, gain, loss, deductions, and credits are allocated to the shareholders based on their percentage of stock ownership and the number of days in the tax year the shareholders owned their stock. These items also retain their character when passed through to the shareholders (Code Secs. 1366(a) and (b)).

Pass-through items must be separately stated if the items could affect the shareholder's tax liability (Code Sec. 1366(a)(1)(a)).

S corporation shareholders report their pro rata share of the corporation's gross income and deductions in the shareholders' tax year that coincides with the end of the S corporation's tax year.

Employment taxes. S corporation shareholders are not subject to self-employment tax on dividends or pass-through income received from the corporation. However, when the shareholder is also an employee of the S corporation, then the employee-shareholder must be paid "reasonable compensation."

> **COMMENT**
>
> In this context, the S corporation reduces the employee-shareholder's compensation in order to avoid wage-based employment taxes. However, if the IRS believes that the employee-shareholder's compensation is too low, it will attempt to reallocate dividend income to compensation.

An S corporation shareholder's loss deduction is limited to the shareholder's basis in the S corporation's stock. The shareholder's basis in S corporation stock is calculated using these steps:

1. Cash contributed in exchange for S corporation stock; plus
2. Shareholder's basis in property contributed to the S corporation in exchange for stock; minus
3. Shareholder liabilities assumed by the S corporation; minus
4. Encumbrances on shareholder property contributed to the S corporation.

To deduct losses, a shareholder's basis also includes any loans made by the shareholder to the corporation (Code Sec. 1366(d)(2)). This includes amounts shareholders borrow from a bank and relend to the S corporation. However, an S corporation shareholder's basis is not increased by loans made to the corporation by others or by the shareholder's guarantees of such loans or by other corporate liabilities.

An S corporation shareholder's basis is increased by pass-through items of income and decreased by distributions and pass-through losses and expenses (Code Sec. 1367(a)). Pass-through deductions and losses reduce a shareholder's stock basis and then reduce a stockholder's debt basis.

> **COMMENT**
>
> A shareholder with insufficient basis may not deduct a pass-through loss; however, the loss may be carried forward indefinitely.

> **CAUTION**
>
> S corporation losses may also be limited by the *at-risk rules* (Code Sec. 465). After the at-risk rules are applied, the S corporation's losses may still be limited by the passive activity loss rules. The passive activity loss rules apply if the shareholder does not materially participate in the S corporation's business. Material participation means regular, continuous, and substantial involvement in the S corporation's trade or business (Code Sec. 469).

Fringe benefits. A more-than-2-percent S corporation shareholder must include the value of any fringe benefits provided by the S corporation in income as wages. A *more-than-2-percent shareholder* is any person who owns more than 2 percent of the S corporation's outstanding stock or more than 2 percent of the total combined voting power of all S corporation stock on any day during the S corporation's tax year.

> **COMMENT**
>
> Under the fringe benefit rules, the spouse of a more-than-2-percent S corporation shareholder is also a more-than-2-percent shareholder (Rev. Rul. 91-26).

Taxes imposed on S corporations. Generally, as a pass-through entity, an S corporation is not subject to corporate level tax on its income. However, in certain circumstances S corporations may be liable for corporate level taxes. S corporations may be subject to corporate-level tax for built-in gains on C corporation property transferred to an S corporation in a conversion, on excess passive investment income, and in LIFO recapture.

The built-in gains tax on C to S conversions. The built-in gains tax applies to C corporations that convert to S corporations. Through this tax, the new S corporation may not avoid corporate-level tax on gain in appreciated assets acquired before the conversion. The built-in gains tax may apply to the accumulated gain in all assets held on the date the C corporation elects to be taxed as an S corporation.

The built-in gains tax is triggered when a converted S corporation disposes of appreciated C corporation assets within a specified period of time. Generally, that period is 10 year from the C to S conversion date. However, the *American Recovery and Reinvestment Act of 2009* shortened the holding period temporarily for dispositions in tax years beginning in 2009 and 2010. The *Small Business Jobs Act of 2010* shortens that period even more, to five years but only in the case of dispositions in any tax year beginning in 2011, provided the fifth year in the recognition period precedes the tax year beginning in 2011. The disposition may be a sale or exchange of capital assets, inventory, and other property.

It is also triggered when cash-basis C corporation accounts receivable are collected by the converted S corporation.

The applicable holding period begins with the first day of the S corporation's first tax year.

The built-in gains tax rate is the highest tax rate under Code Sec. 11(b) (currently at 35 percent), without taking into account the 5-percent surcharge.

> **COMMENT**
>
> In order to avoid overpaying the built-in gains tax, a converting C corporation should value all of its assets, including goodwill and going concern value, as of the date of conversion. It may also be prudent to value these assets regularly after the conversion.

Generally, C corporation loss carryforwards cannot be used to offset S corporation income earned after the date the S election becomes effective. However, such carryforwards may be used to offset taxable built-in gains.

Passive investment income tax. The *passive investment income tax* (PIIT) is imposed on a converted S corporation's excess net passive investment income at the highest corporate tax rate, 35 percent. The PIIT may be imposed on a converted S corporation or an S corporation that received carryover C corporation attributes in a reorganization. The tax applies only when the S corporation has earnings and profits; it cannot be imposed in a loss year.

The PIIT does not apply to corporations that have been S corporations since inception.

Passive investment income is gross receipts from dividends, rents, interest, royalties, and annuities (Code Sec. 1362(d)(3)).

> **COMMENT**
>
> Under the *Small Business and Work Opportunity Tax Act of 2007*, gains from the sale or exchange of stock or securities are no longer passive investment income. However, if the sale or exchange occurs within the applicable holding period after the S conversion (10, 7, or 5 years, as discussed above), the built-in gains tax will apply.

Net passive investment income is passive investment income reduced by the deductions allowed for expenses incurred in the production of such income.

Excess net passive investment income arises when gross receipts from passive investment income exceed 25 percent of the corporation's total gross receipts (Code Sec. 1375(b)).

If an S corporation holds C corporation earnings and profits for three consecutive tax years and also has passive investment income in excess of 25 percent of its gross receipts for each of those years, the S election terminates as a matter of law as of the first day of the succeeding tax year (Code Sec. 1362(d)).

> **COMMENT**
>
> To avoid a legal termination, the S corporation should distribute any C corporation earnings and profits.

LIFO recapture tax. A converted S corporation may be subject to the LIFO recapture tax if its predecessor C corporation used the LIFO inventory method for its last tax year prior to electing S status. The tax is imposed on the LIFO recapture amount. The LIFO recapture amount is the excess of the inventory's value under FIFO and the inventory's value under LIFO. The LIFO recapture amount is included in the corporation's gross income in its final C corporation year.

STUDY QUESTIONS

7. Small business C corporations are not subject to corporate alternative minimum tax if their annual average gross receipts total less than:

a. $1 million
b. $7.5 million
c. $10 million

8. The accumulated earnings tax is applied to a C corporation:

a. Having excess undistributed income
b. During its conversion to an S corporation
c. As a means of avoiding double taxation on the corporation's income

DISPOSING OF A BUSINESS

At some point business owners—whether sole proprietors, partners, shareholders, or LLC members—will want or need to dispose of their interest in a business entity. Disposition of a business interest may require careful planning to avoid or reduce any tax liability that may result. Sometimes, as a business matures, reconsideration of the form of doing business may be made precisely for the purpose of looking toward its eventual sale or transfer to a younger family member.

Sole Proprietorships

The owner of a sole proprietorship may sell or transfer the business's *assets* to another person or entity. However, the owner may not sell or transfer his or her *interest* in the business because the business is not a separate entity. Thus, the new owner must establish a new sole proprietorship.

A sole proprietorship has no single asset called "the business." Each asset sold or transferred is treated as if it were sold or transferred separately. The sale price must be allocated among all of the assets sold or transferred. The cost basis of each asset determines whether there is a gain or loss and the character of the asset determines whether the gain or loss is ordinary or capital and whether there is any recapture.

The owner's sale of a sole proprietorship's assets is reported on Form 4797, *Sales of Business Property,* and Schedule D of Form 1040. The selling proprietor also files a final Schedule C for the last year of the business's operation. There are no adverse tax consequences when a sole proprietor simply ceases doing business.

Partnerships

A partner who disposes of a partnership interest disposes of a single asset, not the partner's pro rata share of each of the partnership's assets. Generally, a partner's gain or loss on the disposition of a partnership interest is the difference between the amount realized and the partner's outside basis in the partnership interest immediately before the disposition (Code Sec. 1.741-1(a)).

As a general rule, when a partner sells a partnership interest:

- The selling partner's gain or loss is capital in nature (but, see the later discussion of "hot assets");
- The selling partner's gain is long- or short-term depending on how long the partner held the partnership interest (Code Sec. 1223); and
- The amount of any liability assumed by the purchaser or forgiven is realized on the sale of the partnership interest.

The selling partner counts the partnership's liabilities when computing the amount realized on the sale of a partnership interest and the adjusted basis of the interest sold. The purchaser includes any assumed indebtedness as a part of the consideration paid for the partnership interest (Reg. § 1.752).

> **COMMENT**
>
> This rule applies even if the liability is nonrecourse (Code Sec. 7701(g)).

The sale of a partnership interest by a partner with a negative capital account may result in recognition of a greater amount of gain than the cash or other property received for the interest. A partner's basis in a partnership interest is never negative, so that relief from a negative capital account may be viewed as relief from liability or a distribution of cash (Code Secs. 704 and 752).

Hot assets. When a partner sells an interest in a partnership with Code Sec. 751 property—so-called hot assets—the general rules change. Instead of selling a single asset, a partner selling an interest in a partnership with hot assets is treated as selling the *pro rata* share of the partnership's hot assets separately. The portion of the purchase price received by the seller for the hot assets is ordinary income or loss. The remaining purchase price is capital gain or loss.

Hot assets include:

- The rights to payment for goods delivered or to be delivered to the extent the proceeds do not arise from the sale or exchange of a capital asset;
- The rights to payment for services rendered or to be rendered;
- The amount of ordinary income that the partnership would be required to include in income under the various IRC recapture provisions; and
- Inventory items and other noncapital assets.

> **COMMENT**
>
> When a partnership interest is sold, all inventory items are treated as a hot asset subject to ordinary income treatment, without regard to the relationship of its value to its cost.

A partner's exchange of a partnership interest for an interest in another partnership is a taxable event. The exchange results in the partner's recognition of gain or loss as if the transaction was a sale.

> **COMMENT**
>
> This rule applies even if the two partnerships have similar businesses, assets, and liabilities. Code Sec. 1031, which generally provides for tax-free treatment of like-kind exchanges, does not apply to exchanges of partnership interests (Code Sec. 1031(a)(2)(D)).

Distributions of partnership property (nonliquidating). A partner does not recognize gain upon receipt of a nonliquidating distribution from a partnership of property other than money. However, a distributee partner must recognize gain to the extent that any money distributed exceeds the adjusted basis of the distributee's interest in the partnership.

> **COMMENT**
>
> The fair market value of marketable securities is considered money for these purposes (Code Sec. 731).

Generally, a distributee partner's gain as the result of a current distribution is capital gain. It is treated as a sale or exchange of a portion of the partner's partnership interest. However, if the gain is attributable to hot assets, it is treated as ordinary income (Code Sec. 731(a) and (c)(6)). Similarly, a distribution to a partner within seven years of the partner's contributing appreciated property to the partnership is taxed as if the appreciated property had been sold (Code Sec. 737).

The distributee partner's basis in property distributed in a nonliquidating distribution equals the lesser of:

- The partnership's adjusted basis in the distributed property; or
- The partner's adjusted basis in the partnership interest minus any cash distributed in the transaction.

The distributee partner's adjusted basis in the partnership interest is reduced by any money received and the basis of property distributed to the partner in a nonliquidating distribution (Code Secs. 731, 732, and 733).

Neither the distributee partner nor the partnership may recognize a loss in connection with a current distribution of cash or property (Code Secs. 731(a)(2) and (b)). The partnership does not recognize gain on a distribution of money or other property to a partner (Code Sec. 731(b)).

Corporations

As a general rule, a seller prefers to *sell corporation stock*. This allows all of the business's attributes to pass from seller to buyer, results in liabilities passing to the buyer, and avoids double taxation of the seller.

A buyer prefers to *purchase the assets* of the seller rather than the corporation's stock. This allows the buyer to select those assets of the seller it desires to acquire and the liabilities it is willing to assume, while avoiding any responsibility for liabilities not assumed. From the tax standpoint, the buyer will prefer to purchase assets so as to acquire a basis in the purchased assets equal to the purchase price paid for depreciation purposes.

Taxable asset acquisitions. An asset sale creates a single level of tax to an individual, a sole proprietorship, or a pass-through entity seller. If the seller is a C corporation, there will be immediate tax liability at the corporate level and also likely additional level of tax at the shareholder level when the selling corporation is liquidated and the consideration distributed to the shareholders. When the seller is an S corporation, there is usually one level of tax to the shareholder, but there may also be a corporate level tax if any of the assets sold are C corporation assets to which the built-in gain rules of Code Sec. 1374 apply.

An asset buyer receives a cost basis in the assets acquired. However, the buyer does not receive any of the tax attributes of the selling corporation. These attributes are lost if the selling corporation is liquidated or remain with the seller if there is no liquidation.

Allocation rules. The asset acquisition rules apply to all taxable acquisitions of a trade or business, including deemed asset sales under Code Sec. 338. These rules do not apply to nontaxable asset acquisitions because the buyer's basis in nontaxable acquired assets is determined by the target's basis in such assets (Code Sec. 1060).

Taxable stock acquisitions. In a taxable stock acquisition, the selling shareholder realizes gain or loss regardless of whether the corporation is a C or an S corporation. The buyer in a taxable stock acquisition acquires a cost basis in the acquired stock. However, the acquired corporation's basis in its own assets and its tax attributes—that is, operating or capital losses, deductions, credits, and carryovers—are not affected by the sale. Nevertheless, the buyer may face serious restrictions on using the acquired tax attributes, particularly if they are not net operating loss carryovers.

Because the acquired corporation does not recognize gain or loss on the stock sale, the inherent gain in the corporation's assets remains to be taxed to the buyer. For tax purposes, it may be possible to treat a stock acquisition as an asset acquisition by making a special Code Sec. 338 election. Such an election could require the buyer to recognize an immediate income tax liability as its cost for gaining an increased basis in the targets corporation's assets.

When a buyer acquires a group of assets in a single transaction, the purchase price must be allocated among the acquired assets. Assets acquired in a business purchase typically include:

- Inventory;
- Land;
- Depreciable property such as machinery, equipment, and buildings;
- Intangible property, such as copyrights, patents, trademarks, licenses, and software; and
- Goodwill or going concern value.

Nontaxable asset acquisitions. In a nontaxable asset acquisition, the buyer acquires the seller's assets in exchange for the buyer's stock. In this case, the seller's shareholders do not recognize any gain or loss. Any gain inherent in the acquired corporation's assets remains with the corporation, now owned by the buyer. Where some consideration other than stock is used in the acquisition—that is, boot—the seller is taxed on the amount of boot received.

Nontaxable stock acquisitions. In a nontaxable stock acquisition, the buyer transfers stock of the acquiring corporation to the shareholders of the target corporation in exchange for their stock in the target company. The selling shareholders do not recognize any gain or loss. The tax attributes of the target and the target's basis in its assets are not affected by the transaction. The buyer's basis in the target's stock carries over from the relinquished stock. There may be limitations on the buyer's ability to use the target's tax attributes.

STUDY QUESTIONS

9. A converted S corporation must pay passive investment income tax if:

   a. The S corporation received carryover C corporation attributes during a reorganization

   b. The former C corporation has no earnings and profits as an S corporation

   c. Its gains arise from the sale or exchange of stock or securities

10. In a nontaxable asset acquisition:

    a. The buyer's basis is determined by the target's basis in the assets

    b. The buyer acquires the seller's assets without receiving stock

    c. The seller's shareholders defer recognition of gain or loss

CONCLUSION

It is important to recognize the different types of business entities and their different levels of organizational complexity, owner liability, and tax issues. Each of the five basic types of business entity are organized based on state law and are assigned their federal income tax status by the Internal Revenue Code. These entities may have a different tax status and reporting requirements in their state of organization, which makes choosing a business entity more difficult. Special attention should be given to the type of business owner and business. A high-liability business may want to choose an entity that provides greater liability protection; a low-liability business may want simpler organizational and reporting requirements. Each entity type must be carefully weighed for its benefits and disadvantages before making the final choice.

CPE NOTE: When you have completed your study and review of chapters 1-3, which comprise Module 1, you may wish to take the Quizzer for this Module.

For your convenience, you can also take this Quizzer online at **www.cchtestingcenter.com.**

Wealth Building Under Changing Tax Laws

This chapter explores some of the key provisions of the U.S. tax code that can foster or hinder individual wealth building. As a taxpayer's income increases, the ability to reduce taxes through planning becomes more complex. Adding to the complexity is uncertainty over the long-term fate of reduced individual tax rates and capital gains/dividends tax rates, repeal or modification of the federal estate tax, new Medicare taxes for higher income individuals, and more.

LEARNING OBJECTIVES

Upon completion of this chapter, you will be able to:

- Identify changes to the individual marginal income tax rates scheduled to take effect after 2010 and possible legislative initiatives to mitigate those changes;

- Describe the impact of the alternative minimum tax (AMT) on higher-income taxpayers;

- Understand changes to the Medicare tax effective after 2012 for higher-income taxpayers

- Understand the advantages and disadvantages of converting a traditional IRA to a Roth IRA available to higher-income taxpayers in 2010 and beyond;

- Identify the taxpayer-friendly attributes of health savings accounts (HSAs) and important changes to HSAs in 2011; and

- Describe repeal of the federal estate tax for 2010.

INTRODUCTION

The U.S. tax code has been both praised and criticized for various provisions that may allow taxpayers to build up wealth with minimal or no tax consequences. Despite news stories about taxpayers exploiting so-called loopholes and evading taxation, the vast majority of taxpayers having taxable income report and pay tax on that income. There are, however, legitimate tax reduction strategies. For 2011, several challenges may commence. Individual marginal tax rates are scheduled to rise significantly after December 31, 2010, for higher-income taxpayers. Tax rates on capital gains and dividends likewise are set to increase. Congress may provide for alternative minimum tax (AMT) relief, but its progress is hampered by large federal government deficits. The federal estate tax, abolished for 2010 unless Congress acts to retroactively reinstate it, is set to return for 2011 at dramatically lower exemption amounts. The health care reform package places new limits on health savings accounts (HSAs). Beyond 2012, the health care reform package increases Medicare taxes for higher-income taxpayers.

INDIVIDUAL MARGINAL INCOME TAX RATES

Under the U.S. graduated or progressive system of taxation, taxpayers are taxed at higher marginal tax rates as their taxable income increases. As a point of reference, tax practitioners frequently divide application of individual income tax rates into three periods: pre-EGTRRA, EGTRRA, and post-EGTRRA, with EGTRRA being an abbreviation for the *Economic Growth and Tax Relief Reconciliation Act of 2001*, a tax law that ushered in a 10-year sea change reduction of rates across the board.

Pre-EGTRRA

Between 1993 and early 2001, individuals and estates and trusts were subject to one of five tax rates of 15, 28, 31, 36, or 39.6 percent. Each tax rate applied to a range of income called a *bracket*, with higher rates applying to higher brackets.

EGTRRA

On June 7, 2001, President Bush signed the *Economic Growth and Tax Relief Reconciliation Act of 2001* (EGTRRA) into law. The signing set in motion the gradual reduction of the individual marginal income tax rates through December 31, 2010. Although all of the individual marginal income tax rates were reduced under EGTRRA, the greatest reduction and the reduction (and ultimate elimination) of the overall limitation on itemized deductions benefited taxpayers in the top bracket.

The EGTRRA rates, as continued through 2010, subject individuals and estates and trusts to one of six tax rates of 10, 15, 25, 28, 33, or 35 percent. In addition to an across-the-board reduction in the regular income tax brackets, EGTRRA ushered in an era of lower capital gains rates, reducing the highest rate from 20 to 15 percent and applying that rate to most dividend distributions as well.

> **COMMENT**
>
> EGTRRA should not be confused with JGTRRA, which is short for the *Jobs and Growth Tax Relief Reconciliation Act of 2003*. Basically, JGTRRA did for the capital gains tax rates what EGTRRA did for the individual income tax brackets: lower them significantly. JGTRRA reduced the maximum rate on net capital gains and taxed qualifying dividends at that same low rate.

Post-EGTRRA

As this chapter goes to press, Congress is expected to keep the tax rates for 2011 at 2010 levels for taxpayers in the 10- through 28-percent brackets. Those with taxable income within the two highest rate brackets will likely see their rates jump from 33 and 35 percent to 36 and 39.6 percent.

The dollar brackets to which the 2011 rates will apply basically are anticipated to track the 2010 bracket amounts, adjusted upward for inflation as is done every year, but with two possible changes:

- The Obama Administration wants the new 36-percent bracket to start at a higher amount, not to apply until income reaches $200,000 for single filers and $250,000 for joint returns (rather than what would be an inflation-adjusted bracket levels imposed at $176,000 and $314,250, respectively); and
- Marriage penalty relief provided for filers within the middle-income brackets, which is also scheduled to sunset after 2010, would need to be specifically extended by Congress.

> **COMMENT**
>
> Wealth building for individuals necessarily focuses on tax rates and brackets. Individuals should take a look at their total tax liability projected over a number of years to increase overall wealth.

Additional Rate Increase Post-2012

Higher-income individuals also need to keep in mind changes to Medicare taxation under the health care reform package. The revised Medicare taxation rules apply to tax years beginning after December 31, 2012. The health care reform package imposes an additional 0.9-percent Medicare tax on the wages and self-employment income of qualified taxpayers received with respect to employment for tax years beginning after December 31, 2012. Moreover, the health care reform package also imposes, effective for tax years beginning after December 31, 2012, a 3.8-percent Medicare tax on the lesser of an individual's net investment income for the tax year or modified AGI in excess of $200,000 ($250,000 in the case of married couples filing a joint return). These new Medicare taxes are discussed later in this chapter.

Impact on Business Activities

The individual income tax rates apply to all income received by individuals. This includes wages, pass-through income from S corporations or partnerships, or net earnings of sole proprietorships.

According to Congress' Joint Committee on Taxation (JCT), approximately 750,000 taxpayers with net positive business income (3 percent of all taxpayers with net positive business income) will have marginal rates of 36 percent or 39.6 percent under the president's proposal. Fifty percent of the approximately $1 trillion of aggregate net positive business income will be reported on returns that have a marginal rate of 36 percent or 39.6 percent, JCT predicted.

PLANNING POINTER

The rate increase to 36 percent and 39.6 percent may encourage taxpayers currently doing business as an S corporation to convert to C corporation status. One disincentive to convert to a C corporation is the expected rise in dividend taxes after 2010. The current 15-percent tax rate on dividends received will sunset after December 31, 2010, to be replaced by rates keyed to the taxpayer's regular income tax bracket unless Congress continues the treatment of dividends as taxed at the same rates as capital gains. (At press time, it is anticipated that Congress will respond and extend this dividend treatment, which will call for a 20-percent rate for individuals in the new 36- and 39.6-percent brackets and 15 percent for all others.) The short-term benefits of a switch of entity classification to C corporation status, however, should not be done without consideration of a company's long-term goals. Generally, once an S corporation converts to a C corporation, it cannot switch back within the next five tax years.

COMMENT

Business income for purposes of the JCT's analysis consists of income from:

- Sole proprietorships (Schedule C);
- Rental real estate, royalties, partnerships, S corporations, estates and trusts, and real estate mortgage investment conduits (Schedule E);
- Farms (Schedule F).

Not counted as "business income" is income from interest, dividends, or capital gains that may flow through certain pass-through entities.

IMPACT ON PERSONAL TAX PLANNING

Generally, many traditional planning techniques that apply to individuals expecting to be in a higher tax bracket in a future year because of higher income levels would apply to planning for the projected increase in the 33- and 35-percent rates. Techniques that involve the timing of income or deductible expenses in one tax year or another remain applicable. However, in anticipating the rate and bracket amount changes likely to apply to higher-income taxpayers in 2011, planning should not just follow a traditional guideline that income and deductions generally should be evened out between years so that tax liability is evened out. Added to this calculus is the goal of moving a little more income into 2010 if it is taxed at a lower rate, and deferring more deductions into 2011 if doing so helps offset income anticipated to be taxed at a higher rate.

Accelerating Income

Usually, postponing the recognition of income pays dividends in that "time is money" and postponing income means postponing the payment of tax. If a taxpayer anticipates being in a higher tax bracket in a subsequent tax year, however, income acceleration techniques should be considered. Selling property in an earlier tax year is one way to lock in the income to be recognized on the gain. If the buyer insists on an installment sale, however, the planner should remember that each installment is taxed in the year it is received at the tax rates applicable in that year. Taking qualified withdrawals from retirement savings, either as part of a Roth IRA conversion plan or otherwise, presents still another technique to force the acceleration of income.

Maximizing Deductions

Many individuals find that they have more flexibility in accelerating or deferring expenses that generate tax deductions rather than trying to time income recognition. Among the variables to be considered in manipulating deductions are those described here.

Time of payment. Charged transaction amounts are treated as paid when charged on a credit card, not when the amount is later billed and paid. Thus, payments of charitable contributions or medical expenses, for example, can be deducted in 2010 if they are charged in 2010. If payment is made by check, the amount is deductible when the payer gives up control of the check, not when the check is deposited or when the checking account is debited. If the check is mailed, it can usually be deducted as a payment on the date it is mailed. This assumes that sufficient funds are on hand and that the check is honored in due course. Payment with a debit card is made when the transaction occurs, even if the bank will not debit the account until a succeeding day.

Charitable contributions. Making a charitable contribution is a simple way to increase a taxpayer's itemized deductions. Although a pledge or a contribution of a note is not deductible, charging the contribution or mailing a check qualifies as a payment. A taxpayer that charges a contribution or mails a check in 2010 must deduct the payment in 2010. The calendar year taxpayer anticipating being in a higher tax bracket in 2011 should therefore consider delaying making charitable contributions well into January to avoid any question surrounding its deductibility for the 2011 return.

Gifts. Gifts can be used to divert capital gain income to the recipient (assuming the "kiddie tax"—discussed later in this chapter does not apply— and can be used in conjunction with estate planning. The annual gift tax exclusion provides that no gift tax is imposed on gifts of up to $13,000 per recipient ($26,000 for gifts from a married couple). The exclusion applies separately to each year. An unused exclusion cannot be carried over to the following year, so it is beneficial to make a gift before the end of the year. A gift is generally considered completed when the donor releases ownership and control over the gift.

Medical expenses. Medical expenses can only be deducted (as an itemized deduction) if their total per filer (single or joint) exceeds 7.5 percent of AGI (10 percent if alternative minimum tax is paid). To increase the deduction, taxpayers should consider incurring additional expenses for items such as vision correction and dental work all in a single year.

State and local income taxes. State and local income taxes paid during the year are deductible as an itemized deduction. There is also an additional standard deduction for real property taxes for nonitemizers. Taxpayers that expect to owe state or local income taxes for 2010 can increase their withholding or make an extra payment on their withholding or quarterly estimates. The payment must be made in good faith and be based on a reasonable estimate of tax liability. Taxpayers paying estimated state and local taxes can pay the last installment by the end of 2010, rather than in January 2011, so that the taxes can be deducted on the 2010 return.

STUDY QUESTIONS

1. Individual income tax rates do **not** apply to income from:
   a. Partnerships
   b. S corporations
   c. C corporations

2. Taxpayers and planners anticipating changes to the federal income taxation structure after EGTRRA provisions sunset should:
   a. Accelerate income to be taxed for the 2010 year
   b. Defer recognition of income to 2011
   c. Even out income recognition and deduction claims to fall equally before and after the EGTRRA provisions sunset

Limitation on Itemized Deductions

For taxpayers in the highest rate brackets, another variable to consider in determining how to allocate deductions between 2010 and 2011 in particular is the impact of any reinstatement of the limitation on itemized deductions that had been imposed before 2010.

For the year 2010—and 2010 only—the limitation on itemized deductions for higher-income taxpayers is completely repealed. The limitation (known as the *Pease limitation* after the member of Congress who sponsored the bill enacting it) limits the total amount of otherwise-allowable itemized deductions for higher income taxpayers.

Prior to the enactment of EGTRRA, otherwise-allowable itemized deductions—other than for qualified medical expenses, investment interest, theft and casualty losses and gambling losses—were reduced by 3 percent of the amount by which a taxpayer's AGI exceeded a statutory floor that was indexed annually for inflation but not by more than 80 percent of the otherwise-allowable deductions. For 2009, that statutory AGI floor was set at $166,800. EGTRRA reduced the itemized deduction limitation in three steps.

Under EGTRRA, repeal of the limitation on itemized deductions was gradual. For tax years beginning in 2006 and 2007, the limitation was reduced by one-third. For tax years beginning in 2008 and 2009, the limitation was reduced by two-thirds. For tax years beginning in 2010, the limitation is not applicable. Under EGTRRA's sunset rules, the limitation on itemized deductions will return after 2010.

PLANNING POINTER

If the Pease limitation is reinstated by default, higher-income individuals may want to shift taking at least some of their itemized deductions to 2010 by accelerating payment of deductible expenses. To the extent that the use of a deduction in 2011 would be reduced, it would fail in any reverse strategy to postpone deductions to offset income potentially taxed at a higher rate.

Administration proposal. President Obama has asked Congress to allow the limitation on itemized deductions to return but to modify it for 2011 and beyond. Under the president's proposal, the limitation on itemized deductions would apply to an AGI threshold determined by adjusting a 2009 dollar amount for subsequent inflation. The Obama Administration has proposed a dollar amount for the threshold of $200,000 for single individuals and $250,000 for married couples filing a joint return.

STUDY QUESTIONS

3. Under EGTRRA, the Pease limitation on itemized deductions:

a. Is repealed permanently

b. Is left unchanged

c. Is repealed entirely for the 2010 tax year only

ALTERNATIVE MINIMUM TAX

Because federal tax law gives special treatment to certain types of income and allows special deductions and credits for certain types of expenses, some taxpayers with substantial income can significantly reduce their regular tax. In response, Congress created the alternative minimum tax (AMT) more than 40 years ago to ensure that these taxpayers pay a minimum amount of tax on their income. However, the AMT has had some unintended consequences. These resulted from lowered regular income tax rates and the fact that the AMT exemptions, unlike the regular tax personal exemptions and standard deductions, are not adjusted for inflation.

COMMENT

The AMT is parallel to the regular tax system. Compared to the regular tax system, the AMT has larger exemption amounts and lower tax rates, but has a more inclusive definition of taxable income. Many taxpayers must compute their tax liabilities under both the regular and AMT systems and, in effect, pay the higher amount.

Planning to Avoid AMT Liability

Perhaps the most important planning technique for taxpayers who are borderline candidates for the AMT is to do their best to maintain this situation. Bunching itemized deductions into one year causes the taxpayer to lose the value of these deductions in the regular tax year. If deductions are not evenly distributed, and the taxpayer has AMT and non-AMT years, the taxpayer should shift preference items from the AMT year to the non-AMT year until the taxpayer arrives at the brink of AMT liability, therefore reducing regular tax to the point where it equals the tentative tax. This technique provides the maximum benefit of preference deductions.

Liability for AMT is triggered when the taxpayer's tentative minimum tax exceeds regular tax liability for a particular tax year. Therefore, a taxpayer can recognize AMT adjustments and tax preference items up to the point in which the tentative minimum tax is equal to regular tax without incurring AMT liability—the AMT crossover point. For individual taxpayers, the AMT crossover point generally occurs when 26 percent of the first $175,000 of taxable excess (AMTI minus the applicable exemption amount, reduced by the AMT foreign tax credit) is greater than the taxpayer's regular tax.

Timing Strategies

Timing strategies may be effective for nonpreference adjustments. If the taxpayer is subject to the AMT in one year and not in the next, the marginal rate for the regular tax year should be determined. If the rate is more than 26 or 28 percent, nonpreference deductions should be shifted to the regular tax year. If the regular tax rate is 15 percent, this strategy should be reversed with nonpreference deductions shifted to the AMT year. One way to take advantage of the rate differentials between an AMT year and a non-AMT year is to accelerate items of income into the AMT year and postpone deductions into the non-AMT year.

Accelerating income. Among other strategies, income can be accelerated by:

- Making prepayments of salary and bonuses;
- Redeeming Series EE savings bonds;
- Recognizing short-term capital gains;
- Converting tax-free bonds to higher yielding taxable bonds; and
- Withdrawing money from IRAs and other retirement funds.

Deferring deductions. Deductions can be deferred by:

- Depreciating rather than expensing business furniture and equipment; and
- Delaying the payment of non-AMT deductible items to a year when the AMT does not apply.

Medical expenses. Taxpayers with itemized medical expenses should determine whether their employer has a pretax medical deduction plan or cafeteria plan. Medical expenses paid on a pretax basis are not included in taxable wages or deducted as itemized deductions, and such payments reduce both AMT and regular tax. Furthermore, itemized medical expenses are only deductible for AMT purposes to the extent they exceed 10 percent of adjusted gross income (AGI), rather than at the 7.5-percent floor set for regular tax purposes.

Real estate and state income taxes. In a year in which the taxpayer is subject to AMT, prepaying real estate or state income taxes does not provide any benefit. If the taxpayer lives in a state where income taxes are high, then the taxpayer is likely to be subject to the AMT. Instead of prepayment, payment should be delayed to another year, if possible.

Mortgage interest. Because interest on mortgage borrowings used for purposes other than to buy, build, or improve the taxpayer's home is not deductible under the AMT, taxpayers subject to the AMT achieve no advantage from using a home equity line of credit to purchase a car or make some other expenditure. However, if the car is used in the taxpayer's business, a taxpayer may be able to deduct some of the auto loan interest or other costs as a business expense on Schedule C.

Employee business expenses. Taxpayers with unreimbursed employee expenses who are subject to the AMT should consider asking their employer to start reimbursing them for their business expenses. If the employer refuses this request, the taxpayer may be better off negotiating a lower salary in exchange for payment of the business expenses.

Other miscellaneous itemized deductions. A taxpayer who is not subject to AMT each year should keep in mind that miscellaneous itemized deductions do not reduce AMTI. However, some itemized deductions—such as cash charitable contributions, home mortgage and other qualified interest, medical expenses, casualty and theft losses, gambling losses, and estate taxes—act to reduce AMTI. Consequently, a taxpayer should attempt to maximize the allowable deductions in any tax year in which AMT might be imposed.

> **COMMENT**
>
> The nondeductibility of miscellaneous itemized deductions for AMT purposes can become a problem for taxpayers who take significant deductions on Schedule C claiming to be independent contractors and who are later recharacterized by the IRS to be employees. The amounts previously deducted on Schedule C become miscellaneous itemized deductions on Schedule A, *Itemized Deductions*, and often result in AMT liability. This can also occur if a taxpayer takes deductions based on the existence of an active trade or business that is later recharacterized to be an investment activity.

Qualified Small Business Stock

Under Code Sec. 1202, a portion of the gain from the sale of qualified small business stock held for more than five years may be excluded from income. The gain on the sale of this stock is 50 percent excludable for regular tax purposes, but 42 percent of the excluded gain is added back for AMT purposes. In a year in which qualified small business stock is sold, other AMT adjustments should be reduced or eliminated as much as possible to receive the maximum gain exclusion on the sale of the stock.

AMT Liability

A taxpayer's AMT liability is the excess of the taxpayer's tentative minimum tax over the taxpayer's regular tax liability. The starting point for determining the taxpayer's tentative minimum tax is the taxpayer's alternative minimum taxable income (AMTI), which is computed by increasing or decreasing the taxpayer's regular taxable income by:

- AMT adjustments;
- Tax preference items; and
- Certain gains and losses.

Adjustments and Preferences

The favorable tax benefits available under the regular tax are curtailed for the AMT by a system of adjustments and preferences. Adjustments and preferences are similar in that both involve modifications to deductions or exclusions that are preferential in the sense that they permit the taxpayer to pay tax on an amount less than his or her economic income. The primary distinction between the two categories of modifications is that adjustments may increase or decrease AMT income relative to taxable income, whereas preferences can only increase AMT income.

> **COMMENT**
>
> One tax preference item is tax-exempt interest earned on certain private activity bonds, although private activity bonds do not include bonds issued after July 30, 2008, that are:
>
> - Exempt-facility bonds that are part of a bond issue in which 95 percent or more of the proceeds are used for qualified residential rental projects;
> - Qualified mortgage bonds; or
> - Qualified veterans' mortgage bonds.
>
> Any bond issued after December 31, 2008, and before January 1, 2011, is not treated as a private activity bond.

AMT patch. In 2009, because of the AMT patch (temporary fix) enacted by Congress, all nonrefundable personal credits could be used to offset AMT liability.

Nonrefundable personal credits. In 2010, unless Congress enacts an AMT patch or other legislation, the only available nonrefundable personal credits are those described here. As a general rule, nonrefundable personal credits are allowed only to the extent that the taxpayer's regular tax liability exceeds tentative minimum tax However, Congress has waived this tax limitation rule for tax years beginning in 2000 through 2009 by allowing nonrefundable personal credits to offset regular tax liability (as reduced by the Code Sec. 27(a) foreign tax credit) plus the taxpayer's AMT liability (Code Sec. 26(a)(2)). In other words, for tax years beginning during 2000 through 2009, nonrefundable personal credits are fully allowable against both regular tax (reduced by the foreign tax credit) and the AMT.

The nonrefundable personal credits include:

- Child and dependent care credit (Code Sec. 21);
- Elderly and disabled credit (Code Sec. 22);
- Credit for adoption expenses (Code Sec. 23);
- Child tax credit (Code Sec. 24);
- Hope and Lifetime Learning credits for higher education expenses (Code Sec. 25A);
- Retirement savings credit (Code Sec. 25B);
- Nonbusiness energy property credit (Code Sec. 25C);
- Residential energy efficient property credit (Code Sec. 25D);
- District of Columbia homebuyer's credit (Code Sec. 1400C); and
- Personal portion of the plug-in electric motor vehicle credit (Code Sec. 30D).

COMMENT

AMT liability in one year can generate a credit against a taxpayer's regular tax liability in a later year. This is called the *minimum tax credit* (MTC). Generally, the MTC cannot be used to reduce any tax owed below the tentative minimum tax in later years.

COMMENT

For 2009 and 2010, the Hope credit was enhanced and temporarily renamed the American opportunity tax credit. Depending upon whether Congress extends certain enhancements into 2011, the name may revert to the hope credit. In any event, the "Hope" designation is the name retained within the official title of Code Section 25A, Hope and Lifetime Learning Credits.

AMT Rate Schedule

The AMT's rate schedule is two-tiered and graduated:

- A 26-percent tax rate applies to the first $175,000 of AMTI in excess of the applicable exemption amount;
- A 28-percent tax rate applies to AMTI more than $175,000 above the exemption amount; and
- For married individuals filing separately, the rate changes when AMTI reaches $87,500 rather than $175,000.

> **COMMENT**
>
> The 26- and 28-percent AMT rates are not subject to any post-EGTRRA sunset. Because the end computation in determining AMT liability, however, is comparing it to regular tax liability and paying the higher amount, the anticipated 36- and 39.6-percent regular income tax rate increases for 2011 will have the probable impact of having slightly fewer individuals in those brackets becoming subject to AMT.

Exemption Amounts

The AMT exemption amounts for 2010 (unless adjusted by Congress) are:

- $45,000 in the case of married individuals filing a joint return and surviving spouses;
- $33,750 in the case of single individuals; and
- $22,500 in the case of married individuals filing separate returns.

> **COMMENT**
>
> Because of the AMT patch for 2009, the exemption amounts were higher for 2009:
>
> - $70,950 for tax years beginning in 2009 in the case of married individuals filing a joint return and of surviving spouses;
> - $46,700 for tax years beginning in 2009 in the case of other unmarried individuals;
> - $35,475 for tax years beginning in 2009 in the case of married individuals filing separate returns.
>
> If Congress enacts an AMT patch for 2010, the exemption amounts will be comparable to the 2009 exemption amounts with appropriate adjustment for inflation.

Phaseout

Under phaseout rules, the exemption amount is reduced by 25 percent of the amount by which AMTI exceeds a threshold amount.

**Table 1. AMTI Phaseout Amounts for
AMT Exemptions by Filer Status**

Filer	25% Reduction on AMTI Amounts
Single individuals and heads of households	> $112,500
Married couples filing jointly and surviving spouses	> $150,000
Married individuals filing separately and estates and trusts	> $75,000

Administration proposals. President Obama has asked Congress to provide that individual AMT exemption amounts, the thresholds for the phaseout of the exemption amounts, and the threshold amounts for the beginning of the 28-percent bracket be indexed for inflation from the levels that were in effect for 2009. The proposal allows an individual to offset the entire regular tax liability and alternative minimum tax liability by the nonrefundable personal credits. According to the Obama Administration, these proposals will reduce the number of taxpayers affected by the AMT.

> **COMMENT**
>
> President Obama's proposal is different from Congress' AMT patches that have become common in recent years. The patches are temporary remedies to limit the growing reach of AMT liability affecting increasing numbers of middle-income taxpayers. The president's proposal is intended to be a more long-term fix that is short of repealing the AMT.

STUDY QUESTIONS

4. To achieve the maximum benefit of preference deductions to avoid imposition of the AMT, taxpayers should:

   a. Shift preference items from the non-AMT year to an AMT year
   b. Reduce regular tax to equal the tentative tax
   c. Ensure that tentative minimum tax under AMT exceeds regular tax liability

5. In a year in which the taxpayer is subject to AMT, prepaying real estate or state income taxes helps to minimize the AMT liability. *True or False?*

COMING CHANGES FOR CAPITAL DIVIDENDS AND CAPITAL GAINS

At the same time taxpayers are looking at higher individual marginal income tax rates, the capital gains and dividend tax rates likely will increase after December 31, 2010, especially in the case of higher-income taxpayers. Under the *Jobs and Growth Tax Relief Reconciliation Act of 2003* (JGTRRA) and subsequent legislation, the maximum capital gains and dividends tax rate is 15 percent (zero percent for taxpayers in the 10- and 15-percent tax brackets) for 2010. Effective January 1, 2011, because of sunsets in JGTRRA and subsequent legislation, the tax rate on qualified long-term capital gains will likely rise to 20 percent for taxpayers in the two highest regular income tax brackets. Furthermore, there also is the possibility at press time that these higher-bracket individuals, if not everyone, will pay tax on dividends at the same rates that apply to ordinary income.

PLANNING POINTER

When investments are managed using taxable accounts, the measure of success is the net return after taxes, rather than the gross return. Some strategies that could be used to maximize returns while minimizing taxes include:

- Using dividend-paying stocks, which are taxed at a maximum rate of 15 percent for 2010;
- Postponing long-term capital gains in tax years that generate short-term capital losses for a more favorable tax year;
- Recognizing losses from worthless investments;
- Evaluating the tax ramifications of municipal as opposed to government bonds;
- Capturing losses without violating the *wash sale rules* by purchasing a replacement security in the same industry, or a mutual fund that invests in substantially the same investments;
- Considering the tax impact of original issue discount bonds; and
- Deducting investment interest expense to the extent of net investment income.

PLANNING POINTER

Among the most significant costs that higher-income families encounter are education for children and grandchildren, and often at the same time, support of elderly parents. Taxpayers can reduce costs by prefunding expenses, for example, by transferring income-producing property to a person on whose behalf they would eventually have spent after-tax dollars. This transfer of property is called *income shifting* because, after the transfer, the income will be taxed to the new owner, who may have a lower tax bracket than the client. Keep in mind that children are taxpayers in their own right for any money that they actually earn as well as for their investment income; but special rules, called the *kiddie tax,* apply to the investment income. Once the young people reach age 18 (24 for students who are dependents), their separate tax status permits investment income to be taxed at rates that may be significantly below their parents' rate, but not much benefit exists before that age.

Dividends

Recent tax background. Generally, dividends are included in the recipient's gross income and traditionally had been taxed at ordinary income rates. However, Congress enacted lower rates starting in JGTRRA for qualified dividend income received by noncorporate shareholders. The lower rates for 2010 are zero percent for taxpayers in the 10- and 15-percent brackets and 15 percent for all other taxpayers. Qualified dividend income is taxed at the same reduced rates that apply to net capital gains, for both regular and alternative minimum tax purposes. Because of sunset provisions in JGTRRA and subsequent legislation, this treatment expires after December 31, 2010, and dividends will be taxed at ordinary income rates.

Qualified dividend income. *Qualified dividend income* for purposes of the lower rates consists of dividends received during the tax year from domestic corporations and qualified foreign corporations. However, if a shareholder does not hold a share of stock for at least 61 days during the 121-day period that began 60 days before the ex-dividend date, dividends received on the stock are not eligible for the reduced rates. In the case of dividends attributable to periods of more than 366 days that are received on preferred stock, the taxpayer must hold the stock for at least 91 days during the 181-day period that began 90 days before the ex-dividend date.

Capital Gains

Recent tax background. If a noncorporate taxpayer has a net capital gain, the tax rates imposed on that gain depend on the type of asset, the individual's tax rate bracket, the length of time the asset was held, and when the asset was sold. Under JGTRRA and subsequent legislation, prior to January 1, 2011, the maximum rate of tax on the adjusted net capital gain of an individual taxpayer is 15 percent. Additionally, any adjusted net capital gain otherwise taxed at the 10- or 15-percent individual income tax rate is taxed at a rate of zero percent. However, the 15-percent and the zero-percent rates will expire for tax years beginning after December 31, 2010, and the maximum capital gains rate will be 20 percent, unless Congress extends the lower rates.

Administration proposal. President Obama has asked Congress to impose a 20-percent capital gains and dividends tax rate on individuals with incomes that subject them to the two highest regular income tax brackets; that its, above $200,000 (less the standard deduction and one personal exemption indexed from 2009). The 20-percent rate would also apply to married couples filing a joint return with income above $250,000 (less the standard deduction and two personal exemptions indexed from 2009). All other taxpayers would pay capital gains and dividends taxes of 15 percent unless they qualify for the zero-percent tax rate.

> **COMMENT**
>
> If Congress takes no action and the 20-percent rate on capital gains returns after 2010, capital gains will effectively be taxed at a 33.33-percent higher rate (20 percent instead of 15 percent).

Recapture of depreciation deductions. If a taxpayer realizes a capital gain on the sale or other disposition of property used in the taxpayer's trade or business, the taxpayer generally will not enjoy the benefit of the special capital gains tax rate on the entire amount of the gain. This is because the tax code wants to first *recapture* (take back) some of the benefits of the depreciation deductions the taxpayer has been claiming for all the years he or she owned the property. The tax rules for recapture differ, depending on whether the property is real estate or personal property. For business real estate, there is a special, more generous rule applied to home offices.

Recapture rules for personal property. If a taxpayer has a capital gain on any depreciable personal property other than real estate, the taxpayer must report all or part of the gain as ordinary income to reflect the amount of depreciation, and any first-year expensing deductions that were claimed on the asset. The amount that must be reported as ordinary income (recaptured) is not eligible for the special long-term capital gains rates described above and is equal to the lesser of the total of depreciation and expensing deductions allowable on the asset, and the total gain realized.

If the total gain realized is more than the amount that must be recaptured, the excess will be taxed at the long-term capital gain rate, provided that the asset has been held for more than one year. If the total of the depreciation deductions is greater than the gain realized, the entire amount of the gain is reported as ordinary income.

Recapture of real estate depreciation. For sales of real estate used in a trade or business after May 6, 1997, including home offices, the recapture rules apply to real estate as well as personal property. If a taxpayer realizes a capital gain on the disposition of real estate after that date, the taxpayer must report all or part of the gain as recaptured depreciation to reflect the amount of accelerated depreciation, claimed on the asset. This recaptured amount is taxed at a special maximum rate of 25 percent. The amount that must be recaptured is equal to the lesser of the total depreciation allowable on the asset (except that for home offices, only depreciation for periods after May 6, 1997, counts), and the total gain realized.

If the total gain realized is more than the amount that must be recaptured, the excess may be reported as a capital gain (with its lower rate) provided that the asset has been held for more than one year. If the total of the depreciation deductions is greater than the gain realized, the entire amount of the gain is taxed at the 25-percent rate.

PLANNING POINTER

A taxpayer may wish to time the sale of a depreciable asset to coincide with a loss year. Such timing can enable the taxpayer to be hit with a recapture in a year in which the taxpayer's business has an operating loss (which can be used to offset the recapture amount), rather than in a profitable year, when the recapture liability will increase the taxpayer's taxable income and possibly even move the taxpayer into a higher tax bracket.

STUDY QUESTIONS

6. To qualify for taxation as qualified dividend income, common stock yielding the dividends must be held for at least _____ before the ex-dividend date.

   a. 61 days
   b. 91 days
   c. 181 days

7. A maximum rate of _____ applies to recaptured depreciation upon the sale of real estate.

   a. 25 percent
   b. 35 percent
   c. 50 percent

MEDICARE TAX CHANGES

The health care reform package (the collective title for the *Patient Protection and Affordable Care Act of 2010* and the *Health Care and Education Reconciliation Act of 2010*) imposes a 0.9-percent additional Medicare tax on higher-income taxpayers and a 3.8-percent Medicare contribution tax on *qualified unearned income* of higher-income taxpayers. The new Medicare tax treatment is effective for tax years beginning after December 31, 2012.

Background

The *Federal Insurance Contributions Act* (FICA) imposes two taxes on employers and employees:

- One finances the federal old-age, survivors and disability insurance (OASDI) program, more commonly known as Social Security; and
- The second is to finance hospital and hospital service insurance (HI) for those 65 years of age or older, more familiarly known as Medicare.

The employee's portion of the Social Security tax is 6.2 percent of his or her wages, up to the Social Security wage base. The employer's portion also equals 6.2 percent of the employee's wages, up to the Social Security wage base. Thus, the equivalent of 12.4 percent of the employee's wages is contributed to the OASDI fund. The wage base for the Social Security portion of the FICA tax is $106,800 for 2010. The Medicare tax on an employee's wages also consists of an employee's portion and an employer's portion. The employee's portion is 1.45 percent of the employee's wages. The employer's portion of the Medicare tax also equals 1.45 percent of the wages. Thus, the equivalent of 2.9 percent of the employee's wages is contributed to Medicare.

Self-employment tax. Individuals engaged in trade or business as sole proprietors or partners must pay self-employment tax on net earnings from self-employment. Self-employment tax has two components:

- The OASDI component (Social Security) is imposed on net self-employment earnings up to the Social Security wage base; and
- The HI component (Medicare) is imposed on net earnings from self-employment without limitation.

The Medicare rate is 2.90 percent of all net earnings from self-employment. Thus, the combined self-employment tax rate is 15.3 percent (12.40 + 2.90). A self-employed individual is permitted to deduct one-half of the self-employment tax liability for the year as a business expense in arriving at adjusted gross income (AGI). Alternately, a self-employed individual is allowed to reduce self-employment income by an amount equal to one half of the combined self-employment tax rate, or 7.65 percent (0.5 × 15.3%) multiplied by the taxpayer's self-employment income.

Additional Medicare Tax

The 0.9-percent additional Medicare tax is imposed on single individuals who receive wages with respect to employment in excess of $200,000 during any tax year beginning after December 31, 2012. The threshold for imposition of the 0.9-percent additional Medicare tax is $250,000 for a married couple filing a joint return ($125,000 for a married taxpayer filing separately).

> **COMMENT**
>
> The definition of *employment* for purposes of the 0.9-percent additional Medicare tax tracks the definition of *employment* in Code Sec. 3121(b) and generally includes any service, of whatever nature, performed by an employee for the person employing him, or her, regardless of the citizenship or residence of either.

Wage earners. The additional 0.9-percent Medicare tax is imposed on the combined wages of the married couple if they file a joint return. However, the responsibility to withhold the additional Medicare tax is only imposed on an employer if the employee receives wages from the employer in excess of $200,000. The employer is permitted to disregard the amount of wages received by the taxpayer's spouse.

> **CAUTION**
>
> If the employer does not withhold the 0.9-percent additional Medicare tax, the taxpayer is liable for paying the tax.

> **EXAMPLE**
>
> Rachel Benes is employed by ABC Co. Rachel's annual wages in 2013 total $164,000. Rachel's spouse, Brandon, is employed by XYZ Co. Brandon's annual wages in 2013 are $97,000. Rachel and Brandon traditionally file a joint federal income tax return. Combined, their wages are more than the $250,000 threshold for the 0.9-percent additional Medicare tax. Neither ABC Co. nor XYZ Co. will be required to withhold the 0.9-percent additional Medicare tax because neither Rachel nor Brandon receives wages from their respective employers in excess of $200,000. Both employers may disregard the amount of wages received by their employee's spouse.

Self-employed taxpayers. The 0.9-percent additional Medicare tax also applies to an individual with self-employment income in excess of $200,000 ($250,000 for married couples filing a joint return and $125,000 for married couples filing separately). A self-employed individual may deduct one-half of the self-employment tax liability for the year as a business expense in arriving at adjusted gross income (AGI). The 0.9-percent additional Medicare tax is excluded from this calculation. Alternately, a self-employed individual may reduce self-employment income by an amount equal to one half of the combined self-employment tax rate, or 7.65 percent (0.5×15.3 percent) multiplied by the taxpayer's self-employment income. The 0.9-percent additional Medicare tax is also excluded to compute the election to reduce self-employment income by an amount equal to one half of the combined self-employment tax rate.

Medicare Contribution Tax

The health care reform package imposes a 3.8-percent Medicare contribution tax on qualified unearned income of higher-income individuals. The 3.8-percent Medicare tax is imposed on the lesser of an individual's net investment income for the tax year or any excess of modified adjusted gross income (MAGI) in excess of $200,000 for an individual. The threshold for married couples filing a joint return and surviving spouses is $250,000 ($125,000 in the case of a married taxpayer filing separately). *MAGI* for purposes of the 3.8-percent Medicare contribution tax is an individual's AGI for the tax year increased by otherwise-excludable foreign earned income or foreign housing costs under Code Sec. 911 (as reduced by any deduction, exclusions, or credits properly allocable to or chargeable against the foreign earned income).

EXAMPLE

Julie Collins is single and has $250,000 of wage income and $40,000 of qualified net investment income for 2013. Julie will be liable for the 3.8-percent Medicare contribution tax on the lesser of her qualified net investment income ($40,000) or the difference between her MAGI of $290,000 and the $200,000 threshold ($90,000). In this case, Julie will be liable for the 3.8-percent Medicare contribution tax on $40,000 because her $40,000 of qualified net investment income is less than her MAGI of $290,000 reduced by her $200,000 threshold amount.

> **EXAMPLE**
>
> Kevin and Annie Winston are married. Their MAGI for 2013 is $335,000, reflecting a combined income of $270,000 in wages and $65,000 of qualified net investment income, in 2013. Kevin and Annie file a joint federal income tax return. Kevin and Annie will be liable for the 3.8-percent Medicare contribution tax on the lesser of their qualified net investment income ($65,000) or the difference between their MAGI of $335,000 and the $250,000 threshold ($85,000). In this case, Kevin and Annie will be liable for the 3.8-percent Medicare contribution tax on $65,000 because their $65,000 of qualified net investment income is less than their MAGI of $335,000 reduced by the $250,000 threshold.

Net Investment Income. *Net investment income* is the excess of the sum of the following items less any otherwise allowable deductions properly allocable to such income or gain:

- Gross income from interest, dividends, annuities, royalties, and rents unless such income derived is in the ordinary course of any trade or business. For this purpose, income derived in the ordinary course of a trade or business excludes any trade or business that is either a passive activity of the taxpayer (within the meaning of Code Sec. 469), or involves trading in financial instruments and commodities (as defined in Code Sec. 475(e)(2));
- Other gross income from any passive trade or business; and
- Net gain included in computing taxable income that is attributable to the disposition of property other than property held in any trade or business that is not a passive trade or business.

> **EXAMPLE**
>
> Ashleigh Smythe is a limited partner in the Celtic, Ltd., partnership that operates an equipment leasing business. Celtic also owns nondividend-paying stock that it holds solely for future capital appreciation. The stock was purchased with borrowed funds for which Celtic incurs an annual interest expense. Ashleigh does not materially participate in any of Celtic's activities. In 2013, Ashleigh's distributive share of the partnership's rental income from its equipment leasing business is $60,000, which is her only source of investment income in that year. In 2013, Ashleigh's distributive share of Celtic's interest expense incurred in connection with its ownership of the stock is $20,000. All of Ashleigh's 2013 gross income for purposes of the unearned income Medicare contribution tax is derived from rents. Her share of Celtic's interest expense would not be considered allocable to such gross income and, therefore, may not be used in computing her net investment income for the year.

Exceptions. Certain items and taxpayers are not subject to the 3.8-percent tax. A significant exception is provided for distributions from qualified plans, 401(k) plans, tax-sheltered annuities, individual retirement accounts (IRAs), and eligible 457 plans (although these distributions continue to be taxed as ordinary income rather than capital gains, even to the extent of investment earnings). There is no exception for distributions from non-qualified deferred compensation plans subject to Code Sec. 409A. However, distributions from these plans (including amounts deemed as interest) are generally treated as compensation, not as investment income.

Estates and trusts. The 3.8-percent Medicare contribution tax also reaches estates and trusts. Estates and trusts also must pay the 3.8-percent unearned income Medicare contribution tax on the lesser of their undistributed net investment income for the tax year or any excess of their AGI (as determined under Code Sec. 67(e)) over the dollar amount at which the highest tax bracket for estates and trusts begins for the tax year.

STUDY QUESTIONS

8. Effective after December 31, 2012, the health care reform package will impose an additional Medicare tax for higher-income taxpayers equal to _____.

   a. 0.9 percent
   b. 1.45 percent
   c. 6.2 percent

---

9. All of the following are included in calculating the modified adjusted gross income of taxpayers subject to the Medicare contribution tax *except:*

   a. Foreign earned income

   b. Credits chargeable against foreign earned income

   c. Foreign housing costs

ROTH IRAS

Beginning in 2010, Roth IRAs are a very attractive savings vehicle. The traditional $100,000 AGI ceiling for converting a regular IRA to a Roth IRA has been removed for 2010 and future years. The AGI limit, in addition to filing status preclusions, generally prevented individuals with AGI of $100,000 or more or married couples filing a joint return from contributing to, or converting another qualified plan account to, a Roth IRA. Roth IRAs and traditional IRAs share many features, but there are important differences.

Features of the Traditional IRA

Contributions to a traditional IRA are generally tax deductible. The deduction is taken from gross income to compute AGI. However, no deduction is allowed if the individual has attained age 70½ before the end of the year in which the contribution is made. The amount of deduction contributions to an IRA is generally limited to the lesser of the individual's taxable compensation for the year or a specific dollar amount. Distributions from a traditional IRA are taxed as ordinary income. When an individual reaches age 70½, he or she is required to begin taking distributions.

Features Unique to the Roth IRA

Contributions to a Roth IRA are not tax deductible. However, qualified distributions are free from taxation. Additionally, an individual can continue to make contributions to a Roth IRA after age 70½. Moreover, a Roth IRA may be passed to the owner's heirs income tax-free at death.

Contributions. Taxpayers can make two types of contributions to a Roth IRA:

- An annual contribution; and
- A conversion contribution.

In 2010, an individual can make an annual maximum contribution to a Roth IRA of the smaller of $5,000 or the amount of the individual's taxable compensation. Individuals age 50 and older by the end of the year can make an additional catch-up contribution of $1,000. The same maximum contributions apply to traditional IRAs.

Distributions. Qualified distributions from a Roth IRA are not included in income. Unlike a traditional IRA, Roth IRA owners are not required to take minimum distributions. Qualified distributions may be made after five tax years beginning with the first tax year for which the taxpayer contributed any amount to the Roth IRA. A Roth IRA distribution will be treated as a qualified distribution after the five-year holding period has passed and may be made upon the occurrence of any of the following:

- On or after the date the IRA owner turns age 59½;
- To a beneficiary or the estate of the IRA owner on or after the death of the IRA owner;
- As a result of the IRA owner becoming disabled; or
- For a qualified first-time home purchase.

EXAMPLE

Keisha Washington contributes $5,000 to a Roth IRA on May 22, 2011. Keisha turns 60 years old on June 1, 2011. The five-year holding period would begin on January 1, 2011, and end on December 31, 2015. Keisha may take a qualified distribution from her Roth IRA anytime after the expiration of the required five-year holding period because she will be over age 59½ at the time of the distribution.

EXAMPLE

Nicholas Knightly contributes $5,000 to a Roth IRA on July 3, 2011. At the time of the contribution, Nicholas is 31 years old and will turn 32 on September 12, 2011. The five-year holding period would begin on January 1, 2011, and end on December 31, 2015. On January 31, 2018, Nicholas purchases his first home. A distribution from Nicholas' Roth IRA at that time to be used toward the purchase of his first home is a qualified distribution.

CAUTION

Nonqualified distributions from a Roth IRA are subject to a 10-percent tax, federal income tax on any appreciation of assets deemed withdrawn, and possible state and local tax.

> **PLANNING POINTER**
>
> Roth IRA owners are not subject to the required minimum distribution rules; therefore, the funds in the Roth IRA grow tax-free. Over a period of years, this growth can be significant. Further, although Roth IRA beneficiaries are required to take required minimum distributions each year, these withdrawals are tax-free. These factors make Roth IRAs attractive vehicles to transfer the greatest amount of wealth.

Conversions

Until 2010, a taxpayer's eligibility to convert a traditional IRA to a Roth IRA depended on the individual's AGI and filing status. If a taxpayer's AGI exceeded $100,000, the taxpayer was ineligible to make a conversion. Married couples who filed a joint return were held to the same $100,000 AGI limit based on the couple's combined income. Additionally, individuals who filed their return as married filing separate returns were ineligible. These limits are abolished for 2010 and future tax years.

> **PLANNING POINTER**
>
> Three factors to consider when contemplating a Roth conversion are:
>
> - Tax rate differential;
> - Use of outside funds to pay income tax; and
> - Time horizon.
>
> If the taxpayer's current and future tax rates are the same, and the income tax liability is paid with funds inside of the IRA, the taxpayer is in the same economic position when converting to a Roth IRA as if no conversion took place. However, a taxpayer who uses outside funds to pay the income tax liability on a Roth IRA conversion is in a better economic position than if the funds were kept in a traditional IRA. The time horizon is critical, because the longer that funds can grow in a tax-deferred environment, the better the economic result.

Recognition of income. Taxpayers making a Roth conversion in 2010 may recognize the conversion amount ratably in their taxable income on 2011 and 2012 returns, unless the taxpayer elects to recognize the amount all on a 2010 return.

> **EXAMPLE**
>
> Hannah Jensen has a traditional IRA with a value of $10,000 consisting of deductible contributions and earnings. Hannah converts her traditional IRA to a Roth IRA in 2010, and as a result of the conversion, she has $10,000 in gross income. Unless Hannah elects otherwise, $5,000 is included in income in 2011, and $5,000 is included in income in 2012.

> **PLANNING POINTER**
>
> Before converting a traditional IRA to a Roth IRA, individuals should consider whether they will be in lower or higher tax brackets after conversion. The tax deferral rules for traditional IRAs are generous to individuals who anticipate being in a lower tax bracket because the distributions will be subject to the ordinary tax rates in effect at the time the distributions are made. Individuals who anticipate being in the same tax bracket or a higher tax bracket would benefit from conversion because the distributions from a Roth IRA would be tax-free.

DESIGNATED ROTH ACCOUNTS

A retirement plan may include a designated Roth contribution program, such as a 401(k) plan (or for public school employees and employees of tax-exempt organizations, a 403(b) plans and for employees of governmental units, a 457(b) plan). Generally, designated Roth contributions in one of these plans can be rolled over to another designated Roth account or to a Roth IRA. It all cases, it is up to the discretion of the employer that sponsors the plan to change it to allow for designated Roth accounts. Most sponsors choose to do so, however, because the administrative costs involved are generally minor in comparison to the benefits—funded basically by Uncle Sam—to those employees who opt to use a designated Roth account.

Intraplan Rollovers

On September 27, 2010, President Obama signed the *Small Business Jobs Act* (H.R. 5297) into law. The *Small Business Jobs Act* makes an important, retirement-savings friendly change to intraplan rollovers. Under the new law, a 401(k), 403(b), or governmental 457(b) plan that includes a qualified Roth contribution program may now permit a qualified rollover contribution from a participant's non-Roth account to the participant's designated Roth account within the same plan. The distribution to be rolled over must be otherwise allowed under the plan. Accordingly, an employer may have to amend its non-Roth plan to allow in-service distributions or distributions prior to normal retirement age. The new law also allows governmental 467(b) plans to offer a qualified Roth contribution program.

> **PLANNING POINTER**
>
> The new intraplan rollover rules provide a convenient way to move pretax contributions into a Roth account.

Income

The taxpayer must include the converted amount gross income as a distribution for the tax year in which the amount is distributed or transferred. This amount is reduced by any after-tax contributions included in the amount rolled over. The 2010 *Small Business Jobs Act* includes a special rule for rollovers accomplished in 2010. If the rollover is done in 2010, the amount the taxpayer would have to include in gross income in 2010 is instead included in equal installments in 2011 and 2012. A taxpayer may elect to include it all in 2010.

PLANNING POINTER

Taxpayers anticipating being in a higher income tax bracket after 2010, because of the expected rise in the top two individual income tax rates or because of another change in circumstances, may want to consider including any amount in income in 2010. Conversely, taxpayers anticipating being in a lower income tax bracket after 2010, because of retirement or other events, may want to not opt out the two-year spread available under the new law.

COMMENT

The 10-percent additional tax under Code Sec. 72(t) does not apply to rollover distributions under the special rollover provisions in the 2010 Small Business Jobs Act. However, the 10-percent additional tax would apply if the amount rolled over is subsequently distributed from the Roth account within the five-tax-year period beginning with the tax year in which the contribution was made.

HEALTH SAVINGS ACCOUNTS

Health savings accounts (HSAs) are savings vehicles for qualified medical expenses. HSAs are attractive because qualified contributions to an HSA are tax deductible and qualified distributions are excluded from income. Income from investments made in HSAs is not taxable and the overall income is not taxable upon disbursement for medical expenses. However, not everyone can open or invest in an HSA. Eligible individuals must have a high-deductible health plan (HDHP), among other criteria.

> **COMMENT**
>
> In addition to an HDHP, an eligible individual may be covered by a health plan that provides permitted coverage and permitted insurance. A plan provides only permitted coverage if it covers only accidents, disability, dental care, vision care, or long-term care. Eligibility for an HSA is not affected by participation in an employee assistance program (EAP), disease management plan, or wellness program, as long as the program does not provide significant medical care benefits or treatments.

> **PLANNING POINTER**
>
> Only one person can be the "beneficiary" of an HSA. That person is either the *eligible individual* who initially sets up the account or, upon death, the person named in the HSA instrument as the beneficiary. Spouses cannot share an HSA, so each spouse who is an eligible individual must open a separate account. However, if both spouses are eligible, they may be able to choose how they allocate the annual limit on deductible contributions. An eligible individual may have more than one HSA, but all of the accounts are aggregated for purposes of the annual contribution limit.

> **PLANNING POINTER**
>
> Although only one person may be the beneficiary of an HSA, account distributions are not limited to that person's expenses. Tax-free HSA distributions can also be used to pay medical expenses incurred by the beneficiary's spouse or dependents.

STUDY QUESTIONS

10. A key advantage of Roth IRAs compared to traditional IRAs is that:

    a. Contributions to Roth IRAs are untaxed

    b. Qualified distributions are tax-free

    c. The annual maximum contribution to Roth IRAs is higher than to traditional IRAs

11. Qualified distributions from Roth IRAs:

    a. May begin when the owner turns age 59½

    b. Are required by the time the owner reaches age 70½

    c. May not be taken to fund a qualified first-time home purchase

High-Deductible Health Plan

Generally, an HDHP for individual (self-only) coverage is a health plan that has an annual deductible of at least $1,200 (for tax years beginning in 2010) and an out-of-pocket expense limit of no more than $5,950 (for tax years beginning in 2010). An HDHP for family coverage, which is anything other than self-only coverage, is a health plan that has an annual deductible of at least $2,400 and an out-of-pocket expense limit of no more than $11,900 (for tax years beginning in 2010).

> **EXAMPLE**
>
> For 2010, Tamwar and Abby Baruch have family HDHP coverage with a $6,000 deductible. Tamwar has no other coverage. Abby also has self-only coverage with a $200 deductible. Abby, who has coverage under a low-deductible plan, is not eligible and cannot contribute to an HSA. Tamwar may contribute to an HSA.

> **EXAMPLE**
>
> For 2010, Drake and Emma have family HDHP coverage with a $7,000 deductible. Drake as no other coverage. Emma also has self-only HDHP coverage with a $3,000 deductible. Both Drake and Emma are eligible individuals. Drake and Emma are treated as having only family coverage. Their combined HSA contribution may be divided between them by agreement.

Contributions

For tax years beginning in 2010, the maximum HSA contribution is $3,050 for self-only coverage and $6,150 for family coverage. Individuals who have attained age 55 by the end of the tax year can make additional contributions (*catch-up contributions*) of $1,000. Once an individual is enrolled in Medicare, contributions cannot be made. Contributions to an HSA must be in cash.

> **CAUTION**
>
> Excess contributions to an HSA are subject to an excise tax of 6 percent.

> **PLANNING POINTER**
>
> Self-employed persons may not contribute to an HSA on a pretax basis and may not take the amount of their HSA contribution as a deduction for self-employment tax purposes. However, they may contribute to an HSA with after-tax dollars and take the above-the-line deduction.

Distributions

HSA distributions that used for qualified medical expenses are excluded from income. Distributions that are not used for such expenses are included in income and are subject to a 10-percent additional tax as well. The additional 10-percent tax does not apply, however, if the distribution is made after death, disability, or attainment of age of Medicare eligibility.

Health Care Reform Impact

The health care reform package (the *Patient Protection and Affordable Care Act of 2010* and the *Health Care and Education Reconciliation Act of 2010*) make two important changes to HSAs. The health care reform package increases the additional tax on nonqualified distributions from an HSA and places new limits on the uses of distributions from an HSA.

Additional tax. For tax years beginning in 2010, the additional tax on nonqualified distributions from an HSA is 10 percent. Effective for distributions made in tax years beginning after December 31, 2010, the additional tax on nonqualified distributions increases to 20 percent.

> **COMMENT**
>
> Unlike reimbursements from a flexible spending arrangement or health reimbursement arrangement, distributions from an HSA are not required to be substantiated by the employer or a third party for the distributions to be excluded from income. The determination of whether the distribution is for a qualified medical expense is subject to individual self-reporting and IRS enforcement.

Distributions. The health care reform package modifies the definition of *qualified medical expense* for HSAs to conform it to the definition used for the Code Sec. 213 medical expense deduction. Over-the-counter medications are excluded unless prescribed by a health care professional or are insulin. This new definition applies to tax years beginning after December 31, 2010.

> **EXAMPLE**
>
> Carey Grobowski used HSA dollars to purchase over-the-counter allergy medication on October 2, 2010. The expenditure is allowed under pre-health care reform package law and is excluded from Carey's gross income. If Carey uses his HSA dollars to purchase the same allergy medication on April 12, 2011, the expenditure is not allowed and will not be excluded from Carey's gross income, and so will be subject to the additional 20-percent penalty.

STUDY QUESTIONS

12. Only one person may be named the eligible individual for an HSA, but the distributions may pay the medical expenses of the beneficiary's spouse and dependents. *True or False?*

13. Which of the following is *not* a change to health savings accounts made by the health care reform package?

a. HSA funds may be used to purchase nonprescribed over-the-counter medications

b. Nonqualified distributions from an HSA are subject to additional tax

c. New restrictions apply to the scope of qualified medical expenses

FEDERAL ESTATE TAX

The purpose of the federal estate tax is to tax transfers of wealth from one generation to another. The estate tax is applied to property transfers at death and is separate from the federal income tax. EGTRRA repealed the federal estate tax for 2010. In its place, EGTRRA imposes a carryover basis regime.

> **COMMENT**
>
> At the time this course was published, Congress was considering several pieces of estate tax legislation, including bills to extend the 2009 estate tax into 2010. Pending estate tax legislation is discussed later in this chapter.

Carryover Basis

Under the traditional stepped-up basis at death rules, the income tax basis of property acquired from a decedent at death generally is stepped up (or stepped down) to equal its value as of the date of the decedent's death (or on the date six months after date of death, if alternate valuation is elected on the decedent's estate tax return). Under EGTRRA, the traditional stepped-up basis at death rules do not apply to decedents dying after December 31, 2009, and before January 1, 2011.

Effective for property acquired from a decedent dying after December 31, 2009, and before January 1, 2011, the income tax basis of property acquired from a decedent is generally carried over from the decedent. The recipient of the property receives a basis equal to the lesser of the adjusted basis of the property in the hands of the decedent or the fair market value of the property on the date of the decedent's death.

> **EXAMPLE**
>
> Barbara Atherton died on February 1, 2010, bequeathing stock in XYZ Co. to her son, Jacob. At Barbara's death, the stock had a fair market value of $45 per share. Jacob will receive his mother's basis of $20 per share in the stock. If Jacob subsequently sells the stock for $50 per share, Jacob will incur a $30 per share gain ($50 − $20). Under the stepped-up basis rules, Jacob would only have had a $5 gain ($50 − $45).

> **EXAMPLE**
>
> Ameera Khan's father died on January 2, 2009, and left her 1,000 shares of ABC Co. stock. At the time of his death, Ameera's father had a basis of $100 per share and each share had a fair market value of $1,000. Therefore, Ameera's basis per share will step up to its date of death value of $1,000. Assuming no further appreciation in the value of the stock prior to sale, when Ameera sells the stock she will avoid tax on $900 per share in capital gains. Under a carryover basis regime, assuming the general basis step-up amount of $1.3 million is not available, the father's basis of $100 would become Ameera's basis. Ameera would pay tax on the $900 per share of gain when he sells the shares.

Unless Congress retroactively revives the estate tax for 2010, as a partial replacement for the repealed basis step-up, executors will be able to increase the basis of estate property by up to $1.3 million or $3 million in the case of property passing to a surviving spouse. The executor generally can increase the basis of assets of the executor's choosing by a total of $1.3 million (a *general basis increase*). This general basis increase provision can be allocated to assets passing to any property recipient. For properties passing to the decedent's surviving spouse, an additional $3 million in basis increase is available (a *spousal property basis increase*).

> **PLANNING POINTER**
>
> Both of the basis increase provisions can be applied to property passing to a surviving spouse. Up to $4.3 million in date-of-death-basis increase can be allocated to property received by a surviving spouse.

> **EXAMPLE**
>
> Francine O'Hara died on March 3, 2010, leaving an estate that consisted entirely of 100,000 shares of Manso Inc., having an aggregate date-of-death value of $7.5 million and an aggregate basis (determined under the

carryover basis rules) of $2.2 million. Francine is survived by her husband, David, to whom she bequeaths all of her stock in Manso Inc. Francine's executor can increase the total basis of the stock to $6.5 million ($2.2 million carryover basis + $1.3 million general basis increase + $3 million spousal property basis increase).

Property acquired during three years preceding death. The basis increase provisions of the carryover basis at death rules do not apply to property acquired by a decedent by gift or by lifetime transfer for less than adequate and full consideration in money or money's worth during the three-year period ending on the date of the decedent's death. This prohibition does not generally apply to property received by the decedent from his or her spouse during the three-year period.

Pending Legislation

On December 3, 2009, the House approved the *Permanent Estate Tax Relief for Families, Farmers, and Small Businesses Bill of 2009* (H.R. 4154), which would permanently extend the top federal estate tax rate of 45 percent with a $3.5 million exclusion ($7 million for married couples who fully use their exclusions). However, the bill has stalled in the Senate as of the date this course was published.

PLANNING POINTER

If Congress does not pass an estate tax bill, the pre-EGTRRA estate tax provisions will return for decedents dying on or after January 1, 2011. The exemption amount will be $1 million and the maximum tax rate will be 55 percent.

STUDY QUESTIONS

14. The income tax basis of property acquired from a decedent dying between December 31, 2009, and January 1, 2011 is:

   a. Stepped up or down to its value as of December 31, 2010
   b. Generally carried over from the decedent
   c. Changed automatically to its value under the alternate valuation election

15. Carryover basis at death rules do not apply to property that the decedent acquired by gift or lifetime transfer within _____ years of his or her death.

a. Two
b. Three
c. Five

CONCLUSION

The tax code can appear daunting to wealth building, but a careful and focused review of its provisions can, in fact, complement a taxpayer's wealth-building strategy. Preservation of existing assets also must be taken into account. Into this process, moreover, must be added uncertainty over key provisions such as the reduced individual income tax rates and capital gains/dividend tax rates, the fate of the estate tax, and more.

Individuals: Handling Losses and Debts

Individuals engage in a variety of economic activities: starting a business, investing, purchasing property, or initiating loans. People strive to earn income and generate financial gains. But some of these activities may instead result in losses. Individuals may suffer business losses, investment losses, or casualty losses. Property is damaged or stolen. Although economic losses are never desirable, they generate tax losses that can be used to offset other taxable income and to reduce overall tax liabilities. However, there may be limits on the available loss deduction. This chapter will look at the sources and proper treatment of tax losses as they affect individuals. The chapter will not focus on corporations, although many loss deductions may be common to both individuals and corporate entities.

LEARNING OBJECTIVES

Upon completion of this course, you will be able to:
- Identify sources of tax losses and determine the deductible loss;
- Calculate and claim net operating losses (NOLs) and other loss carryovers;
- Recognize limits on deducting business and investment losses; and
- Determine when to recognize cancellation of indebtedness income.

INTRODUCTION

Losses can stem from many sources: operating a business; selling property used in a business; investing in stock or securities; writing off bad debts or worthless securities; or suffering a theft, fraud, or other casualty loss. These losses can be used to offset current year income, and excess losses (especially net operating losses) may be available to be carried over to a past or future tax year.

Individuals' ability to deduct business losses may be limited. For example, the deduction may be limited to the amount "at risk," if the individual (or the business) has borrowed funds and is not personally liable for the loan. An individual who does not "materially participate" in a business may be engaged in a "passive activity," and any loss may be limited to passive gains and used only to offset his or her passive gains. One person's activities may be a business, whereas another person's activities, being more casual, are treated as a "hobby" that is not considered a business. Hobby loss deductions are limited to offsetting income from the hobby. A variation of the hobby loss issue is the treatment of gambling losses.

An individual suffering economic losses (or unexpected financial circumstances) may have trouble paying off a loan or other debt. If the creditor decides to reduce or cancel the debt, the reduction will be income to the debtor, unless the tax code provides an exception.

TAX LOSSES

Business Losses

A *trade or business* is an activity carried on as a livelihood or with the intent to make a profit (even if it does not actually produce a profit). The business does not have to be incorporated; an individual can operate a business as an unincorporated sole proprietorship. Whereas a corporation's business income and losses are taxed to the entity on Form 1120 (under Subchapter C of the tax code), an individual's business income is computed on Schedule C of Form 1040 and included in gross income reported on Form 1040.

If overall business expenses exceed business income for the tax year, the business incurs a loss. A C corporation's business losses do not flow to the shareholders, but an individual's business losses can reduce the individual's gross income from other sources.

> **COMMENT**
>
> The deductible portion of the loss may be limited by the at-risk rules of Code Sec. 465 or the passive activity loss rules of Code Sec. 469.

If, after offsetting his or her nonbusiness income, the individual has a net loss for the year, the individual may have a net operating loss (NOL). An NOL can be carried over to another tax year to offset income in that year.

> **CAUTION**
>
> An individual's NOL calculation differs from that for a corporation. The individual also must make adjustments to the loss amount, disregarding certain expenses and deductions.

Capital Losses

Income and losses are either capital or ordinary. Business gains and losses are ordinary and therefore taxed at "ordinary" rates. Many property items—both tangible and intangible—are capital assets. Capital gains and losses can be long-term or short-term. Long-term capital gains (gains on capital assets that are inherited or that are held for more than a year) are taxed at lower rates than ordinary income. Their tax rates generally are 15 percent for 2010, but may be as low as 5 percent for lower-income taxpayers. These lower rates are set to expire after 2010 and may increase to 20 percent in subsequent years, depending on congressional action. Short-term capital gains (on property held for one year or less) are taxed at ordinary income rates.

Capital losses generally can offset capital gains. Individuals can deduct an additional $3,000 of capital losses against that year's other, ordinary income. Any excess capital losses above $3,000 can be carried forward to the following year or years, where they can offset capital gains in that year and another $3,000 of ordinary income. Married couples are limited to deducting an additional $3,000 in capital losses ($1,500 per person for married individuals filing separately). The couple is not entitled to a $6,000 deduction.

COMMENT

An individual cannot carry back excess capital losses. Corporations cannot deduct any excess capital losses in the same year but can carry back capital losses three years and carry them forward up to five years.

PLANNING POINTER

Capital gains in excess of capital losses cannot be used to calculate an NOL.

Under Code Sec. 1221(a), a *capital asset* is defined as "property held by the taxpayer (whether or not connected with his trade or business)." The regs state that a capital asset does *not* include:

- Inventory and property held primarily for sale in the ordinary course of business;
- Supplies regularly used in a trade or business;
- Depreciable property used in the trade or business and real property used in the trade or business, if they are held for more than one year;
- Accounts and notes receivable acquired in business;
- Copyrights and artistic compositions held by the taxpayer who created the property;
- U.S. government publications that were not acquired by purchase; and
- Commodities derivatives.

Most items of personal property are capital assets, such as a car, home, or furniture. A *capital gain or loss* is the difference between the sales price of the asset (less selling expenses) and the individual's basis in the asset. *Basis* is the taxpayer's cost or investment in the asset (purchase price plus fees and capitalized costs).

Although gains on personal property are taxable, losses on the sale of personal property are not deductible, even against capital gains. Items purchased for investment or for the production of income, such as stocks and bonds, are capital assets. Capital losses from the sale or exchange of stocks and bonds can offset other capital gains.

> **NOTE**
>
> Securities held by a dealer in securities are not a capital asset.

Denial of stock losses. A taxpayer that sells stock at a loss and buys identical stock within 30 days before or after the sale has engaged in a *wash sale* and cannot deduct the loss from the sale. Instead, the taxpayer must increase his or her basis of the purchased shares, thus delaying recognition of the loss until the purchased shares are eventually sold. A taxpayer who sells stock to a related party also cannot deduct any loss on the sale.

Section 1231 property. Gains and losses on the sale of inventory and property held primarily for sale in the ordinary course of business are ordinary gains and losses. Gains and losses from property used in the trade or business (primarily depreciable property and real estate held more than one year) get special treatment under Code Sec. 1231, even though they are not considered capital assets. If gains from this *Section 1231 property* exceed losses from Section 1231 property, then all gains and losses are capital. As a result, the net gains are capital gains and are taxed at the lower long-term capital gain rates. If losses exceed gains, all gains and losses are ordinary. Thus, the net losses are ordinary losses and can offset other ordinary income.

This special treatment applies to the sale or exchange of capital assets held in connection with a trade or business or with a transaction entered into for profit. It also applies to the involuntary conversion of property used in the trade or business. However, if the taxpayer had Section 1231 losses within the previous five years, then Section 1231 gains from the current year must be treated as ordinary income to the extent of the losses.

> **COMMENT**
>
> Property used in the trade or business includes:
> - Cattle, horses, and other livestock held for draft, breeding, dairy, or sporting purposes;
> - Unharvested crops on land used in the business and sold and sold at the time (and to the same person) as the land; and
> - Timber and coal.

It does not include:

- Copyrights;
- Artistic and musical compositions; and
- U.S. government publications that were not purchased.

Gains and losses from compulsory or involuntary conversions of property not used in the trade or business can also qualify for Section 1231 treatment if the property is:

- A capital asset;
- Held for more than one year; and
- Held "in connection with" a trade or business or a transaction entered into for profit.

Worthless securities. Generally, losses cannot be *recognized* (reported on a tax return) until they are *realized*. If the value of an investment declines, but the owner still retains the investment, no deduction is allowed, because the loss is unrealized. However, Code Sec. 165(g) allows an exception for worthless stock and securities.

COMMENT

A security includes a bond or other evidence of indebtedness and a right to subscribe to or receive a share of stock.

If the security becomes worthless, the individual can take a capital loss for the year of worthlessness, as if the security had been sold. The loss is treated as a loss from a sale of the asset on the last day of the tax year. The deduction must be taken in the year the securities become worthless, even if the taxpayer was not initially aware of the worthlessness. No deduction is allowed for a mere decline in value, if the stock still has any recognizable value.

COMMENT

Because securities held by a securities dealer are not capital assets, any losses from a dealer's wholly worthless securities are ordinary. Losses on stock of a *small business corporation* (Code Sec. 1244) or a *small business investment company* (Code Secs. 1242 and 1243) are also ordinary losses.

A security can be treated as wholly worthless when:

- The taxpayer abandons the security—permanently relinquishing and surrendering all rights in the security without receiving any payment in exchange; or
- It has no value or potential value.
  The taxpayer must show that the stock:
  - — Had some value in the previous year;
  - — Is now totally worthless; and
  - — Became worthless by an identifiable event.

> **CAUTION**
>
> The IRS has ruled that a taxpayer did not have a loss when he disposed of stock he did not believe was worthless, in a transaction characterized as a gift or a capital contribution.

Sufficient to establish the worthlessness of securities are certain identifiable events:

- Cessation of the corporation's business;
- Commencement of liquidation;
- Appointment of a receiver; and
- Actual foreclosure.

A corporation and its securities may be worthless even though the corporation has not dissolved, liquidated, or ceased doing business.

> **NOTE**
>
> Although bankruptcy can be an identifiable event, a company's stock is not automatically worthless when the company declares bankruptcy in response to a lawsuit.

The value or worthlessness of securities depends on the securities' current liquidation value and the potential value the securities may acquire through the foreseeable operations of the corporation. A security is completely worthless only if both elements of value have disappeared.

STUDY QUESTIONS

1. Which of the following is a capital asset?
   a. Stocks and bonds purchased for investment
   b. Supplies used in a trade or business
   c. A copyright held by the taxpayer who created the property

---

2. A deduction for a security that becomes worthless is taken by the individual:

    a. For the tax year in which he or she purchased the security, by filing an amended return

    b. In the tax year in which the security becomes worthless

    c. After the security declines in value by 75 percent

Bad Debts

An individual may loan money to another party or sell property subject to a mortgage. If the borrower/buyer stops paying the debt and lacks the resources to make payments, the debt may become worthless. *Worthlessness* is not defined in the tax regulations but is a question of fact; it does not necessarily require a legal determination. Creditors must exercise sound business judgment and cannot be unduly optimistic or pessimistic.

For a debt to be considered a bad debt, the creditor must have no reasonable expectation of collecting the debt, based on circumstances at the time of the determination, without taking into account subsequent events. The lender must be able to demonstrate that the debt is wholly without value and that the debt became worthless during the tax year for which the lender is claiming the deduction. The lender cannot take the deduction in another tax year.

An inconsistent act, such as the extension of further credit to the debtor, may nullify a bad debt deduction. The deduction may be disallowed if the debtor could satisfy the debt with an offset or counterclaim against the creditor. No deduction is allowed if the debt is secured by collateral having more than a nominal value, until all collateral has been sold. If a taxpayer may be reimbursed for part of a debt, the debt still has value, regardless of the source of potential reimbursement, unless the source of funds is totally unforeseeable (e.g., winning the lottery).

Under Code Sec. 166, the treatment of this loss depends on the context of the transaction:

- If the debt arose in connection with a trade or business, the loss is an ordinary loss and can be deducted against ordinary income; and
- If the creditor is not a corporation, and the debt did not arise (and was not acquired) in a trade or business, the loss is treated as a short-term capital loss. The loss is equal to the creditor's basis in the loan.

The bad debt rules do not apply to worthless debt evidenced by a security and covered by Code Sec. 165(g) (described earlier).

Casualty Losses

Under Code Sec. 165(c)(3), individuals can take an ordinary loss for non-business property losses from casualty, theft, or disaster. Casualty includes fire, storm, and shipwreck. There must be complete or partial physical destruction of the property (not merely a decrease in its value) from a sudden, unexpected, or unusual event.

Generally, losses caused by insects, plant diseases, or drought are not deductible. Events include earthquake, hurricane, and flood. Automobile accident losses are deductible. The casualty loss must be permanent. A temporary condition, such as loss of drinking water due to contamination, is not deductible. Damage to a beach in front of a residence may be temporary in part if the beach will regenerate.

Some related expenses are deductible, such as cleanup and removing debris from damaged property, and amounts paid to recover lost property or mitigate the loss. However, expenses to prevent casualty losses (including insurance premiums), appraisals, and temporary living arrangements and similar expenses are not deductible, even if incurred in connection with a casualty.

Disaster loss. A disaster loss can occur in a disaster area designed by the president. A loss on personal property can be a disaster loss only if it also qualifies as a casualty loss, but a loss on property used in a trade or business or a for-profit transaction can qualify as a disaster loss without being a casualty loss. A home that is ordered demolished or relocated as a result of a disaster qualifies as a disaster loss.

Deductible loss. The casualty or theft loss is limited to the lesser of the decrease in value or the basis of the property. For nonbusiness property, the loss is only deductible to the extent each loss exceeds $100 and all losses for the year exceed 10 percent of the taxpayer's adjusted gross income (AGI). (The $100 amount was increased to $500 for 2009, but the 10 percent AGI limitation did not apply to disaster losses for 2008 and 2009.) Casualty losses must be offset by casualty gains (e.g., payments for damaged property that exceed basis). The separate AGI limits on itemized deductions do not apply to casualty and theft losses.

Under Code Sec. 165(h), these dollar and AGI limits do not apply to casualties involving business property or a transaction entered into for profit. Moreover, any gains from the involuntary conversion of Section 1231 property are treated as capital gains under Code Sec. 1231, rather than as ordinary gains. Section 1231 treatment also applies to any capital asset held for more than one year in connection with a transaction entered into for profit.

Year of deduction. Generally, the loss is deductible for the year the casualty loss occurs or the theft is discovered. A theft loss cannot be taken in the year of the taxpayer's investment. However, if the loss occurred in a presidentially declared disaster area, the loss can be deducted in the immediately preceding year, allowing the taxpayer to claim a quick refund. A casualty loss may be deductible in a subsequent year if damage to the property worsens after the year of the casualty (e.g., trees suffering insect infestation following damage by fire).

A deduction for casualty or theft is treated as a business deduction under the NOL rules and can be carried back 3 years and forward 20 years. If the loss was discovered in 2008, and the taxpayer qualifies as a small business, the carryback can be 4 or 5 years, as described later.

Investment theft or fraud. The IRS does not allow theft losses for declines in stock value that are attributable to corporate misconduct or bad investment advice, because there is no specific intent to deprive the shareholder of money or property. However, in Rev. Rul. 2009-9, the IRS allowed taxpayers who sustained investment losses from Ponzi schemes, such as the Bernard Madoff fraud, to claim ordinary losses from a theft loss, rather than a capital loss from an investment transaction. The loss must be considered a theft under state law, but there does not have to be a conviction for theft.

> **EXAMPLE**
>
> In the Madoff transactions, the promoter received cash and property from investors, supposedly invested the funds in stocks, and reported fictitious earnings to the investors (and to the IRS). Payments of "income" were made to investors upon request, using amounts contributed by other investors. The IRS concluded that the losses qualified for the theft loss deduction because they arose from a criminal act.
>
> The IRS concluded that the dollar thresholds for personal casualty losses ($100/$500 floor and 10 percent of AGI) did not apply because the transactions were entered into for profit. As a theft loss, the losses were itemized deductions. However, the limits on overall itemized deductions (based on a percentage of adjusted gross income) and miscellaneous itemized deductions (2 percent of AGI threshold) did not apply. Rev. Rul. 2009-9 determined that the loss was sustained in the year the taxpayer discovered the loss.

The amount deductible for these Ponzi schemes equaled the amount invested plus the any fictitious income reported by the taxpayer and reinvested in the scheme. Taxpayers had to reduce the loss by amounts withdrawn, reimbursements, and recoveries (including claims for potential recovery). The IRS provided a safe harbor to determine the deductible portion of the losses, allowing taxpayers to deduct up to 95 percent of their losses if they were not pursuing third-party recoveries, and up to 75 percent if they were pursuing third-party recoveries. Investors also had to reduce their loss for any potential recovery from personal insurance or from the Securities Investor Protection Corporation.

Taxpayers have the option of amending returns to recover taxes paid on the fictitious income, but this option applies only to "open" tax years (generally, the last three years) and may not provide the tax benefits that the IRS ruling gives.

STUDY QUESTIONS

3. A bad debt:
   a. Is deductible as an ordinary loss regardless of whether it arises from business or personal loans
   b. May not be deducted if the loan is secured by unsold collateral
   c. Is currently deductible even when the lender reasonably expects to collect the debt in a subsequent tax year

4. Under net operating loss rules, a deduction for casualty or theft of property may be carried back _____ years and forward _____ years.
   a. 2; 10
   b. 3; 20
   c. 6; 25

Net Operating Losses

A trade or business incurs an NOL when its allowable deductions exceed its gross income for the tax year. Both individuals and corporations can have NOLs. For example, a trade or business operated as an unincorporated sole proprietorship and taxed at the individual level can generate an NOL. A corporation must deduct its NOL at the entity level; the shareholders cannot take it. However, NOLs from a business that operates as a passthrough entity (a partnership or S corporation, for example) flow through to the partners and shareholders, and cannot be used by the entity.

Individuals (and corporations) can use an NOL by carrying it back two years and carrying it forward up to 20 years. The taxpayer must use the NOL in the earliest year available; however, the taxpayer can waive the carryback period and immediately carry forward the NOL. If the NOL deduction amount is not exhausted in the first year, it can be carried over to multiple years.

> **EXAMPLE**
>
> Tom Hastings operates an unincorporated landscaping business. In 2009, Tom had net income of $20,000. In 2010, he had a net loss of $10,000. Tom can carry back the $10,000 loss to 2009 and offset it against the income for that year. When he files an amended 2009 return, the IRS will refund Tom the taxes he paid on the $10,000 of income.

Taxpayers can claim a longer carryback period for some types of losses.

Table 1. Loss Carryback Periods

Type of Loss	Maximum Carryback Period
NOL from casualty or theft	3 years
NOL from presidentially declared disaster affecting farming business	3 years
Farming loss	5 years
Specified liability loss	10 years

A *specified liability loss* includes losses from product liability, workers' compensation, and reclaiming land.

Five-year carryback. Congress amended Code Sec. 172 twice to allow both individuals and businesses to carry back an NOL three, four, or five years. For small businesses (sole proprietors as well as entities with average gross receipts of $15 million or less over three years), the *American Recovery and Reinvestment Act of 2009* allows the extended carryback for NOLs incurred in tax years beginning in 2008. For all taxpayers, the *Worker, Homeownership, and Business Assistance Act of 2009* allows the extended carryback for NOLs incurred in one tax year beginning in either 2008 or 2009.

Taxpayers who wanted to use the extended carryback must have made an election on their returns by six months after the due date of their return for the last tax year beginning in 2009. Thus, the election was due September 15, 2010, for a calendar year corporation and October 15, 2010, for a calendar year taxpayer (individual) with an unincorporated business. A taxpayer using a fiscal year for 2009 may have a later due date for the election. If the election was timely made, for example, taxpayers have another three years after the loss year to file an amended return (Form 1040X or 1120X) to actually claim the NOL for a prior year.

Individuals. Individuals can have an NOL for amounts other than trade or business losses. An individual may include the following deductions in his or her NOL computation:

- Employee business expenses;
- Casualty and theft losses, even if not incurred in a trade or business;
- Moving expenses for a job relocation; and
- Expenses of rental property held for the production of income.

Income and deductions from separate businesses are aggregated to determine the NOL for the year. An item that is otherwise excluded from gross income is also excluded in the NOL computation.

In contrast, certain deductions are excluded in computing the NOL. These include deductions for personal exemptions, net capital losses, the exclusion for small business stock under Code Sec. 1202, the Code Sec. 199 domestic production activities deduction, and NOLs from other years. Other nonbusiness deductions are also excluded, such as contributions to an individual retirement account or self-employed individual's retirement plan, and health savings account deductions.

The starting point for determining whether an individual has an NOL is the line on Form 1040 that represents adjusted gross income minus itemized deductions or the standard deduction. If the result is a negative number, the individual may have an NOL and should make further computations and adjustments. The computation of the NOL is determined under the law for the year the NOL arose, disregarding the law for the year to which the NOL is carried.

> **COMMENT**
>
> A married couple can apply an NOL incurred during the marriage against their joint income. However, if a divorced spouse incurs an NOL after the divorce, the NOL can be carried back to a year the spouse was married, but can only offset the spouse's separate income, as if the couple had filed separate returns.

Refund claims. Individuals can claim NOL carrybacks on IRS Form 1045, *Application for Tentative Refund,* or Form 1040X, *Amended U.S. Individual Income Tax Return.* Schedule A of Form 1045 can be used to calculate the NOL. Form 1045 must be filed within one year of the end of the tax year generating the NOL. To claim an NOL carryback, an individual must file an amended return within:

- Three years of the due date of the return for the year the NOL arose, or
- Two years from the time the tax was paid.

An NOL carryover is deducted with the return for the year to which it is carried.

STUDY QUESTION

> **5.** Which of the following may *not* be included in an individual's NOL computation?
>
> **a.** Expenses of rental property held for the production of income
>
> **b.** Net capital loss deduction
>
> **c.** Aggregated deductions from separate businesses

LIMITATIONS ON DEDUCTING BUSINESS LOSSES

"Hobbies"

Sometimes a person engages in a financial or business activity for enjoyment, or on a casual (rather than full-time) basis, without concern for whether the business generates a profit. If an individual, S corporation, or partnership does not engage in the activity for profit, Code Sec. 183 limits deductions from the activity to the income from the activity. This is commonly known as the *hobby loss limitation* and is aimed at activities primarily carried on as a sport, hobby, or recreational activity. The for-profit restrictions do not apply to C corporations; they are aimed at individuals.

For partnerships and S corporations, the determination whether an activity is for profit is made at the entity level, regardless of the partner's or shareholder's (profit) motive in investing in the entity.

COMMENT

For many entities—especially limited partnerships—the determination applies to tax shelters and may be used to deny deductions to the partners or shareholders if the entity was set up primarily to generate large tax losses and not to make a profit.

An activity not engaged in for profit is any activity that is not a trade or business or that is not engaged in for the production or collection of income. This characterization is based on the presence or absence of a profit motive for the taxpayer's involvement in the activity. To treat the activity as a business, the taxpayer must have a good faith expectation of making a profit. In addition, the IRS and courts weigh other factors to evaluate whether the taxpayer engaged in the activity for profit.

Factors considered. The regulations prescribe nine factors that are traditionally considered. The factors are not exclusive, and no single factor (or its absence) is decisive. The IRS can look at other factors and will consider all the facts and circumstances in making its determination. The factors are:

- The manner in which the taxpayer carries on the activity;
- The expertise or experience of the taxpayer's advisors;
- The taxpayer's time and effort spent on the activity;
- Whether assets used in the activity may appreciate in value;
- The taxpayer's success in carrying on other business activities;
- The taxpayer's history of losses from the activity;
- The history of occasional profits from the activity;
- The taxpayer's financial status; and
- The pleasure and recreation derived by from the activity.

The tax code establishes a presumption for determining whether the activity is engaged in for profit. If the activity's gross income exceeds its deductions for three or more years in the five-year period ending with the current tax year, the taxpayer is presumed to engage in the activity for profit, unless the IRS establishes to the contrary. Moreover, a taxpayer can elect to wait until the end of the fourth year after initiating the activity to test whether the presumption applies.

> **NOTE**
>
> For activities involving the breeding, training, showing, or racing of horses, the presumption applies if profits are generated in two years of the seven-year period ending with the current year. An election to defer the testing of the presumption applies until the end of the sixth year in the period.

Allowable deductions. When taking deductions for an activity not engaged in for profit, the taxpayer must first deduct amounts that are deductible under other provisions, such as real estate taxes. These amounts remain fully deductible, regardless of the income from the activity. After deducting these items from the activity's income, the taxpayer can take other expenses related to a business or the production of income, such as wages, advertising, or supplies, up to the balance of the income. If any income from the activity remains, the taxpayer can take depreciation adjustments on depreciable property used in the activity.

These deductions must be taken as itemized deductions on Schedule A of Form 1040, rather than Schedule C or E of Form 1040. Deductions other than those allowable regardless of profit motive must:

- Be taken as miscellaneous itemized deductions; and
- Exceed the threshold of 2 percent of adjusted gross income.

STUDY QUESTION

---

6. The tax code presumes that an activity is engaged in for profit if the activity's income exceeds its deductions for _____ or more years in the _____ period ending with the current tax year.

  a. Two; four-year
  b. Three; five-year
  c. Five; six year

Gambling Losses

Gambling winnings are taxable income but may be reduced by gambling losses, whether the underlying transactions are legal or illegal. However, Code Sec. 165, which deals with losses, limits losses from "wagering transactions" to the gains from such transactions. Thus, the deduction for gambling losses under Code Sec. 165(d) cannot offset taxable income from nongambling sources.

Offsets. Professional gamblers, unlike casual gamblers, are not limited to claiming offsetting gambling deductions as Schedule A miscellaneous itemized deductions. Instead, professional gamblers may take loss deductions and any related gambling expenses "above-the-line" as part of a Schedule C separate trade or business. Nevertheless, professional gamblers that show a net loss from gambling activities cannot use any excess to offset nonwagering income.

COMMENT

Congress was concerned that gamblers tended to deduct their gambling losses but failed to report gambling winnings. One purpose of Code Sec. 165(d) was to force taxpayers to report their winnings if they want to deduct gambling losses.

Gambling losses can offset all gains from wagering transactions, not merely gambling winnings.

EXAMPLE

Complimentary items received from a casino as an inducement to gamble are gambling gains from which the taxpayer can deduct gambling losses. For a professional gambler, gambling losses include related business expenses, such as admission fees, meals, and lodging.

> **COMMENT**
>
> A number of court decisions establish limits on deducting gambling losses to gambling professionals. Some taxpayers have tried (usually unsuccessfully) to work around these rules by characterizing certain gambling-related expenses (e.g., state taxes, meals, supplies, and travel) as nongambling expenses, which would allow the individuals to deduct the expenses against nongambling income.

Gambling losses may only offset gambling winnings from the same year. Excess gambling losses and expenses from one year are lost and cannot be carried forward or back to offset gambling winnings from another year, even by a professional gambler.

> **COMMENT**
>
> The combined gambling losses of a husband and wife who file a joint return can be deducted against the couple's combined gambling winnings.

Required elements. The IRS requires that a wagering transaction have three elements:

- Consideration;
- A chance to win a prize; and
- A prize.

Raffle and lottery winnings are treated as gambling winnings that can be offset by gambling losses. However, a prize or contest award that can be won without an entry fee or other consideration is not gambling income; thus, it cannot be offset by gambling losses. The IRS has also ruled that the cost of a losing raffle ticket paid to a charity is a gambling loss, not a charitable contribution, and can only be deducted according to the gambling loss rules.

> **NOTE**
>
> Gambling losses from one type of activity can be deducted against gambling winnings from another type of activity.

A professional gambler can treat gambling losses as trade or business expenses (Schedule C expenses); thus, the losses that are allowed will in effect reduce AGI. Excess gambling losses by professional gamblers by order of the special gambling-related restriction under Code Section 165(d), however, cannot be used against gambling income from other years or generally as business NOLs. *Professional gambler* status is hard to achieve. Casual gamblers cannot become professional gamblers in the eyes of the IRS simply by gambling frequently. Strict requirements include the ability of the gambler to show activities being treated in a business-like manner using plans, strategies, and schedules.

For nonprofessional gamblers, gambling losses are only deductible as miscellaneous itemized deductions, and individuals' AGI will be higher. A casual gambler who takes the standard deduction cannot deduct gambling losses, although his or her winnings must be reported as income in full. Moreover, those losses that are deducted as itemized deductions are subject to the 2-percent floor on miscellaneous itemized deductions.

Amounts at Risk

The amount of losses that a taxpayer may deduct from many activities is limited to the amount at risk. The purpose of the at-risk rules is to limit the deduction of losses only to the taxpayer's investment in the activity (the amount the taxpayer could actually lose), and to deny losses that exceed the taxpayer's investment.

The at-risk rules apply to:

- Individuals;
- Individual partners of a partnership; and
- Individual shareholders of an S corporation.

The rules generally do not apply to:

- Widely held C corporations; and
- A partnership or S corporation at the entity level.

> **EXAMPLE**
>
> TechnoParts, a general partnership engaged in computer technology, has two partners: Atlas Corporation, a widely held corporation, and Jean Beach, an individual. The at-risk limits apply to Beach but not to Atlas.

The at-risk rules disallow a loss (the excess of deductions over income) to the extent the loss exceeds the amount to which the taxpayer is at risk. If a taxpayer is denied a loss because of the at-risk rules, the loss may be carried over for deduction in subsequent tax years when the amount at-risk increases.

The rules generally apply to a trade or business and to activities engaged in for profit. There is an exception for equipment-leasing activities of closely held corporations (five or fewer individuals having more than 50-percent ownership). The holding of real property was exempt prior to 1986, when this exemption was removed. Nevertheless, the rules are more lenient for real estate activities.

The amount at risk includes the amount of money (whether styled as a contribution to capital or a loan) and the adjusted basis (*not* fair market value) of property contributed to the activity. Income from the activity (or from selling an interest in the activity) increases the amount at risk. If the taxpayer has a loss or makes a withdrawal from the business, that figure reduces the amount at risk.

> **NOTE**
>
> Personal services, though they have value, are not treated as a capital contribution.

The at-risk amount also includes loan balances by the taxpayer for which the taxpayer is personally liable or has pledged property as collateral, other than property used in the activity. Amounts borrowed from related persons or persons having an interest in the activity (other than creditors) are not considered at risk if the activity involves:

- Farming;
- Oil, gas, or geothermal development; or
- Certain other activities.

Amounts are not at risk if they are protected by nonrecourse financing, guarantees, stop-loss agreements, or similar arrangements.

If the taxpayer engages in a real estate activity, the individual is also at risk for *qualified nonrecourse financing.* This applies to financing (or a portion of the financing):

- For which there is no personal liability;
- That is secured by real property used in the activity; and
- That is loaned by a government or "qualified person" (an unrelated person who is in the business of lending money and who was not the seller of the property).

The exception for nonrecourse financing does not apply to amounts borrowed from a person holding an interest in the activity or a person related to the interest-holder.

> **COMMENT**
>
> The at-risk rules are applied to partners and S corporation shareholders before the passive activity loss rules. A loss that is denied under the at-risk rules is not a passive loss.

Passive Activity Losses

If a taxpayer does not materially participate in a trade or business, the activity is a passive activity. Unlike the at-risk rules, which focus on financial contributions to the business, the passive activity loss (PAL) rules focus on the individual's participation in the business.

The PAL rules apply to:

- Individuals;
- Personal service corporations;
- Closely held C corporations;
- Partners; and
- S corporation shareholders.

The rules do *not* apply to partnerships, S corporations, or widely held C corporations.

Activities (and income) are divided into active (nonpassive), passive, and portfolio types. Losses from a passive activity can only be deducted against income from the same or another passive activity; such losses cannot offset active or portfolio income. Deductions that are disallowed in the current year under the PAL rules can be carried forward indefinitely and used to offset passive activity income in succeeding years.

PLANNING POINTER

Whether an activity is passive is determined each year. If a taxpayer has a carryover of PALs from a prior year, and the same activity generates active income in the current year, the PAL carryover can be used against active income from the current year.

Passive income includes gain from the disposition of property used in a passive activity. If the taxpayer disposes of the passive activity in a taxable transaction, the PAL limitations are removed. Any suspended PALs can be deducted against active and portfolio income.

Nonpassive income. Portfolio income generally includes interest, dividends, royalties, and annuities, although portfolio income derived in the ordinary course of a passive trade or business may be passive income. To prevent the deduction of PALs against nonpassive income, a number of items are categorized as active. Passive activity income does not include income from:

- Personal services and covenants not to compete;
- A working interest in oil and gas property;
- Intangible property significantly created by the taxpayer;

- Certain low-income housing projects;
- Income tax refunds; and
- State of Alaska dividend payments.

> **COMMENT**
>
> The oil and gas working interest exception applies regardless of the level of the taxpayer's participation in the activity.

Antiabuse provisions prevent active and portfolio income from being converted into passive income and soaking up PALs. Thus, passive income also does not include income from:
- Significant participation passive activities;
- Rental and sale of property developed by the taxpayer;
- Rental of property to a trade or business in which the taxpayer materially participates;
- Rental of nondepreciable property; and
- Equity-financed lending activities and interests in passthrough entities that license intangible property if the taxpayer acquires the interest after the entity creates the property.

Rental activities. Rental activities are passive activities, regardless of the taxpayer's level of participation, unless the individual is a real estate professional. However, individuals who own and "actively" participate in the management of rental real estate can offset up to $25,000 of losses from the rental real estate against active income in any year. Active participation is a lower standard than material participation. The offset is phased out by 50 percent of the amount that the taxpayer's adjusted gross income exceeds $100,000, up to $150,000 of AGI.

Material participation. A taxpayer materially participates in an activity if he or she is involved in the operations of the activity on a regular, continuous, and substantial basis. Although this is a factual determination, there are six safe harbor provisions that deem material participation if the taxpayer spends a certain number of hours on the activity in the current year or if the taxpayer materially participated in the activity in prior years. The six tests require that the taxpayer:
- Participated in the activity more than 500 hours during the year;
- Provided substantially all of the participation by individuals;
- Participated for 100 hours or more, and this equaled or exceeded others' participation;

- Participated for more than 100 hours in several activities and total participation adds up to more than 500 hours annually;
- Materially participated in the activity for 5 of the 10 previous years; and
- Provided personal (professional) services to the business and materially participated in any three preceding years.

> **COMMENT**
>
> Another test asks whether the facts and circumstances of the taxpayer's personal efforts suggest participation on a regular, continuous, and substantial basis.

For closely held C corporations and personal service corporations, there is material participation if shareholders owning 50 percent or more of the value of the outstanding stock materially participate in the activity. For closely held corporations, there is an alternative rule based on the participation of full-time employees.

> **COMMENT**
>
> Limited partners are deemed not to materially participate in partnership activities. The IRS has argued that this same treatment should apply to individuals holding interests in a limited liability partnership or limited liability corporation, but the courts have disagreed and allowed taxpayers to demonstrate material participation. The IRS has indicated that it will no longer litigate these cases but will issue guidance to tighten the material participation standard in this area.

STUDY QUESTIONS

7. Passive activity income includes:

  a. Royalties

  b. Income tax refunds

  c. Gain from the disposition of property used in a passive activity while the activity continues

8. A safe harbor for material participation applies to an individual who does not participate in an activity in this tax year if:

  a. He or she materially participated for the past five years

  b. He or she provided professional services to the business beginning with the previous two years

  c. He or she participated as the activity's business owner through 1998

FORGIVENESS OF DEBT

To purchase property or obtain funds for business or personal spending, individuals often borrow money. From credit card charges to the purchase of a home or a car, people go into debt so that they can use or enjoy an item before they have to pay its full price. Individuals intend to fully pay their debts, but a decline in individuals' economic circumstances may sometimes make this difficult.

To resolve the unpaid debt, creditors sometimes agree to reduce or cancel the liability. Depending on the circumstances, this *cancellation of indebtedness* (COI) can generate taxable income, even though nothing was paid to the debtor and the debtor is likely to be in difficult financial straits.

However, there are exclusions and exceptions to the recognition of income:

- The taxpayer will not have to recognize COI income if the debtor is
  - Bankrupt,
  - Insolvent, or
  - A disaster victim;
- Other exclusions are tied to the nature of the debt, such as
  - Farm debt;
  - Debt from real estate used in business,
  - Principal residence debt; and
- Debt from student loans.

If the income is not recognized, the debtor generally must reduce tax attributes. Some attributes are business related, such as NOLs. A common attribute for individuals is the basis of property—sometimes, the property for which the debt was incurred, sometimes other property. Thus, the excluded income is offset by reducing the basis (cost) of property owned by the debtor. This reduction delays the recognition of the COI income but generally ensures that the income will be recognized on the sale of the property, rather than being permanently excluded.

Discharge of Debt

COI income results from the discharge of debt and is treated as ordinary income. A *discharge* occurs when the creditor accepts less than the full amount of the debt as full payment. The debtor's circumstances, such as filing for bankruptcy, may trigger a discharge. There is no discharge if there is a reasonable expectation that the debt will be paid, although a delay in making payment of 36 months may be treated as triggering a discharge. A creditor who sold property and then reduces the debt is treated as reducing the sales price, not as cancelling any of the debt. If the debt is discharged, the COI income is the difference between the face value of the debt and the amount paid by the debtor that is treated as satisfying the debt.

NOTE

Though a debtor's going into bankruptcy may lead to a discharge, one of the exclusions of COI income applies to a debtor who is bankrupt.

COMMENT

The IRS issued regulations that eliminate reporting of COI income under the 36-month rule for credit card companies and finance companies. As economic conditions have worsened, some companies are giving customers more time to pay their debts. The 36-month rule could trigger reporting by the creditor that the debtor has COI income, even when the debt has not been discharged.

Exclusions

There are a number of potential exclusions that apply to a debtor who has COI income. Exclusions apply for:

- Insolvency—the debtor's total liabilities must exceed the total value of debtor's assets;
- Bankruptcy—a discharge by court order involving a liquidation, reorganization, or wage earner's plan;
- Farm debt—either debt on property or the farmer's personal debt, incurred in the farming business;
- Real property business debt—debt to acquire, construct, or substantially improve property used in a trade or business;
- Principal residence debt—up to $2 million of debt to buy, construct, or substantially improve a principal residence, if the discharge occurs by 2012;
- Student loans—applies to students working in certain professions (law, medicine, teaching) for public employers, charities, and schools;
- Disaster and terrorism victims—temporary exclusions for discharges of personal (not business) debt for victims of specified events during particular dates;
- Gifts and bequests that discharge personal debt—generally not business debt, because there is no donative intent;
- Deductible payments—for example, the discharge of interest expenses or a business debt that would have been deductible by a cash-basis taxpayer (no exclusion for accrual-basis taxpayers); and
- General welfare payments—for some government payments that are not taxable because they promote the general welfare, e.g., housing assistance or job training.

> **COMMENT**
>
> A taxpayer who is not bankrupt or insolvent may qualify for another exclusion.

Reduction of Tax Attributes

To offset the benefit of excluding the COI income, debtors may have to reduce their tax attributes. The most common attributes are net operating losses and the basis of property (depreciable or nondepreciable); others include capital loss carryovers and passive activity loss carryovers. Generally, NOLs are reduced first, followed by capital loss carryovers and basis of property. But a taxpayer may elect to reduce the basis of depreciable property before other attributes.

If the amount of COI income exceeds the taxpayer's total attributes, the excess is excluded from income permanently. The taxpayer does not have to recapture this excluded amount. However, different rules apply to real property business debt and principal residence debt; if the debt exceeds the property's basis, the excess is taxable.

> **COMMENT**
>
> If the taxpayer reduces basis and later sells the property at a gain, the taxpayer must recapture the basis reduction as ordinary income, even if recapture would not ordinarily apply to the sale.

For a debtor in bankruptcy, attribute reduction applies to the bankruptcy estate, not to exempt property or attributes of the debtor that arise after the case began. In general, the reduction of basis applies to property held at the beginning of the year following the year of discharge.

Generally, attributes are reduced dollar-for-dollar for the income excluded. However, for certain credits, such as the passive activity loss credit, attributes are reduced one dollar for every three dollars excluded.

> **COMMENT**
>
> Attributes have to be reduced for most exclusions but not for the exclusions for student loans, gifts and bequests, deductible debts, and general welfare payments.

Foreclosures, Repossessions, and Abandonments

If the debtor fails to make payments on a loan secured by property, the lender may foreclose on the loan or repossess the property. The transaction is treated as a taxable sale that may generate (capital) gain or loss to the debtor, even if the debtor voluntarily returns the property to the lender. The debtor's gain or loss is the difference between the debtor's adjusted basis in the property and the amount realized. If the loan balance exceeds the property's value and the excess is canceled, the debtor will also have ordinary income from the cancellation of debt, assuming the debtor is personally liable for the debt (recourse debt). If the debtor is not personally liable for the debt (nonrecourse debt), the treatment of the transaction as a sale by the debtor applies to the entire debt, even the portion (if any) that exceeds the property's value.

Property is abandoned when the owner voluntarily and permanently gives up possession and use of the property, intending to end ownership without transferring the property to anyone else. Abandonment is a disposition of property; loss from the abandonment is ordinary loss to the debtor, even if the property is a capital asset. The loss is equal to the property's basis. However, as stated earlier, an individual cannot deduct the loss from a home or other personal use property.

STUDY QUESTIONS

9. Which of the following is considered a discharge of debt resulting in cancellation of indebtedness income?
   a. The creditor who sold the property reduces the buyer's debt.
   b. The debtor promises to pay off indebtedness within 14 months, but the amount is not paid off in monthly installment for 20 months
   c. The creditor accepts 50 percent payment on a $100,000 debt

10. When a creditor forecloses on a secured nonrecourse loan and repossesses the debtor's car:
    a. The transaction is a sale for the entire debt amount
    b. The debtor has cancellation of indebtedness income
    c. The debtor has ordinary income or loss

CONCLUSION

Economic losses can provide tax benefits. A taxpayer with current year income can take advantage of tax losses to reduce taxable income and tax liability. A taxpayer with income in a previous or succeeding year can carry over current year losses (such as NOLs) to another year and thus obtain tax benefits. To take full advantage of tax losses, a taxpayer must be aware of the restrictions and special rules on the use of losses, whether from business, investment, hobby, or other circumstances, such as casualty.

CPE NOTE: When you have completed your study and review of chapters 4-5, which comprise Module 2, you may wish to take the Quizzer for this Module.

For your convenience, you can also take this Quizzer online at **www.cchtestingcenter.com**.

MODULE 3: COMPLIANCE AND DISCLOSURE — CHAPTER 6

Business Disclosure Rules in Transition

This chapter explores additional disclosure requirements for businesses exceeding the ordinary income tax return filing requirement. The chapter both provides background in these areas and covers the information taxpayers must report.

LEARNING OBJECTIVES

Upon completion of this chapter, you will be able to:

- Identify reportable transaction disclosure requirements resulting from the IRS's Tiered Issue Process;
- Explain the implications of disclosure requirements under the codified Economic Substance Doctrine;
- Describe reporting requirements for uncertain tax positions;
- Understand the enhanced reporting requirements for foreign assets and accounts; and
- Discuss the role of broker basis reporting and increased information reporting in reducing the federal tax gap.

INTRODUCTION

Any taxpayer with an income tax return filing requirement makes disclosures to the IRS. However, within the last several years, both the IRS and the tax code have begun requiring businesses to provide increasing disclosures above and beyond those required for an ordinary income tax return. To the IRS, large businesses provide the highest risk of noncompliance, whether due to misunderstanding of reporting rules or due to aggressive tax planning. Any business, however, is suspect if it fits certain profiles.

In defense of increasing required disclosures, IRS officials consistently state that the agency is seeking to improve the efficiency of its examinations so that high-priority items are given appropriate amounts of time and resources. They also state that, with its limited resources, the IRS is looking to head off erroneous and noncompliant tax reporting before it occurs.

TIERED ISSUE PROCESS

The IRS's Tiered Issue program is part of the IRS Large Business and International Division (LB&I), whose name was changed in August of

2010 from the Large and Mid-Size Business Division (LMSB) to give it a more international emphasis, but which still covers most businesses having more than $10 million in assets. Through this process, the IRS evaluates tax issues to assess the level of risk they pose for noncompliance. The IRS then assigns each issue to one of three risk tiers. Those tiers, according to descending level of risk, are as follows:

- Tier I Issues—Composed of issues of the highest strategic importance to LB&I, often affecting one or more industries and often involving a large number of taxpayers, significant dollar risk, substantial compliance risk, or high visibility;
- Tier II Issues—Reflecting areas of potential high importance to LB&I or an industry, including emerging issues, where the law is fairly well established, but there is a need for further development, clarification, direction and guidance on LB&I's position; and
- Tier III Issues—Comprising issues representing high compliance risk limited to a particular industry and requiring unique treatment within that industry.

When a Tier I issue is recognized for its abusive nature, the IRS will always address it during an examination. Otherwise, LB&I will examine risk factors such as the adjustment potential, materiality, impact on future years, and available resources before conducting an examination.

Required Transaction Disclosures

Although the Tiered Issue program is a mostly internal process for the IRS's coordination and administration of controversial tax issues, it is important nevertheless for taxpayers from a disclosure perspective. The IRS turns its Tier I or Tier II tax compliance issue into reportable transactions by issuing guidance describing them and designating them as reportable. Taxpayers must disclose their participation in reportable transactions under Reg. § 1.6011-4 along with their income tax returns and provide a copy of this disclosure to the IRS Office of Tax Shelter Analysis.

> **COMMENT**
>
> Although certainly possible for a Tier III issue to become a reportable transaction, that situation is unlikely due to such an issue's limited industry focus.

A reportable transaction encompasses all facts surrounding the expected tax treatment of an investment, entity, plan, or arrangement. A reportable transaction may consist of a series of steps carried out according to a plan, but it may also be a series of transactions entered into in the same tax year. Taxpayers disclose their reportable transactions on Form 8886, *Reportable Transaction Disclosure Statement,* and attach it to their income tax return. There are five categories of reportable transactions:

- Listed transactions;
- Confidential transactions;
- Contractually protecting transactions;
- Loss transactions; and
- Transactions of interest.

COMMENT

Reportable transactions are not limited to LB&I taxpayers. All taxpayers— whether businesses or individuals (or individuals receiving pass-through benefits from a partnership or S corporation)—are subject to the same standards in determining what transactions must be reported.

Listed Transactions

Listed transactions are ones the IRS has determined to have tax avoidance as their main or sole purpose. The IRS identifies them as such in published guidance. Taxpayers are required to report their transactions on Form 8886 that are the same as or substantially similar to those the IRS has determined to be listed transactions.

COMMENT

The IRS's *Internal Revenue Manual* maintains that the agency will request a taxpayer's tax accrual workpapers in special circumstances. According to the agency's policy, taxpayer participation in a listed transaction constitutes such a circumstance.

The IRS will consider a taxpayer to have participated in a listed transaction when the tax return reflects the tax consequences or the tax strategy of a listed transaction identified in IRS guidance. Additionally, the taxpayer must know or have reason to know that tax benefits were derived from those aspects of the listed transaction.

> **EXAMPLE**
>
> Positive Corporation, on the advice of a tax professional, enters into a transaction to reduce its income tax liability from the sale of corporate stock. The IRS released Notice 2005-13 labeling the transaction as a sales-in, lease-out (SILO) transaction and indicating similar transactions or those substantially the same as them to be abusive tax avoidance strategies. The company's chief counsel informed the company of this fact. Positive Corp. must disclose its participation in this transaction on its income tax return, as well as with any subsequent amended return.

Confidential Transactions

Confidential transactions are those offered to taxpayers under conditions of confidentiality and for which the taxpayer has paid a minimum fee to an advisor in order to participate. This occurs when the advisor requests that the taxpayer keep the tax treatment of the transaction or its tax structure confidential. A transaction may fall within this category even if the taxpayer's confidentiality obligation is not legally enforceable. The transaction is not confidential merely because the transaction is considered proprietary or exclusive if the advisor also informs the taxpayer that there is no limit on the taxpayers' disclosures.

Participation. The IRS will consider a taxpayer to have participated in a confidential transaction when the return shows a tax benefit from the transaction and also when the taxpayer's disclosure of its tax treatment or structure to the IRS was so limited by its agreement with the advisor as to qualify the transaction as confidential. When a partnership, S corporation, or trust is limited in its disclosure of the transaction, the partners, S corp shareholders, or beneficiaries of those entities are also generally considered to have participated in a confidential transaction. An exception exists if the participants were free to disclose the transaction to the IRS.

Confidentiality. To be considered confidential, the taxpayer's advisor for the transaction must also charge a minimum amount for his or her fee. The minimum amount is $250,000 for each transaction involving a corporate taxpayer or when the transaction involves a partnership or trust and all partners or beneficiaries are corporations. The minimum fee is $50,000 for all other transactions.

The taxpayer must pay the fee to an unrelated person. Additionally, the fee must qualify as consideration for a tax strategy, services for tax advice, or for implementation of the transaction. It does not include amounts paid to a person in their capacity as a party to the transaction; as a reasonable charge for the use of capital; or for the sale or use of property.

STUDY QUESTIONS

---

1. The Tiered Issue risk level to which emerging issues with established law, but requiring further development or clarification of the IRS's position, are assigned as:

   a. Tier I
   b. Tier II
   c. Tier III

2. By issuing guidance identifying new Tier I and Tier II compliance issues, the IRS turns them into:

   a. Reportable transactions
   b. Unlisted transactions
   c. Undisclosable transactions

Contractually Protected Transactions

Taxpayers are required to report participation in transactions on Form 8886 when the participants have the right to a full or partial refund of fees if all or part of the transaction's intended tax consequences are not sustained upon any government action. This includes arrangements in which an advisor's fees are contingent upon realization of tax benefits. The IRS will consider the taxpayer to have participated in a *contractually protected transaction* if the taxpayer:

- Reports tax benefits from the transaction on a tax return; and
- Retains the right to a full or partial refund of fees or the fees were contingent.

If a partnership, S corporation, or trust has a right to refund of fees from the advisor or establishes a contingent fee arrangement, then partners, shareholders, and beneficiaries of those entities are also considered to have participated in a contractually protected transaction. An exception to this rule applies if the partner, shareholder, or beneficiary does not have a right to a fee refund or contingency fee arrangement.

In determining whether a transaction is contractually protected, the IRS will only examine certain fees. Relevant fees include those paid by or on behalf of the taxpayer or a related party to a person who made a statement concerning the potential tax consequences of the transaction. The advisor's statement may be oral or written.

However, the transaction will not be deemed contractually protected and will not warrant reporting if any party to the transaction has a subsequent right to terminate because of an occurrence that affects the transaction's tax treatment. Additionally, a transaction will not qualify as contractually protected if the advisor made representations concerning the transaction after the taxpayer entered into it and reported its consequences on a tax return.

> **CAUTION**
>
> Although this latter exception may be true, Section 10.27(b) of Circular 230 (regulations governing practice before the IRS) limits contingent fees for tax practitioners to:
>
> - Services in connection with the examination or challenge to a return;
> - Refund/credit claims in connection with the IRS's determination of statutory interest or penalties; and
> - Fees related to any judicial proceeding under the tax code.

Loss Transactions

Taxpayers must disclose their participation in transactions resulting in Code Sec. 165 losses above certain threshold amounts. The IRS will consider taxpayers to have participated in a *loss transaction* if they actually report Code Sec. 165 losses on their own income tax returns in an amount exceeding those thresholds. Partners, shareholders, or beneficiaries are considered to have participated in reportable loss transaction if they receive a flow-through of Code Sec. 165 losses from a partnership, S corp, or trust exceeding the applicable thresholds and report those losses on tax returns. Under this rule, a partner, shareholder, or beneficiary must disregard any netting of the Code Sec. 165 losses against other income at the entity level. Additionally, those investors must report the loss transaction even if the excessive losses are carried over or carried back to other tax years as net operating or net capital losses.

Loss thresholds applicable to reportable loss transactions include the following:
- $10 million during a single tax year or $20 million in a combination of tax years for a corporation;
- $2 million in a single tax year or $5 million in a combination of tax years for partnerships;
- $10 million in a single tax year or $20 million in a combination of tax years for partnerships with only corporations as partners; and
- $2 million in a single tax year or $4 million in a combination of tax years for S corporations.

The combinations of tax years may include loss from the tax year in which the transaction took place and those losses recognized in the five subsequent tax years.

Transactions of Interest

Finally, taxpayers must disclose participation in transactions that are the same as or substantially similar to those designated by the IRS in published guidance as transactions of interest.

STUDY QUESTIONS

3. The IRS considers a taxpayer to have participated in a _____ if his or her tax advisor orally promises to refund fees if the transaction fails to have its intended tax consequence.

   a. Listed transaction

   b. Confidential transaction

   c. Contractually protected transaction

4. A transaction is not considered to be contractually protected if the advisor made representations about the transaction after the taxpayer includes its consequences on a tax return. ***True or False?***

Timing of Disclosure

Generally, taxpayers must include Form 8886 describing their participation in a reportable transaction along with their income tax return for the tax year during which they participated. This holds true for partnerships and S corporations participating in reportable transactions as well. However, taxpayers must also include their disclosure along with each amended return reflecting the tax benefits from a reportable transaction. Additionally, the taxpayer must include Form 8886 with an application for a tentative refund or amended tax return for a prior tax year when claiming a loss carryback resulting from a reportable transaction.

If a transaction becomes a listed transaction after the taxpayer has filed a tax return reporting the tax benefits of a transaction, the taxpayer must disclose participation in the transaction with the next tax return it files after that date. However, the transaction must have become listed within the statute of limitations period for the tax year in which the taxpayer participated in the transaction.

COMMENT

The IRS proposed regulations in September 2007 (NPRM REG-129916-07) that would require taxpayers to disclose the patenting of tax advice or strategies. Such a disclosure would include a situation in which a taxpayer pays the patent holder for the right to use a patent-protected tax-planning method. However, the rules would not apply to patents issued solely:

■ For tax-preparation software;

■ To perform mathematical calculations; or

■ To provide mechanical assistance in the preparation of tax returns.

Penalties

Understatements. By participating in a reportable transaction, taxpayers are subject to penalties. Code Sec. 6662A imposes an accuracy-related penalty upon understatement of tax attributable to participation in a reportable transaction. The penalty is 20 percent of the amount of the understatement.

However, this penalty may be avoided if taxpayers can show reasonable cause and that they acted in good faith. Taxpayers must have:

- Adequately disclosed the transaction;
- Had substantial authority for the position; and
- Reasonably believed that their position was more likely than not the proper treatment.

Nondisclosure. Special penalties apply when the taxpayer fails to disclose participation in a reportable transaction, regardless of whether any understatement penalty is ultimately due. The accuracy-related penalty increases to 30 percent if the taxpayer fails to disclose a listed transaction or other tax avoidance transactions. Additionally, Code Sec. 6707A also imposes a $10,000 penalty against individuals and a $50,000 penalty against other taxpayers for each reportable transaction they fail to report as required by the Code Sec. 6011 regulations. For each listed transaction, the penalty is increased to $100,000 for individuals and $200,000 for other taxpayers.

EXAMPLE

With the assistance of a legal advisor, Granite Corp participates in a lease-in, lease-out (LILO) transaction and a confidential transaction during the tax year, recognizing $5,000 in related tax benefits. The IRS has identified the LILO transaction in published guidance as a listed transaction. Contrary to the advice of its tax preparer, the C corporation does not disclose its participation in these transactions to the IRS.

Upon subsequent discovery by the IRS, Granite would be subject to a $200,000 penalty for its participation in the LILO transaction, as it is a listed transaction. Granite would pay a $50,000 penalty for failing to disclose participation in the confidential transaction, because it is only a reportable transaction.

The IRS is authorized under Code Sec. 6707A(d) to rescind the penalty for reportable transactions that are not listed transactions if doing so would promote compliance with the Tax Code and effective tax administration. This authority is consistent with the IRS's desire to develop and clarify its position on uncertain Tier I and Tier II issues before conducting routine examinations or other enforcement efforts.

COMMENT

In response to congressional requests, IRS Commissioner Douglas Shulman imposed a moratorium on enforcement of Code Sec. 6707A beginning in July 2009 and lasting until June 1, 2010, for certain small businesses. At press time, that moratorium has been informally extended again. Congressional members were concerned about penalties on small businesses failing to disclose participation in a reportable transaction because such a penalty is often largely disproportionate to the transaction's reported tax benefits. Legislation has been introduced to create a penalty equal to 75 percent of the tax benefits reported for a nondisclosed reportable transaction, with a maximum $100,000 penalty for individuals and maximum $200,000 penalty for other taxpayers failing to disclose listed transactions. The amount would drop to a maximum of $10,000 for individuals and maximum of $50,000 for other taxpayers failing to disclose reportable transactions. The *Small Business Jobs Act of 2010* (H.R. 5297) proposed to apply these penalty rates retroactively to penalties assessed after December 31, 2006.

STUDY QUESTION

5. If a transaction becomes a listed transaction after the taxpayer has filed a tax return reporting the tax benefits from the transaction:

a. No penalty accrues

b. The taxpayer must disclose participation in that transaction with the next tax return within a three-year period

c. The taxpayer has no statute of limitations period beginning with that tax year

ECONOMIC SUBSTANCE

Throughout the modern era of U.S. taxation, the judicially created *economic substance doctrine* has been an essential tool in the government's effort to combat tax avoidance. The essence of the economic substance doctrine is that the IRS will not respect the reported form of a taxpayer's transaction if the taxpayer entered into the transaction solely for its tax benefits. Inadequate disclosure of a transaction that is ultimately deemed to lack economic substance in turn carries several penalties for the taxpayer.

Development and Codification

The economic substance originally began as a judicially created legal concept. Its roots, along with several other tax concepts, begin with the landmark decision, ***Gregory v. Helvering.*** In that case, a taxpayer used a corporate reorganization to report ordinary income normally constituting a corporate dividend as capital gains income. The U.S. Supreme Court held that the taxpayer's reorganization was "a disguise for concealing its real character."

During the heyday of marketed tax shelter products, the government successfully used the economic substance doctrine to go after abusive tax shelter participants. For many years, government officials proposed codifying the doctrine and creating a penalties structure for violations to give the doctrine even more legal weight. Finally, in March 2010, the *Health Care and Education Reconciliation Act of 2010* created Code Sec. 7701(o) to encapsulate the economic substance doctrine. To survive IRS scrutiny of its reported tax attributes, the transaction must change the taxpayer's economic position in a meaningful way (an objective standard) and the taxpayer must have a substantial nontax-avoidance purpose for entering into the transaction (a subjective standard).

COMMENT

This rule settles a long standing dispute among the federal circuits about how to apply the economic substance doctrine. Several jurisdictions applied the current form of the rule. However, other courts applied a disjunctive version of the current rule. In those jurisdictions, a taxpayer could prove economic substance for a transaction by only showing having met only one of the two standards.

In determining whether a transaction changes the taxpayer's economic position in a meaningful way, the law allows taxpayers to show that their transaction had the potential to make a profit. However, to do so, the present value of any reasonably expected pretax profit from the transaction must be substantial in relation to the present value of its expected net federal tax benefits. With regard to the objective prong, a taxpayer may not claim a financial reporting benefit as a substantial purpose for entering into the transaction if that benefit is rooted in an effort to reduce the taxpayer's income tax liability.

COMMENT

The economic substance rule applies to both individuals and businesses, but only to individuals if they engage in transactions in connection with a trade or business activity for the production of income. The new codification is also limited to the income tax provisions of the tax code and does not apply to any estate or gift tax transactions.

Finally, the law attempts to keep application of the codified economic substance doctrine similar to its common law form. The provision states that "determination of whether the economic substance doctrine is relevant to a transaction shall be made in the same manner as if this subsection had never been enacted." As a consequence of this fact, codification of the economic substance doctrine is not intended to change the tax treatment of certain basic business transactions that have been respected under a longstanding judicial or administrative practice. This is true even when the taxpayer had the choice between meaningful economic alternatives and made its decision based on the tax consequences for each position.

Penalties

Now that the doctrine has been put into the tax code, taxpayer disclosures of transactions that could potentially lack economic substance are more important than ever to avoid crushing penalties. Although practitioners welcomed the uniformity codification of the economic substance brought, the most controversial portion of codification remains its associated penalties for lack of disclosure.

Code Sec. 6662 imposes accuracy-related penalties for the underpayment of taxes because of:

- Negligence;
- Substantial understatements of tax; or
- Understatements of tax due to valuation misstatements.

The penalty is generally 20 percent of the underpayment of tax. However, the taxpayer may avoid the penalty if it had reasonable cause for the underpayment of tax and acted in good faith. As Congress codified the economic substance doctrine in Code Sec. 7701(o), it also added a new penalty under Code Sec. 6662 for the underpayment of tax attributable to tax benefits disallowed for lack of economic substance. This penalty is also 20 percent of the underpayment amount.

The penalty for participation in a transaction lacking economic substance increases to 40 percent when the taxpayer fails to adequately disclose the transaction on its tax return or in a separate statement.

> **COMMENT**
>
> In determining whether the taxpayer has adequately disclosed the transaction, the IRS will look to the taxpayer's original tax return for the year at issue. The IRS will not consider any amended return or supplement to the tax return filed after the agency has contacted the taxpayer for examination.

However, distinctive from other accuracy-related penalties, the penalty for failing to disclose a transaction lacking economic substance is not subject to any exceptions. Taxpayers cannot dispute the imposition of the penalty using the reasonable cause and good faith defense. As a result, even an outside legal opinion or in-house legal analysis will not protect the taxpayer from the penalty.

> **COMMENT**
>
> The IRS will not impose the Code Sec. 6662A accuracy-related penalty on understatements of tax attributable to reportable transaction if the taxpayer is subject to the 40-percent penalty for failing to disclose a transaction lacking economic substance.

> **COMMENT**
>
> The 40-percent penalty for failing to disclose a transaction lacking economic substance will not apply to any understatement of tax subject to the fraud penalty.

STUDY QUESTIONS

6. The economic substance doctrine was codified in the:
  a. *Health Care and Education Reconciliation Act of 2010*
  b. *Tax Reform Act of 1986*
  c. Circular 230 regulations

7. The accuracy-related penalty for failure to disclose a transaction lacking economic substance will not apply to:
  a. Tax understatements due to valuation misstatements
  b. Substantial understatements of tax
  c. Understatements of tax due to fraud

UNCERTAIN TAX POSITIONS

A relatively new development, the issue of *uncertain tax positions* (UTPs), remains one of the most controversial additional disclosure requirements for taxpayers and practitioners. Publicly traded businesses required by generally accepted accounting principles (GAAP) to produce audited financial statements must report contingent liabilities under certain circumstances. Financial Accounting Standards Board Interpretation Number 48, *Accounting for Uncertainty in Income Taxes* (FIN 48), applies to these taxpayers' contingent tax liabilities. FIN 48 limits the benefits a taxpayer may report as a result of its reported tax position to those benefits more likely than not to be sustained upon an examination by the IRS or through litigation in court. To make the more likely than not determination, taxpayers must often obtain opinions from counsel and compile spreadsheets of relevant data. These are often referred to as the taxpayer's *tax accrual workpapers.*

Financial reporting of uncertain tax positions became an issue with the IRS because taxpayers who must comply with the FIN 48 tax-reporting standard are required to share this information with an independent auditor to obtain an unqualified audit opinion. The IRS takes the position that this disclosure waives any sort of privilege the taxpayer had to this information. The IRS largely bolsters this argument with the U.S. Supreme Court's decision in the *Arthur Young* case (*U.S. Sup. Ct,* 84-1 USTC ¶9305, 465 US 805, 104 SCt 1495). In that decision, the Supreme Court ruled that there is no special auditor–client privilege.

However, given the vast amount of sensitive information contained in tax-payers' tax accrual workpapers, the IRS has self-imposed a "policy of restraint" in its practice of requesting them. As incorporated within the *Internal Revenue Manual,* the IRS will not request submission of tax accrual workpapers as a general practice. Instead, IRS rules state that it will only request these documents in special circumstances. Such situations include where the taxpayer has engaged in transactions the IRS has previously stated have the potential for tax avoidance or actually provide for tax avoidance.

These developments have met much disapproval from the tax practitioner community. Despite the IRS's policy of restraint, many have argued that disclosure of tax accrual workpapers to the IRS places taxpayers at an unfair advantage during a tax dispute. Due the sensitive nature of the information they contain, practitioners argue that the documents provide a "roadmap" for the IRS concerning the taxpayer's position. Workpapers not only provide direction to any potential outstanding tax liability but also reveal potential weaknesses in the taxpayer's defense that the IRS could exploit at trial. The documents provide an unnecessary advantage to the IRS, practitioners claim, for positions in which reasonable minds could differ on interpreting the tax law.

Despite these protests, the IRS continued to press on with its position on disclosure of tax accrual workpapers. As a result of this effort, the IRS won a critical lawsuit in the U.S. Court of Appeals for the First Circuit. After losing at the district court level and a panel hearing from the First Circuit, the government finally prevailed in an en banc decision from the First Circuit. The court ruled that the taxpayer's tax accrual workpapers were not protected from disclosure to the IRS by the work product privilege. The taxpayer appealed the decision to the U.S. Supreme Court, which denied the petition for *writ of certiorari.*

> **COMMENT**
>
> A decision from U.S. Court of Appeals for the District of Columbia Circuit, on the other hand, applied the work product protection to a taxpayer's tax accrual workpapers.

Proposed UTP Disclosures

Spurred by its litigation successes concerning tax accrual workpapers, the IRS released Announcement 2010-9 in January 2010, announcing its plans to require certain publicly traded taxpayers who report uncertain tax positions in their financial statements under FIN 48 to also report them on their income tax returns. The IRS justified this requirement by reasoning that UTP disclosures would improve the effectiveness and efficiency of its examinations of business taxpayers. The announcement stated that, based upon the amount of tax exposures reported in UTP disclosures, examiners could prioritize their selection of taxpayers for review and spend less time identifying issues while spending more time discussing applicable laws. Further, the IRS reasoned that, because it arguably has legal authority to request taxpayers' tax accrual workpapers—those documents at the very core of taxpayers' UTPs—the agency was on secure legal ground in requiring its own version of UTP reporting on returns.

> **COMMENT**
>
> Despite this enhanced reporting requirement, IRS Commissioner Shulman reported that the IRS will still apply its policy of restraint against asking for tax accrual workpapers during an examination.

Although the IRS termed the disclosure requirement as a proposal, the requirement appears to be a certainty. Commissioner Shulman has indicated that the IRS expects to publish regulations requiring taxpayers to report their UTPs. He even suggested that the agency may ask Congress for additional authority to penalize taxpayers failing to adequately meet their UTP filing requirements.

The UTP reporting requirement applies to businesses with total assets exceeding $10 million. Further, although the requirement applies to taxpayers who determine their federal income tax reserves under FIN 48, the taxpayer must actually have one or more UTPs affecting the organization's U.S. tax liability.

> **COMMENT**
>
> As the IRS continued to receive feedback concerning proposed UTP reporting, the government now maintains that taxpayers subject to FIN 48 reporting should file Schedule UTP, *Uncertain Tax Positions*, even if they do not actually have a UTP for the year. IRS officials recognized that, through this practice, taxpayers may avoid arousing suspicion with IRS examiners by acknowledging their UTP reporting requirement to the IRS. The form has a check box indicating that the taxpayer does not have any UTPs.

UTP reporting will begin for the 2010 tax year, the results of which taxpayers report in 2011. The IRS will begin requiring corporations and certain insurance companies to disclose their UTPs on Schedule UTP, *Uncertain Tax Positions*. The form must accompany any of the following returns:

- Form 1120, *U.S. Corporation Income Tax Return;*
- Form 1120-F, *U.S. Income Tax Return of a Foreign Corporation;*
- Form 1120-L, *U.S. Life Insurance Company Income Tax Return;* and
- Form 1120-PC, *U.S. Property and Casualty Insurance Company Income Tax Return.*

> **COMMENT**
>
> IRS officials have stated that 2010 UTP reporting will not apply to flow-through entities, Subchapter S corporations, and partnerships. However, officials have stated that the IRS has not ruled out this reporting possibility for future years. The agency invited practitioners to comment on this issue.

> **COMMENT**
>
> UTP reporting does not apply to personal service corporations (PSCs) because their stock is generally held by current or former employees, as defined by Code Sec. 448(d)(2). Because PSCs are not publicly traded, they do not report audited financial statements and are not required to follow FIN 48.

Schedule UTP

The IRS released Schedule UTP in Announcement 2010-30. On the form, taxpayers must provide a "concise description" concerning those UTPs for which they have recorded a tax reserve in their financial statements. They must also report their maximum tax exposure for each UTP—their outstanding tax liability if the IRS completely disallowed their tax treatment.

> **COMMENT**
>
> Commissioner Shulman has pointed out on several occasions that Schedule UTP does not request taxpayers to disclose their tax reserve amounts or any analysis concerning the merits of their tax position. He has stated that the IRS avoided requesting this information, because the agency was not trying to "get into the heads" of taxpayers.

Schedule UTP also requires a rationale for the UTP and a general statement about why the position is uncertain. Taxpayers must include applicable tax code sections, the affected tax years, and other specifics concerning the UTPs.

Duplicative Disclosures

One of the strongest criticisms of the IRS's proposed UTP reporting requirement is that it creates superfluous reporting. To some extent, the IRS has recognized this fact. Also in Announcement 2010-30, the IRS indicated it will treat taxpayers who file Schedule UTP as having filed Form 8275, *Disclosure Statement,* and Form 8275-R, *Regulation Disclosure Statement.*

Taxpayers use Form 8275 to report items and tax positions that are inadequately disclosed in their tax return in order to avoid certain penalties. These include accuracy-related penalties for substantial understatement of tax and preparer penalties for understatements of tax due to unreasonable positions or disregard of the rules. Taxpayers use Form 8275-R to report tax positions contrary to Treasury regulations. Filing this form allows taxpayers to avoid the same penalties as filing Form 8275. Information reported on these forms, the IRS has recognized, duplicates that required on Schedule UTP.

The IRS also reported it is looking into other potential areas of duplicative reporting. The IRS has mentioned Form 8886, *Reportable Transaction Disclosure Statement.* This form is similar to Schedule UTP in that the IRS may or may not disallow the tax benefits from transactions reported on this form. The form points out controversial or novel transactions to the IRS that the agency may simply study for further understanding rather than for tax enforcement.

The IRS also observed that Schedule M-3 (Form 1120), *Net Income (Loss) Reconciliation for Corporations with Total Assets of $10 Million or More,* may be duplicative to Schedule UTP. This form is somewhat similar to Schedule UTP in that it compares tax information the taxpayer disclosed for financial reporting purposes with the corporation's tax position. Schedule M-3 requires the taxpayer to reconcile the differences between their financial statement net income or loss and reported taxable income.

FIN 48 Differences

Another criticism of the UTP reporting requirement has been that the reporting could confuse IRS personnel regarding the taxpayer's reported position, resulting in unnecessary examinations and adjustments. This critique stems from the fact that reporting requirements on Schedule UTP differ from those required by FIN 48.

Schedule UTP requires taxpayers to report their maximum possible tax liability to the IRS as a result of a UTP. FIN 48 instead limits the tax benefits taxpayers may report on their financial statements, assuming that taxpayers that produce audited financial statements will attempt to maximize their profits reported to shareholders and therefore reduce their tax liabilities. FIN 48 allows taxpayers to account for settlement possibilities in their reporting of tax liabilities. Also, as one practitioner has pointed out, FIN 48 disclosures are often made after the taxpayer has sought professional advice about what tax liability they can realistically expect the IRS to assess. Maximum tax liability amounts do not reflect the advice of a tax professional and could be misleading to IRS personnel when the law is unclear or unsettled.

STUDY QUESTIONS

> **8.** Uncertain tax position (UTP) disclosures reported in taxpayers' financial statements are **not** included on Schedule UTP for the tax returns of:
>
> **a.** Estates and trusts
> **b.** Corporations
> **c.** Life insurance companies
>
> **9.** When taxpayers file Schedule UTP, the IRS will consider them to have filed Form 8275, *Disclosure Statement,* and Form 8275-R, *Regulation Disclosure Statement,* as well. ***True or False?***

FOREIGN ASSET/ACCOUNT REPORTING

In addition to its tax administration duties, the IRS also administers enforcement of the *Bank Secrecy Act* (BSA), as codified by Title 31 to the U.S. Code. Since BSA's enactment in 1970, the government has used the BSA to fight money laundering through recordkeeping and file reporting requirements. These disclosures are used by law enforcement agencies to combat money laundering in furtherance of criminal enterprises, terrorism, and tax evasion.

Under Title 31, U.S. persons must annually report their financial interests in or signatory authority over any type of financial account in a foreign country to Treasury. To report these interests, the taxpayer must file Form TD F 90-22.1, *Report of Foreign Bank and Financial Accounts* (FBAR) on or before June 30 of each calendar year in which the taxpayer possesses the interest.

> **COMMENT**
>
> This reporting requirement does not apply to accounts located in a U.S. military banking or finance facility located abroad or the U.S. territories of Guam, Puerto Rico, or the Virgin Islands.

Penalty for Failure to Report

The *American Jobs Act of 2004* imposes a $10,000 penalty upon taxpayers failing to meet this disclosure requirement. If the taxpayer willfully failed to report their interest, the penalty increases to the greater of $100,000 or 50 percent of the transaction/account.

Tax Return Disclosures

Although foreign interest disclosure requirements have existed for more than 40 years, it is only within recent years that the IRS has made such disclosure a priority in its routine tax compliance administration. This effort began in 2008 when a former senior employee of the Swiss bank, UBS AG, pled guilty to conspiracy to defraud the IRS by assisting U.S. citizens evade reporting their taxable income. The official claimed the bank managed around $20 billion of assets within the accounts of U.S. taxpayers of which the IRS was unaware.

After the U.S. Department of Justice (DOJ) successfully brought suit against UBS in federal court, the parties subsequently entered into a deferred prosecution agreement, under which the bank agreed to pay approximately $700 million in fees. The bank admitted to assisting U.S. taxpayers establish accounts protected from disclosure to the IRS by Swiss banking laws and offshore entities in jurisdictions with little disclosure laws to which the taxpayers transferred income-producing assets. Further, UBS agreed to name its U.S. customers engaging in this activity, whom the IRS estimated were hiding approximately $14.8 billion in securities and cash in offshore jurisdictions. The DOJ petitioned the court to enforce an IRS "John Doe" summons against the bank in the case of noncompliance.

> **COMMENT**
>
> The IRS has authority to issue a summons request on a third party that does not identify whose tax liability is at issue. However, the IRS may only serve this summons after it brings an *ex parte* proceeding in federal court.

In the wake of this success, the IRS launched a temporary Offshore Voluntary Compliance Initiative under which it would not enforce criminal charges against taxpayers hiding assets and offshore accounts in return for:

- Disclosing their foreign interests;
- Paying their taxes owed plus interest; and
- Paying a reduced penalty.

Additionally, legislation from both members of Congress and the Obama Administration's fiscal year 2011 budget was introduced to address this issue as well.

These efforts produced new foreign asset and account disclosure rules in March of 2010 in the form of the *Hiring Incentives to Restore Employment Act* (HIRE Act). Under Code Sec. 6038D, as created by the HIRE Act, taxpayers with financial interests abroad must also meet certain disclosure requirements on their U.S. income tax returns. Effective for tax years beginning after March 18, 2010, taxpayers with foreign financial assets having a $50,000 aggregate value or more must report them on their income tax returns. These assets include:

- Depository, custodial, or other financial accounts maintained by a foreign financial institution;
- Securities issued by a non-U.S. person;
- Financial instruments held for investment with an issuer or counterparty that is a non-U.S. person; and
- Ownership interest in a foreign entity.

Table 1. Asset Reporting Requirements by Type of Asset

Asset Type	Reporting Requirements
Financial accounts	Account number Name and address of the financial institution where the account is maintained
Securities	Information sufficient to identify the class or issue of which the security is a part Name and address of the issuer
Other financial instruments	Information necessary to identify the instrument Name and addresses of all issuers and related counterparties

The taxpayer must disclose the maximum value of these assets during the tax year.

Penalties. Foreign account and asset holders failing to disclose those interests on their tax returns when necessary are subject to a $10,000 penalty under Code Sec. 6038D. They are subject to another penalty if they subsequently fail to disclose their interests after the IRS notifies them of the failure. If the taxpayer fails to disclose for more than 90 days after the day on which the agency mails the notice, the taxpayer is subject to an additional penalty of $10,000 for each 30-day period during which the failure continues, up to a maximum of $50,000.

> **COMMENT**
>
> The IRS may presume that those taxpayers, failing to disclose their foreign financial assets sufficient to allow the IRS to discover their aggregate value, have assets exceeding the $50,000 reporting threshold for purposes of imposing these penalties.

Further, taxpayers subject to these penalties are also subject to the Code Sec. 6662 40-percent accuracy-related penalty for the understatement of tax attributable to an undisclosed foreign financial asset.

Statute of limitations. Code Sec. 6501 generally imposes a three-year statute of limitations on the IRS's prosecution of an outstanding tax liability, but the statute of limitations increases to six years after the taxpayer files a tax return failing to disclose a foreign account or asset. Additionally, the taxpayer must have omitted more than $5,000 of gross income attributable to the foreign interest.

Exceptions. However, similar to most penalties, there are exceptions. The penalties for failure to disclose foreign accounts or assets will not apply if the taxpayer can show the failure was due to reasonable cause and not willful neglect.

> **COMMENT**
>
> Under Code Sec. 6657(d), the taxpayer cannot argue for the reasonable cause exception based on the fact that a foreign jurisdiction would impose a civil or criminal penalty on the taxpayer for disclosing the required information.

STUDY QUESTIONS

10. Under its Offshore Voluntary Compliance Initiative, the IRS would not enforce criminal charges against taxpayers hiding assets and using offshore accounts if the taxpayers:

   a. Disclosed the foreign interest, paid the full tax liability plus interest, and paid a reduced penalty

   b. Disclosed the foreign interest and paid an additional 50 percent penalty

   c. Disclosed full information about other U.S. taxpayers participating in the ventures

---

11. Under the _____, U.S. taxpayers must report foreign financial assets having at least a $50,000 aggregate value on their income tax returns.

a. HIRE Act
b. *American Jobs Act of 2004*
c. *Bank Secrecy Act*

Foreign Trusts

U.S. persons owning and conducting financial transactions with foreign trusts must provide disclosures to the IRS under Code Sec. 6048 along with their income tax return. The taxpayer must complete a Form 3520, *Annual Return to Report Transactions with Foreign Trusts and Receipt of Certain Foreign Gifts,* for each reportable event and for each affected foreign trust. Reportable events include:

- Creation of an inter vivos foreign trust during the tax year;
- The transfer of funds to the foreign trust;
- The death of the taxpayer owning a portion of the foreign trust or including a portion of the trust in his or her gross estate (reported by the executor of the taxpayer's estate); and
- Testamentary transfers to the trust (also reported by the executor of the estate).

COMMENT

To complete the taxpayer's reporting requirements, the foreign trust must also file Form 3520-A, *Annual Information Return of Foreign Trust with a U.S. Owner.* If the taxpayer treats a tax item on its Form 3520 in a manner inconsistent with the foreign trust's treatment on Form 3520-A, the taxpayer must also file Form 8082, *Notice of Inconsistent Treatment or Administrative Adjustment Request.*

PLANNING POINTER

Beneficiaries of a foreign trust are also required to report distributions from the trust received during the tax year.

In making its disclosures on Form 3520, the taxpayer must identify the trust, each trustee, and each beneficiary or class of beneficiaries of the foreign trust. The taxpayer must report the amount of money or property transferred to the trust.

Ownership of a foreign trust. To determine who created the foreign trust and whether a decedent owned a portion of the foreign trust, the grantor trust rules under Code Secs. 671 through 679 apply. The taxpayer is considered to have created a foreign trust when the assets are treated as owned by a person other than the trust. Additionally, only gratuitous transfers to a foreign trust are subject to the Code Sec. 6048 reporting rules.

Gratuitous transfers to a foreign trust include transfers other than those exchanged for fair market value or with respect to an interest held by the trust. Such transfers include, but are not limited to, gift transfers. The determination of whether a transfer to a foreign trust is gratuitous is independent of the gift tax rules. As a result, whereas a taxpayer may not be subject to the gift tax on a transfer to a foreign trust, he or she may still have to report the transfer on Form 3520.

The HIRE Act clarified several aspects of the grantor trust rules in Code Sec. 679 specific to foreign trusts. For purposes of determining whether the foreign trust is a grantor trust, the HIRE Act created a rebuttable presumption that a foreign trust has a U.S. beneficiary if a U.S. person transferred property to the trust. To counter this presumption, the taxpayer must respond to any IRS information requests pertaining to the transfer, demonstrate that no portion of the trust's assets will be used to benefit a U.S. person, and show that no portion of the assets would benefit a U.S. person upon the foreign trust's termination.

The HIRE Act also clarified that a foreign trust will be considered a grantor trust and will require Code Sec. 6048 reporting when:

- A U.S. person has a contingent interest in a foreign trust and is therefore considered a beneficiary; and
- A U.S. person has the discretion to cause the foreign trust to make a distribution to at least one U.S. person.

U.S. persons. Taxpayers must be "U.S. persons" to have a reporting requirement for a foreign trust. A *U.S. person* is a citizen or resident of the United States, a domestic partnership or corporation, or a nonforeign estate or trust. The related-party rules apply in determining whether a U.S. person is considered to have indirectly owned a portion of the foreign trust and to have made a reportable transfer. Although they may not create a reporting requirement for the related party, these rules may come into play in determining when a reportable transfer to the trust has occurred.

Nondisclosure penalties. Taxpayers failing to meet their reporting duties for a foreign trust are subject to penalties under Code Sec. 6677. The penalty is equal to the greater of $10,000 or 35 percent of the gross reportable amount. If the taxpayer subsequently fails within 90 days to make the required disclosures, the penalty is $10,000 for each subsequent 30-day period, up a maximum of the reportable amount.

The reportable amount, as described in Code Sec. 6677, includes the gross value of the undisclosed property transferred to the foreign trust and the portion of the foreign trust's assets treated as owned by the taxpayer.

> **CAUTION**
>
> Beneficiaries of a foreign trust are also subject to a penalty on unreported distributions received from the trust during the tax year.

An exception to the penalty is available when the taxpayer's failure to disclose was due to reasonable cause and was not due to willful neglect. The fact that a foreign jurisdiction would not impose any civil or criminal penalty for failure to disclose does not constitute reasonable cause for purposes of the penalty.

STUDY QUESTIONS

12. Transfers to a foreign trust subject to the Code Sec. 6048 reporting rules include those made:

a. As gifts

b. In exchange for fair market value

c. In respect to an interest that the trust holds

13. If a U.S. person transfers property to a foreign trust, under the HIRE Act rules:

a. The foreign trust is assumed to have a U.S. beneficiary

b. The foreign trust is not deemed to be a grantor trust

c. The foreign trust, as a grantor trust, has no reporting requirements

STOPGAP REPORTING

For many years, the IRS has been pressured by members of Congress to close the infamous $455 billion tax gap—the difference between what taxpayers owe and the amount of tax revenue actually collected. As a result, Congress has created several information disclosure requirements for businesses, not intended to stop their tax abuses, but rather to head off tax noncompliance or abuses by parties with whom the businesses deal.

Basis Reporting

One tool Congress added to the law to assist in closing the tax gap is *broker basis reporting*. Beginning in 2011, Code Sec. 6045(g), as created by the *Emergency Economic Stabilization Act of 2008*, requires that securities brokers report their customers' adjusted bases in certain securities. Brokers are also required to report whether any gain or loss their customer experiences on sales of those securities are long-term or short-term in nature. These rules are intended to help close the annual $11 billion tax gap for all capital gains.

FIFO default. In fulfilling this obligation, brokers are to determine the customer's basis under the *first-in, first-out* (FIFO) method as a default. This cash flow method assumes that, when the customer sells a portion of the securities it owns, it is selling the first portion it purchased through the broker.

> **EXAMPLE**
>
> Fish, John, & Lawrence (FJL) is a securities brokerage firm. During January, its customer, Melissa Jamison, purchased 5,000 shares of a company's common stock at $10. In July, Melissa purchased 3,000 shares at a share price of $15. In November, Melissa instructed FJL to sell 2,000 shares of the company's common stock. In reporting Melissa's stock basis to the IRS, FJL must assume that Melissa shares from her January purchase in November. As a result, at the end of the year, she will have a basis of $75,000 (5,000 × $15 + 3,000 × $10 − 2,000 × $10).

> **COMMENT**
>
> The customer may request that the broker to stop this FIFO treatment by specifically identifying which security is sold.

Average basis alternative. However, if the customer owns mutual fund stock or stock acquired under a dividend reinvestment plan, the broker must use a different method of allocating basis. Basis in these securities is measured according to the *average basis method*. As the name implies, the broker computes the customer's basis per share under this method by dividing the aggregate cost of the securities by the number of shares the taxpayer purchased.

EXAMPLE

In January, Melissa Jamison purchased 10 shares of common stock at $110. In February, she purchased 10 shares at a per-share price of $100. In March, she purchased 10 shares at $90 each. Her basis per share is $100 ([$110 + $100 + $90] ÷ [10 + 10 + 10]). FJL reports her total basis in Melissa's stock of $3,000.

COMMENT

As is the case with the FIFO method, the broker's customers may notify the broker that it is using a different method of valuing its account with these securities, rather than the average basis method.

NOTE

When using the average basis method, the broker must separately report the basis for each customer account as computed under the average cost method.

Increased Information Reporting

Another tool Congress created to reduce the tax gap was increased information reporting for business payments. Code Sec. 6041(h), as added by the *Patient Protection and Affordable Care Act,* requires that taxpayers disclose any payments made to a corporation in the course of a trade or business totaling $600 or more. This reporting requirement is set to begin for taxpayers starting in 2012. This rule is based on the idea that third-party reporting of payments provides more information to the IRS with respect to taxable payments and, therefore, increases the likelihood that the corporate recipient will report the proper amount of taxable income.

COMMENT

This reporting requirement does not apply to tax-exempt corporations under Code Sec. 501(a).

Applicable payments. The payments covered by this reporting requirement include:

- Salaries;
- Wages;
- Rent;

- Annuities;
- Compensation for services; and
- Certain foreign items.

However, there are many exceptions to the rule, including the following:
- Distributions in liquidation;
- Payments of dividends and interest;
- Mortgage interest;
- Broker transactions with customers;
- Royalty Payments;
- Cancellation of indebtedness;
- Payments reported on an S corp return, Employer's quarterly tax return, Form W-3, or Form W-2;
- Tips;
- Payments of bills;
- Rent payments to real estate agents;
- Salaries and profits distributed by a partnership to an individual partner;
- Corporate bond interest payments; and
- Payments to individuals as scholarships or fellowship grants.

Penalties. Taxpayers who fail to comply with the reporting requirement will be subject to penalties, including:
- The Code Sec. 6721 penalty for failure to file an information return; and
- The Code Sec. 6722 penalty for failure to furnish a payee statement.

Criticism. As the 2012 effective date of enhanced information reporting approaches, IRS Commissioner Douglas Shulman has reported that many taxpayers are complaining about the increased costs of compliance. In particular, many have stated that small businesses would be negatively impacted by costly and time-consuming recordkeeping requirements. In reaction, the agency has stated it will implement and uphold the law in a manner that will minimize taxpayer burdens and avoid duplicative information reporting.

COMMENT

As an example, Treasury and the IRS issued proposed regulations (NPRM REG-139255-08) that would exempt business purchases made with credit or debit cards from the reporting requirement because the IRS would already receive notice of them from bank or payment processor reports.

As a result of the IRS's flexibility, although enhanced information reporting will continue as law, reporting requirements under the regime are not likely to be burdensome.

STUDY QUESTIONS

14. Under rules created by the *Emergency Economic Stabilization Act of 2008,* beginning in 2011 securities brokers must calculate the client's basis in nonreinvested shares using the:

a. First-in, last-out (FILO) method
b. Average basis method
c. First-in, first-out (FIFO) method

15. Under the *Patient Protection and Affordable Care Act,* beginning in 2012 third parties must report business payments of $600 or more transferred to:

a. Individuals as scholarships or fellowship grants
b. Corporations
c. Provider reductions in charges for medical services

CONCLUSION

As this chapter has demonstrated, the IRS and the tax code are beginning to request that businesses provide more varieties of disclosures above and beyond those required by the usual income tax return filing requirement. Taxpayers must disclose certain reportable transactions, as determined by the IRS's Tiered Issued Process. The codification of the economic substance doctrine has made disclosure important for affected transactions. The IRS has proposed new disclosure requirements for uncertain tax positions. Taxpayers are required, under recent legislation, to disclose their foreign assets and accounts. Additionally, Congress has imposed tax-reporting requirements to close in on noncompliant tax reporting. Given the success of these efforts and the estimated additional revenues that they are forecast to bring into the federal coffers, it is clear that disclosure rules, information reporting requirements, and enforcement will only continue to increase in coming years.

New Challenges for Nonprofits

Major changes in the federal government's oversight of tax-exempt organizations have tightened the law, increased reporting requirements, and imposed new regulations on nonprofits. In 2008, the IRS completely revised Form 990, the annual information return required of most nonprofit organizations, and continues to update the form. The IRS is also pursuing compliance initiatives that affect hospitals and universities, and it has begun to examine the governance of many nonprofit organizations. Congress has imposed new filing obligations on small nonprofits, rewritten the requirements for organizations that support charities, and tightened the health care obligations of nonprofit hospitals. These developments put pressure on nonprofit organizations to improve their management and operations so that they do not jeopardize their tax exemption or risk penalties for noncompliance. This chapter describes these developments and highlights the IRS activities affecting nonprofit organizations.

LEARNING OBJECTIVES

Upon completion of this chapter, you will be able to:

■ Discuss significant changes to the revised Form 990;

■ Explain the annual filing requirements for small nonprofit organizations and the temporary relief available for organizations that did not file on time;

■ Determine the new requirements for supporting organizations;

■ Identify new rules and important issues for hospitals, medical schools, and colleges and universities; and

■ Describe the IRS's efforts to improve nonprofit governance.

INTRODUCTION

The nonprofit sector continues to grow. In November 2008, the IRS estimated that there were 1.8 million tax-exempt organizations and that they owned $3.4 *trillion* in assets. This growth and vitality provide important benefits to the United States and its people. At the same time, regulators, donors, and the public increasingly question how effectively charitable organizations use their extensive resources for the public benefit.

For example, as health care costs rise, Congress and others have questioned whether charities are operating too much like profit-seeking and profit-making organizations. Congress responded by adopting new requirements for nonprofit hospitals to provide health care in a charitable manner. Another example of challenges to charitable purpose is higher education. As tuition costs rise, Congress has held hearings to consider whether colleges and universities hoard their endowments or in fact use them to benefit students and teachers.

There is an increased demand for transparency in the nonprofit sector. The IRS has required substantially more information from nonprofits by revising Form 990 and continues to make changes to the form. The IRS has also initiated studies of various tax-exempt segments to understand how they operate and identify compliance issues. Smaller organizations that never had to file information returns now have to submit a Form 990 or risk losing their exemption. Like other components of the IRS, the Exempt Organizations (EO) office has become much more proactive in looking for ways to expand both its education and its oversight of the tax-exempt sector.

SIGNIFICANT CHANGES TO FORM 990

Form 990, *Return of Organization Exempt from Income Tax,* is the annual information return that must be filed by:

- Organizations that are tax-exempt under Code Sec. 501(c);
- Political organizations that are exempt under Code Sec. 527; and
- Charitable trusts described in Code Sec. 4947(a)(1).

Smaller tax-exempt organizations may file Form 990-EZ, *Short Form Return (of Exempt Organizations).* The IRS states that each year approximately 550,000 organizations file returns using Form 990 or Form 990-EZ.

Form 990 provides information about an organization's program and activities and is not itself used to report and pay taxes. The IRS uses Form 990 as its primary tax-compliance tool for exempt organizations. According to the IRS, most states also use Form 990 for charitable and regulatory oversight and for organizations to claim an exemption from state income tax. Form 990 is a public document that is made available by the IRS and by the exempt organizations themselves.

> **COMMENT**
>
> An organization that claims to be tax-exempt but has not yet obtained an exemption from the IRS must file a Form 990.

Filing Thresholds

The IRS sets the filing requirements and thresholds for its forms. For tax year 2010 and subsequent years (forms filed in 2011 and later), tax-exempt organizations must file Form 990 if either of these thresholds is met:
- Their gross receipts are at least $200,000; or
- Their total assets are at least $500,000.

Both of these thresholds were reduced from the amounts required for tax years 2008 and 2009, when the IRS engaged in a comprehensive revision of Form 990. For 2009, the Form 990-EZ filing thresholds were gross receipts of less than $500,000 and total assets of less than $1.25 million; for 2008, the thresholds were gross receipts of less than $1 million and total assets of less than $2.5 million. Organizations below both thresholds may choose to file Form 990-EZ. Private foundations, which are tax-exempt charities with narrower funding, must file Form 990-PF.

COMMENT

Every tax-exempt organization, regardless of size, must file an unrelated business income tax (UBIT) return, Form 990-T, for any year that its gross income from an unrelated trade or business is $1,000 or more.

The smallest organizations can file Form 990-N, *Electronic Notice for Tax-Exempt Organizations Not Required to File Form 990 or 990-EZ* (known as the e-Postcard), with a brief statement of identifying information. For tax years 2007–2009, the threshold for filing Form 990-N was having normal gross receipts of no more than $25,000. Starting with tax year 2010, the IRS increased this threshold; organizations can file Form 990-N if their gross receipts normally do not exceed $50,000.

Table 1. Filing Thresholds for Types of Form 990 for the 2010 Tax Year

Form Required	Threshold
990	Gross receipts of $200,000 or total assets of $500,000
990-EZ	Gross receipts of less than $200,000 and total assets of less than $500,000
990-N	Gross receipts of less than $50,000

Some organizations do not have to file Form 990:
- Primarily, religious organizations and religion-affiliated organizations;
- State institutions whose income is tax-exempt under Code Sec. 115; and

- Tax-exempt organizations under Code Sec. 501(c)(1) that are chartered by an act of Congress and are an instrumentality of the United States.

Filing Deadlines

Form 990 is due on the 15th day of the fifth month after the end of the organization's tax year. For a calendar year taxpayer, this is May 15 of the following year. The IRS will extend the due date for three months on request and will extend it another three months if the organization shows reasonable cause. Organizations must pay penalties for late filing; the amounts depend on the size of the organization. The IRS treats an incomplete return as a late-filed return and may impose penalties.

> **CAUTION**
>
> A return is incomplete if an organization fails to attach a required schedule.

Revised Core Form and Schedules

After 30 years of tinkering with Form 990, IRS comprehensively revised the form, beginning with tax year 2008 (returns filed in 2009). The revised form includes a core form with 11 parts that all tax-exempt organizations (other than those qualified to file Form 990-EZ or Form 990-N) must fill out fully. The form also includes 16 schedules to be completed by different organizations, depending on their category and activities. Any part of the old Form 990 that was not used by all exempt organizations was moved to a schedule. The revised form includes two schedules that did not have to be filled out completely until the 2009 tax year: Schedule H, *Hospitals*, and Schedule K, *Tax Exempt Bonds*.

> **COMMENT**
>
> Form 990-EZ was not significantly changed, despite the revision of Form 990. Form 990-EZ is a four-page form containing six parts. Form 990-EZ users may have to complete one or more of the following schedules accompanying the revised Form 990:
>
> - Schedules A, B, C, *Political Campaign and Lobby Activities;*
> - E, *Schools;*
> - G, *Supplemental Information Regarding Fundraising or Gaming Activities;* and
> - L, or N.

The IRS has identified significant changes made to the 2009 Form 990 from 2008. Changes to the core form and its instructions include the following:

- Part III, Statement of Program Service Accomplishments—Filers must now report significant changes in program services in Part III, rather than in a separate letter to the EO Determinations office;
- Part VI, Governance, Management, and Disclosure—Filers must report significant changes to organizational documents in Part VI and in Schedule O, *Supplemental Information.* The fact that officials serve in similar positions with another exempt organization does not create a business relationship between the two (concerning the independence of the governing board);
- Part VII, Compensation—The responsibility test for being a key employee may be met at any time during the calendar year ending within the organization's tax year. The organization must report the entire annual compensation of a person who is a key employee for only part of the year. And, a filer must report all compensation paid to key officials by an organization that is a related organization, even for just part of the year; and
- Part X, Balance Sheet—The filer must report publicly traded stock in a corporation that composes more than 5 percent of the filer's total assets.

Changes to the Form 990 glossary include:
- New definitions of audit, fair market value, and principal officer; and
- Revised definitions of control, fundraising events, related organization (includes government entities), and reportable compensation.

Changes to the schedules and their instructions were substantial. This table summarizes special instructions for completing the schedules, as well as comments and caveats for proper filing.

Table 2. Revised Form 990 Schedules and Rules for Their Proper Completion

Schedule and Title	Instructions	Comments
A, *Public Charity Status and Public Support*	The IRS does not update records on a public charity's status based on a change made on Schedule A. The filer may request a determination letter on its status from the EO Determinations office.	All charities must fully complete Schedule A.
B, *Schedule of Contributors*	The filer should identify a donor, rather than reporting the donor as anonymous.	Despite this instruction, the IRS also instructs organizations not to include nonrequired personal identifying information on the return because the form is made publicly available.

Schedule and Title	Instructions	Comments
D, *Supplemental Financial Statements*	The filer should complete Part X of the core form (Balance Sheet) if its current financial statements included a footnote addressing its liability for uncertain tax positions (UTPs).	The IRS does not initially plan to ask tax-exempt organizations (unlike taxable corporations) to report their UTPs on Schedule UTP. The IRS may use this information to justify expanding the reporting requirements for UTPs.
F, *Statement of Activities Outside the United States*	Foreign financial accounts that are reported on Part V of the core form (regarding other IRS filings and tax compliance) should also be reported on Schedule F. The instructions require enhanced reporting of types of foreign activities, expenditures, and assistance to U.S. individuals for foreign activity.	IRS Tax Exempt and Government Entities (TE/GE) Commissioner Sarah Hall Ingram said that the IRS would expand the reporting of foreign activities on Schedule F. Practitioners found the compilation of data for Schedule F extremely challenging.
L, *Transactions with Interested Persons*	The instructions explain how to report joint ventures with interested persons as business transactions and clarify that governmental units are not interested persons.	Schedule L is also used to report excess benefit transactions, loans to or from key officials, and grants or other assistance to interested persons. Practitioners recommend that the instructions be read carefully.
N, *Liquidation, Termination, Dissolution, or Significant Disposition of Assets*	The filer should report a transaction on Schedule N, rather than in a letter to EO Determinations. The latter no longer issues letters confirming the termination of an organization's tax-exempt status.	The IRS revised Form 990-EZ and its instructions to apply to a "significant disposition of net assets," rather than a "substantial contraction." Unlike a substantial contraction, a significant disposition includes transfers for full consideration.
O, *Supplemental Information*	The filer should use a separate attachment, not Schedule O, to explain any late filing of Form 990.	Every organization filing Form 990 must file Schedule O, because organizations must, at the least, explain certain answers from Part VI (Governance).
R, *Related Organizations*	The instructions explain how the filer can control or be controlled by another organization, for determining related organizations; provide several new examples of control; and explain that governmental units should be treated as tax-exempt organizations on Part II of Schedule R.	The organization must describe how it valued services, cash, and other assets reported on Schedule R.

The IRS has issued drafts of Form 990 components that it is revising for 2010 (forms filed in 2011). These revised forms include Schedules A and L, filed with Forms 990 and 990-EZ; Schedules D, F, J (compensation information), and R, filed with form 990; and Form 990-PF, *Return of Private Foundation or Section 4947(a)(1) Nonexempt Charitable Trust Treated as a Private Foundation.* The IRS did not identify the changes being made to the forms.

STUDY QUESTIONS

1. Although the IRS made substantive changes to Form 990 in 2008 and more for 2009, Form 990-EZ was not significantly revised. *True or False?*

2. Because the content of Form 990 and its schedules is made publicly available, the IRS advises organizations:

   a. To list donors as anonymous on Schedule A, *Public Charity Status and Public Support*

   b. To exclude nonrequired personal information on Schedule B, *Schedule of Contributors*

   c. Not to describe business dealings with key officials on Schedule L, *Transactions with Interested Persons*

SMALL EXEMPT ORGANIZATIONS

Organizations Required to File

The Pension Protection Act of 2006 (PPA) requires all exempt organizations to file an information return (Form 990, *Return of Organization Exempt from Income Tax,* or Form 990-EZ or 990-N for qualifying small exempt organizations) with the IRS, with the exception of churches and church-related organizations. The return must be filed by the 15th day of the fifth month after an organization's fiscal year ends; for a calendar year taxpayer, this means May 15 of the following year.

> **COMMENT**
>
> The sweeping PPA requirement means that very small organizations that have never filed before have to start doing so.

Generally, an organization must file a full return, Form 990. As discussed earlier, smaller organizations with assets and gross receipts below specified thresholds may file Form 990-EZ, *Short Form Return of Organization Exempt from Income Tax.* The smallest tax-exempt organizations may file Form 990-N.

E-Postcard

Forms 990 and 990-EZ are several pages long. For the smallest organizations, the IRS devised an electronic form, Form 990-N, *Electronic Notice for Tax-Exempt Organizations Not Required to File Form 990 or 990–EZ* (known as the e-Postcard). For 2009, the form is available to organizations that normally have gross receipts equal to or less than $25,000 a year. For 2010 (covering filings in 2011) and later years, the threshold is $50,000 or less. The form must be filed online and cannot be filed on paper.

Form 990-N requires eight items, identified on the IRS website:

- Legal name;
- Any other name;
- Mailing address;
- Website address (if any);
- Employer identification number;
- Name and address of a principal officer;
- Tax year; and
- Answers to questions on gross receipts and termination of all activities.

EFFECTS OF NEW RETURN REQUIREMENTS

The new filing requirement was designed to help the IRS maintain current information on tax-exempt organizations. Some organizations that had obtained an IRS ruling granting a tax exemption were not keeping the IRS informed about their current status.

Failure to File

Under the new filing rules, an organization that fails to file the form for three consecutive years automatically loses its tax-exempt status. This filing requirement first took effect in 2007; thus, organizations that did not file a Form 990 for 2007, 2008, and 2009 by May 17, 2010 (the first weekday after May 15) were the first to be affected by the new PPA requirement and were in jeopardy of losing their exemption. Once an organization lost its exemption, it would have to reapply to the IRS to regain its tax-exempt status.

Despite conducting an extensive outreach effort to the tax-exempt sector, the IRS reported that there was a great deal of confusion regarding the new annual filing requirements and that many small organizations were unaware they could lose their exemption if they failed to file for three consecutive years. Although the revocation was supposed to be automatic, the IRS—faced with the potential revocation of tax-exempt status for hundreds of thousands of organizations—developed a relief program with components for both Form 990-EZ filers and e-Postcard filers. (No relief was provided for organizations that had to file Form 990 or to private foundations required to file Form 990-PF.)

E-Postcard Relief

Shortly after the May 17, 2010, deadline, the IRS announced that many small exempt organizations had missed the filing deadline, but indicated that it would provide relief to avoid the automatic loss of exempt status under the three-year rule. On July 26, 2010, the IRS announced that it was extending the Form 990-N (e-Postcard) filing deadline to October 15, 2010, for all eligible organizations (those having gross receipts of $25,000 or less, with a filing deadline by October 15, 2010). There was no compliance fee for Form 990-N filers. An eligible organization could instead file Form 990 or 990-EZ by the October 15 deadline.

To help organizations determine their status, the IRS posted a list of names and last-known addresses for "at-risk organizations." The IRS stressed that the smallest organizations must e-file the electronic postcard by October 15 or lose their tax exemption.

> **COMMENT**
>
> A small exempt organization is not required to file Form 990-N if it is a subordinate of a parent organization and the organization is included on the parent's group information return.

Voluntary Compliance Program

For midsize exempt organizations that are eligible to file Form 990-EZ but had failed to file any returns from 2007 to 2009 by May 17, 2010 (or by October 15, 2010, for fiscal year taxpayers), the IRS developed a voluntary compliance program (VCP). The VCP required that the organization file complete paper Forms 990-EZ (or Form 990 if it chooses) for all three years, 2007–2009, by the extended due date of October 15, 2010. In addition, the organization had to complete a VCP checklist, agreeing to the terms of the VCP, and pay a compliance fee of $100 to $500, depending on the amount of the organization's gross receipts.

Revocation and Reinstatement

The IRS automatically revoked the exemption of an organization that did not meet the October 15, 2010, deadline, effective as of the original due date of their 2009 return. However, the IRS announced that charitable contributors could rely on the organization's exempt status until the IRS published the name of the revoked organization on its website, which would not occur before early 2011.

Once an organization was automatically revoked, it had to file an application for exempt status (Form 1023 for charities; Form 1024 for other exempt organizations) and pay a user fee, even if it was not originally required to submit an exemption application (primarily organizations whose annual gross receipts normally did not exceed $5,000). If the exemption were reinstated, it was generally effective as of the application date. However, if the organization can demonstrate reasonable cause for failing to file a return for three consecutive years, the IRS will reinstate the exemption retroactively to the date of revocation.

STUDY QUESTIONS

3. All of the following types of information are required to complete Form 990-N (the e-Postcard) *except:*

   a. Employer identification number
   b. List of contributors contact information
   c. Name and address of the principal officer

4. Under the Voluntary Compliance Program, organizations that failed to file Form 990-EZ (or Form 990) for the past three years:

   a. Could file completed paper Forms 990-EZ or 990 for 2007 through 2009 before October 15, 2010
   b. Had the compliance fee waived
   c. Could instead commence filing returns for 2010 using the full Form 990

SUPPORTING ORGANIZATIONS

An organization may be tax-exempt as a public charity or as a private foundation under Code Sec. 501(c)(3). Private foundations have only a small number of supporters who may exercise excessive control over the organization. To prevent abuse of its tax-exempt status, a private foundation is subject to excise taxes and other restrictions that do not apply to public charities on self-dealing, excess business holdings, and amounts provided to charities.

Most private foundations are nonoperating foundations that make grants. However, under Code Sec. 509(a)(3), a private foundation that provides support to a public charity will itself be considered a public charity. As a supporting organization, the organization avoids the excise taxes and antiabuse restrictions that otherwise would apply to a private foundation that violates certain requirements.

Requirements for Relationship, Responsiveness, and Attentiveness Tests

The tax code imposes several tests on a supporting organization:

- Organizational and operational test—it must be organized and operated exclusively for the benefit of, to perform the functions of, or to carry out the purposes of, one or more public charities;

- Relationship test—it must be operated, supervised, or controlled by (or in connection with) one or more public charities; and
- Lack of control test—it must not be controlled by disqualified persons other than foundation managers and public charities.

COMMENT

Disqualified persons include:

- A substantial contributor;
- The creator of a trust that is a substantial contributor;
- An owner of more than 20 percent of the voting power of a substantial contributor; and
- A family member of any of these persons.

Relationship test. A supporting organization is classified by satisfying one of three variations of the relationship test:

- Type I—one or more supported organizations (public charities) exercises a substantial degree of control over the supporting organization's programs, activities, and policies (a parent–subsidiary type relationship);
- Type II—the same persons must exercise common control of both the supporting and the supported organization (a brother–sister type relationship); or
- Type III—the supporting organization is operated in connection with one or more supported organizations and is responsive to the needs and demands of the supported organizations *(responsiveness test)*, is significantly involved in the supported organization's operations *(integral part test)*, and the supported organization is dependent upon the supporting organization for the support it provides (also the integral part test).

Type I and Type III organizations will not satisfy the relationship test if they accept contributions from:

- Any person who controls, alone or with related parties, the supported organization's governing board;
- A family member of a person described above; or
- A 35-percent controlled entity, including a corporation, partnership, trust, or estate.

Type III organizations. Congress was concerned that Type III organizations were not sufficiently connected to their supported organizations, so in the *Pension Protection Act of 2006*, it imposed new requirements on the responsiveness test and the integral part test that were already in the regulations, including new payout requirements.

Responsiveness. The responsiveness test requires the Type III supporting organization to demonstrate that it is responsive to the needs or demands of the supported organization. To meet this test, the supported organization usually appoints one member of the governing board of the supporting organization. The supported organization will also put procedures in place to ensure that the supporting organization is responsive to it.

Integral part. The application of the integral part test depends on whether the Type III supporting organization is functionally integrated or nonfunctionally integrated with the supported organization. An organization is functionally integrated if "substantially all" its activities directly further the exempt purposes of the supported organization. The supporting organization must normally engage in those activities, "but for" the involvement of the supporting organization. In proposed regulations, the IRS eliminated an expenditure test and an asset test for functionally integrated organizations. An organization that is not functionally integrated must distribute 5 percent of the fair market value of its previous year's nonexempt-use assets.

Attentiveness. To satisfy an *attentiveness test*, the supporting organization must provide:
- 10 percent of the supported organization's support;
- Sufficient support to avoided an interruption of activities; or
- Sufficient support based on the facts and circumstances.

Charitable trusts. Prior to the PPA, a charitable trust could meet the responsiveness test for being a Type III organization if:
- It was a charitable trust under state law;
- Each supported organization was a beneficiary of the trust; and
- Each beneficiary had the power to enforce the trust and compel an accounting under state law.

The PPA eliminated the charitable trust test. This meant that a charitable trust had to meet a significant voice test under the responsiveness test.

However, the IRS provided relief if a charitable trust filed as a private foundation for 2008 but has continuously operated as a Type III organization under the PPA. The organization can get a refund of excise taxes it erroneously paid on investment income.

HOSPITALS

Tax-exempt hospitals have come under increasing scrutiny by Congress, the IRS, and others who question whether they are living up to their obligations as charitable organizations. IRS revised Form 990 expands the reporting requirements for hospitals. The revised form includes a new Schedule H for hospitals to complete starting in 2010 (for tax year 2009). In 2009 the IRS completed the three-year Hospital Compliance Project, which focused on facilities' provision of benefits to the community and their compensation practices. In 2010, Congress, in the new health care reform package, imposed greater obligations on tax-exempt hospitals, in addition to the existing exemption requirements.

These changes all reflect concerns about whether nonprofit hospitals are satisfying the community benefit standard that applies to tax-exempt hospitals. Although the standard has existed since 1969, the law does not specify all the activities that provide a community benefit, how to measure community benefit, or how much community benefit a hospital should provide. The IRS says it will use the information from Schedule H and its compliance study to quantify and analyze hospitals' current practices. Neither Schedule H nor the compliance study prescribes a community benefit standard or proposes to change the current standard, but with more information on current practices, the IRS will be in a better position to evaluate and revise the standard.

The new Congressional mandates reflect good practices for a nonprofit hospital. The most important obligation is for each hospital to conduct a community health needs assessment (CHNA) at least once every three years and to adopt an implementation strategy to meet those needs. The hospital then must report on Form 990 its efforts to satisfy the identified needs. The Joint Committee on Taxation says that the new requirements (including the CHNA) are in addition to, and not in place of, the requirements that otherwise apply to a Code Sec. 501(c)(3) organization. Do these new requirements, including the CHNA, implement the community benefit standard, take it in a new direction, or apply independently? It remains to be seen.

Community Benefit

The tax code does not provide a per se exemption for hospitals. The IRS has recognized the promotion of health as a charitable purpose if it is beneficial to the community as a whole. Unlike rules for some charities, the IRS does not specifically require that a hospital provide special care to a charitable class of people—"the poor or distressed," to quote a 2009 speech by Steven Miller, then commissioner of the IRS TE/GE division.

In 1969, the IRS devised the community benefit standard for charitable hospitals to satisfy, and this application of the standard continues. The IRS identified five factors for such hospitals:

- A community board of trustees;
- An open medical staff;
- A full-time emergency room open to all, regardless of ability to pay;
- The admission of all types of patients; and
- The use of excess funds to improve the facility, medical training, education, and research.

The willingness to provide charity care to indigent patients is not required but indicates that the hospital benefits the community.

Over the years, some of these factors have become characteristic of for-profit hospitals and no longer distinguish them from nonprofit hospitals:

- An open medical staff;
- Treatment of all emergency room patients; and
- Participation in Medicare and Medicaid.

What remains are the requirements for a community board, the use of excess funds, charity care, and other uncompensated or other undercompensated care. In practice, each hospital measures community benefit in its own manner.

Congress has proposed minimum standards for charity care, such as 5 percent of expenses or revenues, plus penalties for violations, but these standards have not been adopted. The only penalty for violating the community benefit standard is the drastic step of revoking the hospital's tax exemption. The IRS on audit may inquire as to a hospital's practices, but it rarely challenges the exemption.

STUDY QUESTIONS

5. Private foundations are subject to excise taxes and restrictions that do not apply to public charities. *True or False?*

6. Under the *Pension Protection Act of 2006,* Type III supporting organizations are subject to increased requirements using each of the following tests *except:*
   a. Responsiveness test
   b. Integral part test
   c. Charitable trust test

Schedule H of Form 990. New Schedule H attempts to identify and quantify a hospital's provision of charity care and community benefits. It is a four-page form, has 15 pages of instructions, and—like other parts of Form 990—is open to public inspection. It asks about charity care, unreimbursed costs from government programs, and community health improvement, among other issues. It also asks about bad debt expenses, collection practices, and "community-building activities"— items not necessarily treated as community benefits. The IRS expects to obtain significant data in 2010 and 2011, when Schedule H is filed in substantial numbers.

According to the IRS, Schedule H provides clear standards on:
- The types of activities reportable (or not) as community benefit;
- The requirement to report the benefit at cost (not the amount charged); and
- Reporting by tax identification number.

Schedule H enhances transparency and will provide the IRS with a wealth of information, but it does not provide a bright-line standard for assessing whether a hospital should be tax-exempt.

Hospital study. The IRS obtained information from almost 500 non-profit hospitals on their 2005 operations. Although the hospitals community benefits averaged 9 percent of total revenues, the IRS found great variation among the amounts provided. Sixty percent of the community benefits provided were reported by only 9 percent of the hospitals. High-population urban hospitals provided the largest percentage; very small rural hospitals provided the lowest percentage of community benefits. The IRS concluded that modifying the existing standard would have a significant impact on certain hospitals, depending on size and location, but little impact on others.

Steven Miller has said that the IRS needs to consider whether the community benefit standard needs to be refined. Lois Lerner, the Director of the IRS Exempt Organizations office, stressed that the IRS needs to work with others to determine what guidance might be needed, and that the information in the study will inform those discussions. Again, the direction taken by the IRS remains to be seen.

Congress. The Government Accountability Office issued a study in October 2008 that compared how hospitals measured and reported community benefit activities. At the time, Sen. Charles Grassley, R-Iowa, the top Republican on the Senate Finance Committee, commented that IRS audits through 2006 did not examine community benefit, that the community benefit standard is weak, that the IRS needs a bright line to determine whether hospitals are meeting the standard necessary to maintain their tax exemption, and that Congress may need to intervene.

Grassley has noted that many officials believe there is no discernible difference between for-profit and tax-exempt hospitals. He has pushed for legislative changes to increase the accountability of tax-exempt hospitals.

New law. Several of Grassley's proposals were included in the *Patient Protection and Affordable Care Act* (PPACA), enacted in March 2010. Congress imposed several new requirements on nonprofit hospitals. Starting with tax years beginning after March 23, 2012, each hospital must:

- Conduct a community health needs assessment (CHNA) every three years;
- Adopt an implementation strategy to meet the community needs identified; and
- Report on its efforts on Form 990.

The IRS must review the community benefit activities of every hospital at least once every three years. The agency can impose a $50,000 excise tax on any hospital that fails to meet these requirements. The IRS requested comments in 2010 on the appropriate requirements for the CHNA.

The new law imposes three other requirements on hospitals:

- A financial assistance policy;
- Limits on charges; and
- Limits on collection activities.

The hospital must adopt, implement, and widely publicize a financial assistance policy that indicates the criteria for patients to receive financial assistance and whether the assistance includes free or discounted care. The hospital cannot charge patients who qualify for financial assistance more than the amount generally billed to insured patients. Finally, the hospital cannot take certain extraordinary collection actions (such as lawsuits or liens) without first making reasonable efforts to inform the patient of its financial assistance policy and determining whether the patient is eligible for assistance. These requirements generally apply to tax years beginning after March 23, 2010.

> **COMMENT**
>
> The Treasury Department is required to provide an annual report to Congress on charity care, bad debt expense, and unreimbursed costs of government programs.

State Law Challenges

Hospitals are also being challenged by state authorities. The Illinois Supreme Court ruled in March 2010 that a hospital was not entitled to a state property tax exemption because it did not provide enough charity care. The state said that the medical center's charity care was less than 1 percent of its revenue, amounting to less than $1 million against revenues of $113 million. The hospital argued that it provided more than $38 million in free care and other community benefits. The ruling is seen as an incentive for hospitals to engage in a discussion of how to define charity care and how to ensure that people get the care they need.

MEDICAL RESIDENT FICA CLAIMS

FICA Payments by Tax-Exempt Organizations

Employers and employees both pay FICA (Social Security) taxes on wages from employment. Employers normally withhold the employee's shares from the employee's wages and pay a separate excise tax as the employer's share. Although tax-exempt organizations do not pay income tax, they still must pay FICA taxes on the wages of their employees, and these taxes can be substantial.

Student FICA Exception

There are numerous exceptions to the FICA tax requirement in Code Sec. 3121(b). One statutory exception to the definition of employment, enacted in 1939 and found at Code Sec. 3121(b)(10), is known as the *student exception.* The student exception excludes "service performed in the employ of a school, college, or university...if such service is performed by a student who is enrolled and regularly attending classes at such school, college, or university."

The IRS has been in a long-term FICA tax dispute with medical institutions that employ medical residents. This dispute dates back to the 1990s and is scheduled to be heard by the U.S. Supreme Court in its 2010–2011 term.

Applying the exception to medical residents. A *medical resident* is an individual who has earned an MD degree and is participating in a residency program for additional medical training in a specialty field, such as internal medicine or surgery. In the case going to the Supreme Court involving the Mayo Clinic, the clinic operates nationally accredited graduate medical education programs. Residents enroll in the programs, register for courses, attend lectures, perform research, and participate in "teaching rounds" and patient care. Residents receive grades or written evaluations, may be terminated for poor academic performance, and receive formal certification for completing the program. Residents receive a stipend "for the purpose of providing a minimum level of financial support during their enrollment."

COMMENT

Though the stipend may be "minimal," the FICA taxes at issue are not. The Mayo Clinic claimed a refund for FICA taxes of $1.6 million paid for one three-month period in 2005.

The IRS has attempted through regulations and other guidance to impose additional requirements on the student exception:

- The employment must be less than full time;
- The student's service must be incident to and for the purpose of pursuing a course of study, so that the educational aspect predominates, rather than the service aspect;
- The students cannot be "professional employees" whose duties require advance knowledge and cannot be "career employees" who are licensed or who are eligible for the employer's retirement plan;
- In the case of student nurses, the IRS also requires that the total compensation be nominal;
- The school must be a nonprofit institution, as described in the law for charitable contributions; and
- The school's "primary function" must be educational, to distinguish it from a hospital, clinic, or museum.

The IRS maintains that medical residents do not qualify for the student FICA exception under the IRS's additional requirements. The institutions maintain that the student exception clearly applies and that the IRS's additional requirements are improper and illegal.

Regulations and court decisions. After a 2003 district court decision awarding a FICA tax refund to the Mayo Clinic, the IRS amended the regulations that apply to the student FICA exception, effective April 1, 2005 (T.D. 9167). Among other requirements, the amended regulations specifically provide that an individual who works full-time (40 or more hours per week normally) for the school is a "career employee" and is not performing services incident to and for the purpose or pursuing a course of study. The regulations state that the determination of a normal work schedule is not affected by the educational, instructional, or training aspect of the services.

Subsequently, the IRS lost several district court decisions that overturned the 2005 regulations and that applied the student FICA exception to medical residents. However, in 2009, the IRS won a major victory. The Eighth Circuit Court of Appeals upheld the 2005 regulations (2009-1 USTC ¶50,432) and reversed two lower court decisions, one involving the Mayo Clinic (2007-2 USTC ¶50,577), the other the University of Minnesota (2008-1 USTC ¶50,262). The Eighth Circuit found that the statute was ambiguous on the treatment of a medical resident working full-time for a teaching hospital/medical school and that the IRS regulations were consistent with the statute.

> **COMMENT**
>
> Regardless of this decision, litigation is expected to continue in other circuits for post-April 1, 2005, claims.

Administrative relief. Nevertheless, with the issue looking better for the IRS, the IRS made an "administrative decision" in March 2010 to honor the medical resident FICA refund claims for tax periods ending before April 1, 2005, the effective date of the amended regulations. The IRS reported that its decision would resolve more than 7,000 claims that were in suspense while the issue was litigated, potentially involving hundreds of millions of dollars. Although the IRS did not reopen the statute of limitations and allow new claims for the pre-April 1, 2005, period, the IRS agreed to honor any employer or employee claims filed timely for that period and still pending either administratively or in court. In many cases, the employer claims would cover medical residents' employee claims for the same period. The IRS issued procedures and frequently asked questions on its website to address to processing of these claims.

Supreme Court hearing. With the Eighth Circuit upholding the 2005 regulations, the IRS may have taken this approach with the expectation that it could safely deny post-April 1, 2005, claims while honoring older claims made under prior law. But the U.S. Supreme Court intervened, deciding in June 2010 to hear an appeal from the 2009 Eighth Circuit decision. The taxpayer seeking Supreme Court review argued that the circuit courts of appeal are split on the application of FICA taxes to medical residents. The government countered, unsuccessfully so far, that there was only one appeals court decision addressing the validity of the 2005 regulations and that the circuits were not split.

> **COMMENT**
>
> If the Supreme Court upholds the 2005 regulations, the IRS would appear to have clear sailing to continue to deny FICA claims under the new rules. Any other decision, depending on its details, potentially leaves the door open for more litigation and further IRS action.

COLLEGES AND UNIVERSITIES

Organizations that are organized and operated exclusively for educational purposes are tax-exempt charities under Code Sec. 501(c)(3). Colleges and universities with a regular faculty, student body, location, and curriculum, clearly qualify for tax-exempt status.

Colleges and universities comprise one of the largest U.S. nonprofit segments in revenue and assets. IRS initiated a study (which it labeled a compliance project) in October 2008 and sent a 33-page questionnaire to colleges and universities. The study focused on exempt and unrelated business activities:

- Unrelated business income tax (UBIT);
- Endowments;
- Executive compensation; and
- Governance.

IRS Report

The IRS issued an interim report in May 2010, based on information from 2006 provided by 344 organizations (177 private, 167 public). According to Lois Lerner, EO director, the study will enhance the IRS's enforcement and customer outreach efforts.

Business activities. The report divided organizations into three groups based on student size:

Small	Fewer than 5,000 students
Medium	5,000 to fewer than 15,000 students
Large	15,000 or more students

Organizations conducted up to 47 different types of activities listed in the questionnaire; activities could be exempt or taxable, depending on the facts and circumstances, the IRS said. A much larger percentage of organizations reported conducting a particular activity than reported the activity as taxable (on Form 990-T). Nearly half of small schools did not file a Form 990-T, compared to 29 percent of medium-sized schools and only four percent of large schools.

COMMENT

"That is one area we are going to focus on in our ongoing analysis of the data," Lerner reported. "We need to understand if this apparent disparity is appropriate or whether it indicates a broader compliance concern in the unrelated business income area."

Endowment funds. Endowment funds are maintained by nearly all higher-education organizations:

- 87 percent of small organizations;
- 97 percent of medium-sized organizations; and
- 100 percent of large organizations.

Regardless of school size, most organizations reported annual spending rates of 5 percent of endowment assets.

Compensation. Organizations reported on their compensation for the highest paid officers, directors, trustees, and key employees. A majority of organizations in each size category used rebuttable presumptions (comparability data, contemporaneous documentation, and approval by an independent governing body) allowed by the IRS to establish that the level of compensation was reasonable.

Additional study. The IRS is conducting additional analyses of certain areas, particularly:
- Transactions between related organizations and with controlled entities;
- Differences in treatment of activities as exempt or unrelated;
- Cost allocation practices;
- The reporting of losses from exempt and unrelated business activity;
- The use of comparability data to set executive compensation;
- The impact of the initial contract exception on the setting of compensation; and
- The impact of governance policies and practices on potential UBIT activities.

The IRS also is concerned about potential reporting inconsistencies, such as organizations that have controlled entities but did not report income from those entities, and will compare responses against other sources, such as Forms 990 or 941. The IRS will also separately analyze responses by 11 colleges and universities that responded on a system-wide basis (rather than campus-only). The IRS will issue a final report with additional information and analysis.

Audits

In the meantime, the IRS launched follow-up audits of 30 organizations. The exams will look principally at:
- UBIT, including
  - Controlled entities,
  - Expense allocation,
  - Losses, and
  - Debt-financed property; and
- Executive compensation, including the use of
  - Rebuttable presumptions,
  - The initial contract exception, and
  - Comparability data.

The audits will also collect data on governance policies and practices. The IRS will summarize the audits in the final report.

Congressional Oversight

The IRS is not the only party looking at colleges and universities. Senate Finance Committee ranking member Sen. Charles Grassley, R-Iowa, keeps tabs on higher education organizations and has expressed concern about their policies involving endowments, salaries, and tax arbitrage (schools with large untaxed investment portfolios borrowing funds using tax-exempt debt).

Tax-free bonds can be issued to raise funds for charitable organizations. Grassley commissioned a report by the Congressional Budget Office that found that the majority of tax-exempt bonds are held by schools with large investment assets. "The report raises questions...about universities' issuing bonds and going into debt when they have money in the bank," Grassley said.

Grassley has questioned whether universities might rely on double-digit investment losses as a reason to raise tuition or freeze student aid when the schools still have a large endowment. He also questioned the increase in salaries of college presidents and the high amounts paid former officers, stating that increased salaries are "out of sync" with the reality of costs for parents and students struggling to pay for college. Grassley suggested that universities be subject to a minimum payout requirement, such as 5 percent of their assets a year, like rules applied to private foundations. Some colleges announced more generous student aid policies after Grassley questioned their practices.

Grassley applauded the IRS compliance study for colleges and universities. "Colleges and universities should be much more transparent about their activities. Transparency brings accountability," he said. He recommended that the IRS quickly create a separate Form 990 schedule for educational institution reporting. "The questions the agency is asking...should be asked of all tax-exempt colleges and universities as soon as possible."

> **COMMENT**
>
> Form 990 includes Schedule E, *Schools*. This form requires private schools wishing to retain exempt status to state that they do not engage in racial discrimination.

STUDY QUESTIONS

7. Which of the following is *not* a new requirement of nonprofit hospitals under the *Patient Protection and Affordable Care Act* (PPACA)?

a. Publicizing their financial assistance policy

b. Waiving charges for patients who have no health care insurance

c. Limits on collection activities

---

8. Under the 2005 regulations by the IRS regarding the student exception to paying FICA taxes, medical residents are considered:

  a. Employees for whom employer payment of FICA taxes is waived
  b. Career employees for whom institutions should pay FICA taxes
  c. Students eligible for the student exception and thus requiring no payment of FICA taxes

---

GOVERNANCE

The IRS states that a well-governed charity is more likely to obey the tax laws, safeguard charitable assets, and serve charitable interests than a charity having poor or lax governance. According to the IRS, a charity with a clear mission, a knowledgeable governing body and management, and sound management practices is more likely to operate consistent with tax law requirements. According to Sarah Hall Ingram, as of 2010 the TE/GE commissioner, good governance is a tool that advances both an organization's charitable goals and the IRS's objective to ensure compliance with the tax code.

Tax Code and Governance

The IRS concedes that the tax code does not require good governance practices, but Ingram notes that good governance is implicit in the tax law requirements. To be tax-exempt, Code Sec. 501(c) requires that an organization be organized and operated for tax-exempt purposes. Ingram says "How is the organization organized? How is it operated? These questions inevitably involve a consideration of how the organization is governed."

Ingram also points out that the tax code imposes limits and penalties not only on the exempt organization but on the:

- Individual managers of these organizations;
- Tax on a charity's political expenditures;
- Excess benefit tax for self-dealing transactions;
- Tax on prohibited tax shelter transactions; and
- Excise taxes imposed on private foundations for self-dealing, jeopardy investments, and taxable expenditures.

By penalizing bad practices, the tax code implicitly prescribes good practices.

There is no single set of good governance practices, the IRS acknowledges. It has instructed its reviewers and examiners that "one size does not fit all." Governance issues vary depending upon the type, size, structure, and culture of an organization, the IRS advises in its training materials. The IRS says it is not its job to mandate a particular size governing board or to require a particular policy or practice, or to make decisions for the organization. Its goal is not to mandate specific practices but to encourage and recommend items of governance.

> **COMMENT**
>
> The IRS does not want to stamp out the diversity and variety of exempt organizations beneath a cathedral of rules, Ingram says. But it is important for each charity to be thoughtful about the governance practices that are most appropriate in ensuring sound operations and compliance with the tax law.

At the same time, the IRS believes that the risk of tax noncompliance is lower for organizations with good governance practices. As a consequence, the IRS will be less inclined to focus on transactions of organizations with good governance practices and structures in place, and more inclined to scrutinize transactions undertaken by organizations with poor government practices.

IRS Compliance Actions

The IRS is looking at governance at all phases of its interaction with a charitable organization:

- When the organization first applies for its tax exemption;
- As the organization operates from year to year and files its annual Form 990 information return; and
- During an audit, when the IRS may discover that a problem has occurred.

The IRS website posted an extensive and detailed discussion of good governance practices. The IRS revised Form 990 to require that every organization fill out Part VI, Governance, Management, and Disclosure. The IRS devised a check sheet for its examining agents to gather data about the governance practices and related internal controls of organizations being examined.

The IRS intends to use the check sheet to identify instances of noncompliance found during an exam and information about the use of internal controls. For each instance of noncompliance, the IRS will ask "Who made the decision to do it or allow it? Was there a policy in place concerning the transaction or activity, and if so, was it followed?"

> **COMMENT**
>
> The IRS will use the data gathered on audit as part of a long-term study to gain a better understanding of the interaction between governance practices and charities' tax compliance. This study will include several segments involving different activities.

IRS Governance Recommendations

The IRS believes in transparency, accountability, and disclosure. The IRS training materials on the determination letter process (that considers the initial application for tax-exempt status) focus on:

- Mission;
- Organizational documents;
- The governing body;
- Governance and management policies;
- Financial statements and Form 990 reporting; and
- Transparency and accountability.

Form 990, Part VI, on governance is divided into three sections:

- Governing Body and Management,
- Policies ("Not Required by the Internal Revenue Code"); and
- Disclosure.

Mission, documents. An organization should clearly understand and publicly express its mission, Ingram says. Form 990 requires a statement of the organization's mission (Part III). The organizational documents prescribe the framework for its governance and management and include a trust agreement or articles of incorporation, and corporate bylaws. The IRS reviews the documents to ensure that an organization applying for tax-exemption is organized exclusively for exempt purposes and that its activities are consistent with its documents.

Governing body. The IRS says that the governing body manages the charity on behalf of the general public. The IRS encourages a governing board that is active, engaged, knowledgeable, and independent. The board may be large or small. The IRS does not mandate a particular size but notes that a small board may not represent a broad public interest and may lack skills needed to govern the organization. A large board, it suggests, may have trouble making decisions.

Boards should include independent members and not be dominated by employees or by others who are not independent because of family or business relationships. Form 990, Part VI, Section A, asks about the governing body and its independence.

Managing assets. The board is also responsible for safeguarding assets and ensuring their charitable use. The IRS believes that an organization should maintain policies relating to the proper use and safeguarding of assets. On Form 990, Part VI, Section B, the IRS asks whether the organization has a conflict of interest policy (that it monitors and enforces), a whistleblower policy, and a document retention policy. Form 990 asks about executive compensation on Part VI, as well as on Part VII and Schedule J. The IRS through Form 990 is also concerned about investment practices, fundraising, and maintenance of governing body minutes and records.

COMMENT

Executive compensation continues to be a focus of IRS audits, including errors and omissions in reporting compensation and proper withholding of income and employment taxes.

Financial statements. The IRS encourages the organization's board to ensure that financial resources are appropriately accounted for, whether through internal accounting or outside accountants. State law may impose audit requirements. The IRS also recommends that any auditor be independent. Form 990, Part XI, asks about auditing practices and policy.

Governing body use of Form 990. Form 990 asks whether an organization provides a copy of Form 990 to its governing body and whether management or the board review the form before it is submitted to the IRS. According to Ingram, many organizations are using Form 990 as the agenda for board meetings, to expand the board's knowledge and promote their thorough oversight of the organization.

Transparency and accountability. Completed Form 990, Form 990-T, *Unrelated Business Income Tax,* and Form 1023, *Application for Charitable Exemption,* must be available for public inspection. The IRS partnered with Guidestar to make Form 990 information available on the Internet. Form 990, Part VI, asks about disclosure practices and policies.

COMMENT

The IRS wants to incorporate Form 990 questions and answers into compliance initiatives. The EO office has created new compliance units— the Review of Organizations (ROO) unit and the Exempt Organizations Compliance Area (EOCA)—to introduce and expand EO's use of compliance checks.

Future of Governance

Clearly, the IRS is serious about seeking, through both encouragement and additional oversight, to improve the governance of tax-exempt organizations, particularly charities. Ingram states that in the past, a widespread failure of governance led to serious problems within particular segments of the tax-exempt community, such as credit counseling organizations, which departed from their tax-exempt purpose of aiding debtors and converted into fee-earning loan consolidators. The IRS audited every credit counseling organization and revoked the exemption of over 40 percent (based on revenues). Similarly, the IRS has looked at mortgage assistance organizations and foreclosure assistance programs.

Ingram promised that TE/GE has no intention of walking away from governance and will stay engaged with the tax-exempt community in what she hopes is the "right" discussion, about those principles of good governance that contribute to a vibrant and compliant tax-exempt sector.

STUDY QUESTIONS

9. The IRS examines the governance practices of tax-exempt organizations:
   a. Primarily when the organization is new and prepares its mission statement
   b. Upon the organizations' filing for tax-exemption, on annual Form 990 filings, and during audits
   c. Because it is required by the tax code

10. The IRS recommends that tax-exempt organizations keep their governing boards small and consisting primarily of employees and members who have business relationships with the organizations. *True or False?*

CONCLUSION

Tax-exempt organizations are a dynamic and expanding sector of the economy. The IRS does not want to second-guess the activities of exempt organizations, but it does not want to ignore them either. As administrator of tax-exempt status under the Internal Revenue Code, the IRS believes it has a responsibility to the American public to ensure that organizations are not abusing their tax exemptions. This applies most strongly for charitable organizations, because the tax code encourages and rewards charitable contributions. Nonprofit organizations should expect the IRS Exempt Organizations office to continue and expand its interaction with the sector, as a source of information and education, a provider of services, and as an overseer of questionable activities.

MODULE 3: COMPLIANCE AND DISCLOSURE — CHAPTER 8

Retirement Plan Compliance Rules

The recession that started in 2008 hit defined benefit pension plans hard. Congress responded with funding relief, but many employers are choosing to terminate their plans if they can comply with the termination requirements. The hard times for defined benefit plans reinforce the general trend away from offering defined benefit plans and toward 401(k) plans as the retirement plan of choice.

The IRS has recognized the trend toward use of 401(k) plans, and has surveyed employers to identify common compliance issues with an eye toward improving compliance assistance.

Employee benefit plans (especially retirement plans) have annual reporting requirements, and many of these requirements have recently changed due to adoption of a new electronic filing system.

LEARNING OBJECTIVES

Upon completion of this chapter, you will be able to:

- Recognize the recent changes in compliance required under the annual Form 5500 series for employee welfare and benefit plan reporting;

- Describe how a fall in retirement plan asset values affects the employer's funding obligations;

- Describe the funding relief available for plans and how the relief can help a plan's cash flow;

- Describe how it helps a plan comply if it can use asset-to-liabilities ratios from a lookback year;

- Identify the purpose and scope of the 401(k) Compliance Questionnaire Project, and how the IRS is enforcing it;

- Describe the role of the PBGC (if any) in defined benefit plan terminations in contrast to defined contribution plan terminations;

- Describe the conditions under which an employer is allowed to terminate a defined benefit plan;

- Understand the consequences for vesting for purposes of plan termination; and

- Describe how multiemployer plans are terminated.

INTRODUCTION

Retirement plans must file annual reports using the Form 5500 series. The series was recently revised to accommodate changes brought about by a new electronic filing system and to reflect additional reporting requirements.

FORM 5500 COMPLIANCE

Employee pension and welfare benefits plans are generally required to file a comprehensive annual report disclosing information relating to the plan's qualified status, financial condition, and operations. Annual reports are filed on the Form 5500 series information returns. Form 5500 underwent substantial changes for 2009, including rules for a new electronic filing system, issuance of a new Form 5500-SF, *Short Form Annual Return/Report of Small Employee Benefit Plan,* revised Form 5500-EZ, and a number of revised schedules. These Form 5500 changes are carried forward for 2010, along with other anticipated changes to reflect the *Preservation of Access to Care for Medicare Beneficiaries and Pension Relief Act of 2010* (here known as the Pension Relief Act of 2010) and other developments.

> **COMMENT**
>
> Depending on the number and type of participants covered, most 401(k) plans must annually file a Form 5500, Form 5500-SF, or Form 5500-EZ. A plan need not file an actuarial schedule (SB or MB) for a 401(k) feature because 401(k)s are defined contribution plans. Most one-participant plans (sole proprietor and partnership plans) with total assets of $250,000 or less are exempt from the annual filing requirement. A final return/report must be filed when a plan is terminated, regardless of the value of the plan's assets.

Form 5500 Series

The Form 5500 series consolidates the annual report forms of the IRS, the Department of Labor (DOL), and the Pension Benefits Guaranty Corporation (PBGC). The Form 5500, *Annual Return/Report of Employee Benefit Plan,* is filed with the DOL's Employee Benefits Security Administration (EBSA), which forwards relevant information to the IRS and the PBGC.

Large and small plan reporting requirements. The Form 5500 reporting requirements applicable to large plans, small plans, and direct filing entities (DFEs) vary. Generally, the Form 5500 for a pension or welfare benefit plan that covered fewer than 100 participants as of the beginning of the plan year should be completed in accordance with the *small plan rules.* The Form 5500 report filed for a pension or welfare plan that covered 100 or more participants as of the beginning of the plan year should comply with the *large plan rules.*

> **COMMENT**
>
> Some plans (both large and small) participate in pooled investment arrangements that file Form 5500 as a DFE. A DFE Form 5500 must be filed for each master trust investment account (MTIA). An MTIA is a trust for which a regulated financial institution serves as a trustee or custodian and in which assets of more than one plan sponsored by a single employer or by a group of employers under common control are held. Filing is optional for other types of pooled investment arrangements. The schedules that must accompany a DFE Form 5500 vary depending on the filer's type of pooled arrangement. One Form 5500 is filed for each DFE for all plans participating in the DFE.

Schedules for small plans. The following schedules (and any additional information required by the instructions to the schedules) must be attached to a Form 5500 for a small pension plan that is neither exempt from filing nor filing Form 5500-SF:

- Schedule A (if funded in whole or in part by insurance contracts);
- Schedule SB or MB (if it is a single-employer or multiemployer defined benefit plan subject to minimum funding standards or a certain type of money purchase plan);
- Schedule D (if reporting as a direct filing entity);
- Schedule I (financial information); and
- Schedule R (unless the plan is, among other things, not a defined benefit plan, nor subject to the minimum funding rules, and no benefits were distributed during the year).

Schedules for large plans. The following schedules (and any additional information required by the instructions to the schedules) must now be attached to a Form 5500 for a large pension plan:

- Schedule A (if funded in whole or in part by insurance contracts);
- Schedule SB or MB (if it is a single-employer or multiemployer defined benefit plan subject to minimum funding standards or a certain type of money purchase plan);
- Schedule C (if a service provider was paid $5,000 or more in direct or indirect compensation and/or an accountant or actuary was terminated);
- Schedule D (if reporting as a Direct Filing Entity);
- Schedule G (if there financial transaction to report);
- Schedule H (financial information); and
- Schedule R (unless the plan is, among other things, neither a defined benefit plan nor subject to the minimum funding rules, and no benefits were distributed during the year).

Significant Changes

There are a number of important changes for Form 5500 filers starting with the 2009 reporting year that will carry over into future plan years due in large part to the shift to the EFAST2 filing system and because of new reporting requirements for plan costs. These include:

- Form 5500 and schedules must be filed through the EFAST2 electronic filing system;
- Form 5500-SF is a new streamlined version of Form 5500 that is filed through EFAST2 and takes the place of Form 5500-EZ for most small plans;
- Form 5500-EZ is now exclusively used only for one-participant plans and can only be filed on paper with the IRS;
- The schedules have been revised. Schedules E and SSA are removed. Schedule B has been replaced by Schedules SB and MB. Schedule C has been substantially revised to handle information regarding indirect payments to service providers. The IRS has introduced a new Form SSA that is filed separately from Form 5500;
- Nearly all 403(b) plans must file Form 5500; and
- Plans need no longer file Form 5558, *Application for Extension of Time to File Certain Employee Plan Returns,* to obtain an extension.

COMMENT

Anticipated changes for 2010 include the arrival of eligible combined plans (authorized by the *Pension Protection Act of 2006*), which include both defined benefit and defined contribution features. Such plans will have to report all relevant information for both the defined benefit and defined contribution parts of the plan. As a result, the plan will have to provide actuarial information regarding the defined benefits part (Form SB for a single-employer plan) and identify the features of both parts of the plan on Form 5500.

STUDY QUESTIONS

1. Annual reports using a form from the 5500 series are filed with the:
   a. Department of Labor's Employee Benefits Security Administration
   b. Internal Revenue Service Center
   c. Pension Benefits Guaranty Corporation

2. Form 5500-SF, a new streamlined version of Form 5500 filed using EFAST2, replaces Form 5500-EZ for small plans except one-participant plans, which must use paper Form 5500-EZ. ***True or False?***

Filing deadlines. The filing deadline for plans is the last day of the seventh calendar month after the end of the plan year for Form 5000, 5500-SF, and 5500-EZ. Generally this is July 31 for a calendar year plan. Deadlines that fall on the weekend or a federal holiday are postponed until the next week day.

> **EXAMPLE**
>
> The plan year for the ABC Retirement Plan is the fiscal year beginning on July 1. The end of the 2009 plan year for the ABC Retirement Plan is June 30, 2010. The filing deadline for ABC's 2009 Form 5500 is January 31, 2011.

For DFEs except group insurance arrangements (which use the plan deadline), the filing deadline is nine and one-half months after the end of the DFE year. A Form 5500 filed for a DFE must report information for the DFE year (not to exceed 12 months) that ends with or within the participating plan's year.

For a short plan year, deadline is the last day of the seventh calendar month after the short plan year ends. If the short plan year is caused by a change of plan year, the end of the plan year is the date of the change in accounting period. If the short plan year is caused by a plan termination, the short plan year ends upon complete distribution of plan assets.

Extensions. A plan or GIA may obtain a one-time extension of up to two and one-half months by filing IRS Form 5558, *Application for Extension of Time to File Certain Employee Plan Returns,* before the normal due date (not including any extensions) of the Form 5500. The IRS will acknowledge receipt of the Form 5558 by letter, and a copy of the Form 5558 should be kept with the plan's records but need not be included with the electronic filing.

An automatic extension of time to file Form 5500 until the due date of the federal income tax return of the employer will be granted if:

- The plan year and the employer's tax year are the same; and
- The employer has been granted an extension of time to file its federal income tax return to a date later than the normal due date for filing the Form 5500.

EFAST2

For plan years beginning on or after January 1, 2009, the Form 5500 filer must use the EFAST2 processing system. Plan administrators and direct filing entities must maintain an original copy of the Form 5500 annual return/report, with all required signatures, as part of their records. Filers may use electronic media for record maintenance and retention, as long as they meet the applicable requirements.

> **CAUTION**
>
> All information filed with EFAST2 is subject to immediate publication on the Internet.

> **COMPLIANCE POINTER**
>
> Prior year delinquent or amended Form 5500s must be filed electronically.

> **COMMENT**
>
> The EFAST2 system requires a substantial learning curve on the part of a new user.

Signing Form 5500. A filing signer credential is required to file through the EFAST2 system. The system was set up so that the plan administrator would have the credential and sign the return. However, a practitioner can sign on behalf of a plan sponsor client if the plan sponsor gives the practitioner written authority to file through the EFAST2 system on its behalf (DOL FAQ #33A, May 13, 2010). If the practitioner goes this route, the client does not need any EFAST2 credentials. A .pdf copy of the form with the plan sponsor's actual signature must be attached as part of the filing.

> **COMMENT**
>
> This alternative signing procedure is a work-around devised by the DOL rather than a change in the system itself. Consequently, when a practitioner signs for a client, the practitioner's name goes out on the public disclosure website in place of the sponsor's. That can be confusing and the DOL is in the process of creating a statement to explain why the practitioner's name appears as the signature of the plan sponsor.

Attachments. Attachments for EFAST2 system must be .pdf or text-only files. The filer must attach a document for every line that requires one. EFAST2 will not accept a secured file.

> **COMMENT**
>
> An auditor's report is typically provided by the auditor in a secured file that nobody can change. The auditor might be willing to provide an unsecured file for EFAST2 under the circumstances. If not, the filer will have to print and scan the pages.

STUDY QUESTIONS

---

3. The information filed on each of the following reports is subject to immediate publication on the Internet *except:*

   a. Form 5500

   b. Form 5500-EZ

   c. Form 5500-SF

4. Which method is *not* used to provide the IRS with a filing signer credential for Form 5500?

   a. Written authority given to practitioner by the plan sponsor to file the form

   b. Submission of a notarized document that the sponsor's official signature was properly witnessed

   c. Inclusion of a .pdf file

Form 5500-SF

Form 5500-SF, *Short Form Annual Return/Report of Small Employee Benefit Plan,* is available for certain small plans that invest solely in easily valued assets such as readily tradable stocks, bonds, and mutual funds.

Plans that can file Form 5500-SF. The EBSA, the PBGC, and the IRS have adopted the two-page Form 5500-SF as a new simplified report for certain small plans. A pension plan is eligible to file the short form if the plan:

- Covers fewer than 100 participants at the beginning of the plan year, or filed as a small plan for 2008 and did not cover more than 120 participants at the beginning of plan year 2009;
- Is eligible for the waiver of the annual examination and report of an independent qualified public accountant (but not by reason of enhanced bonding);
- Holds no employer securities;
- Invested 100 percent of its assets in investments with a readily ascertainable market value such as
  - Mutual funds,

— Investment contracts with insurance companies and banks valued at least annually,
— Publicly treated securities held by a registered dealer,
— Cash and equivalents, and
— Participant loans; and
- Is not a multiemployer plan.

Schedules. Most Form 5500-SF filers will not be required to file any schedules, although defined benefit pension plans will continue to be required to fill out Schedule MB or SB, where applicable.

Form 5500-EZ

A Form 5500-EZ, *Annual Return of One-Participant (Owners and Their Spouses) Retirement Plan,* may be filed for one-participant plans that satisfy the applicable conditions, and must be filed for certain foreign plans. Form 5500-EZ can only be filed on paper with the IRS.

One-participant plans. A *one-participant plan* is a pension benefit plan:
- That covers only an individual or an individual and his or her spouse who wholly own a trade or business, whether incorporated or unincorporated; or
- For a partnership that covers only the partners or the partners and the partners' spouses.

One-participant plan filing options. A one-participant plan may not file an annual return on Form 5500 for the 2009 plan year. One-participant plans must either file Form 5500-EZ or, if eligible, Form 5500-SF. Advantages of filing Form 5500-EZ rather than 5500-SF are:
- Form 5500-EZ is filed on paper with the IRS rather than through EFAST2 system, thus avoiding a steep learning curve for the filer; and
- The information on Form 5500-EZ is not published on the Internet.

Thus, a one-participant plan can cover more than one participant, although just because the plan covers only one participant does not mean it qualifies as a one-participant plan for this purpose.

Foreign plans required to file Form 5500-EZ. A pension benefit plan maintained outside the United States primarily for the benefit of persons substantially all of whom are nonresident aliens is not subject to Title I of ERISA and may not file an annual return on Form 5500 for 2009. Every such plan that is required to file an annual return for 2009 and thereafter must instead file Form 5500-EZ.

Revised Form 5500 Schedules for 2009 and Thereafter

As part of the move to an all-electronic filing system for the Form 5500 series, Form 5500 no longer includes any form or schedule that has been required only for the IRS. As a result, Schedules E (for ESOP reporting) and SSA (identifying separated participants with deferred vested benefits) are eliminated. New IRS Form 8895-SSA, *Annual Registration Statement Identifying Separated Participants with Deferred Vested Benefits,* takes the place of Schedule SSA and is filed directly with the IRS. Three of the questions on the old Schedule E now appear on Schedule R. Form 5500-EZ is not eliminated from the Form 5500 series, but it is to be filed directly with the IRS.

New IRS Form 8955-SSA. Filers required to submit information on participants who have a deferred vested benefit and who separated from the service covered by the plan must file an annual registration statement identifying those participants for the IRS. Historically, filers included this information on Form 5500 Schedule SSA. However, because the information includes Social Security numbers, it cannot be supplied through EFAST2 in that electronic filing would publish protected Social Security information on the Internet. Accordingly, the IRS will issue Form 8955-SSA to replace Schedule SSA.

> **COMMENT**
>
> The practitioner should not file any SSA data in EFAST2, but should wait and file when the form is released. Delinquent Schedule SSAs should be sent to the IRS.

Schedule A. Schedule A, which requires the reporting of insurance and annuity contracts, now requires filers to distinguish between allocated and unallocated contracts. An *allocated contract* for these purposes is one that guarantees a particular benefit for a particular participant at a particular age.

> **COMMENT**
>
> Such contracts are unusual for purposes of reporting. Not even individual life insurance contracts would qualify as allocated.

Schedule C. Schedule C, which requires reporting of service provider information, has been substantially revised to distinguish between direct compensation received from the plan and indirect compensation received from sources other than the plan or the plan sponsor (for example, compensation charged against investment assets).

> **COMMENT**
>
> Starting with 2009 filings, service providers are required to provide notice of indirect fees to plans, but reporting can be inconsistent and not always helpful. Practitioners are only expected to work with what they have.

Schedule H. Schedule H, which requires reporting of financial information for large plans and DFEs, now requires the filer to identify mutual fund dividends separately rather than as part of net mutual fund returns. This requirement applies, however, only if the plan owns the funds directly rather than through a collective or pooled fund. Also, if a defined benefit plan pays PBGC premiums from the plan, it is no longer reported as an expense but as a transfer.

Compliance questions. A new question on Schedule H questions whether the plan failed to provide any benefit when due. This question goes to situations where the funds are not liquid or just are not there as opposed to circumstances in which a required minimum distribution was missed. Schedule H also asks whether there was a blackout period and if so, whether notice was provided (with substantial penalties imposed for failing to provide the required notice).

> **COMMENT**
>
> A new required attachment is required if there are late deposits reported on Schedule H or I (financial information for small plans). The attachment may be included with Form 5500-SF as well, although it is not required.

403(b) Plans

Special limited financial reporting rules for 403(b) plans have been eliminated through regulatory changes. Thus, 403(b) plans that are subject to Title I of ERISA are to follow the same annual reporting rules that apply to other ERISA-covered retirement plans.

STUDY QUESTIONS

> **5.** Which of the following schedules to Form 5500 was **not** eliminated beginning in the 2009 tax year?
>
> **a.** Schedule A (for reporting insurance and annuity contracts)
> **b.** Schedule E (for ESOP reporting)
> **c.** Schedule SSA (for separated participants with deferred vested benefits)

6. Form 8955-SSA is replacing Schedule SSA because:

   a. Participants who separated from service covered by the plan are no longer required to be reported

   b. The schedule cannot be published on the Internet because it includes protected information such as the participant's Social Security number

   c. Schedule SSA did not contain information pertinent to participants with deferred vested benefits

PENSION PLAN FUNDING RELIEF

ERISA and the IRC have long required minimum contributions from employers to fund defined benefit plans. The rules balance two considerations. First, plan assets have to be sufficient to cover future accrued benefits. The countervailing concern was that employers might overfund to park assets in tax-advantaged plans, and so limits needed to be placed on overfunding.

During the past several decades, plans became increasingly underfunded. In recognition of an impending long-term funding crisis, Congress passed the *Pension Protection Act of 2006* (PPA) (P.L. 109-280) to toughen funding requirements. Effective for the 2008 plan year, the PPA substantially rewrote the rules for single-employer plans doing away with the funding standard account (FSA) altogether. The PPA kept the FSA rules largely intact for multiemployer (union-negotiated) plans, however. In addition, a handful of single-employer and multiemployer plans have delayed PPA effective dates and temporarily continue to operate under the old rules.

COMMENT

Currently, there are three funding regimes:

- The single-employer plan rules under the PPA;
- The multiemployer plan funding rules under the PPA; and
- The pre-PPA rules for plans that have a delayed PPA effective date.

The Need for Additional Funding Relief

The bursting of the asset bubble in 2008 and 2009 hit defined benefit pension plans hard. Not only was cash hard to come by for many employers to make their annual contributions, but plans themselves suddenly became poorer as the fair market value of their assets shrank. Under both the old rules and the PPA rules, the ratio of assets to liabilities suddenly lurched into seriously underfunded territory. As a result, employers had to start making up the difference or cutting back benefits. In response to these concerns, Congress passed the *Preservation of Access to Care for Medicare Beneficiaries and Pension Relief Act of 2010* (Pension Relief Act of 2010) (P.L. 111-192).

Funding Relief Under the Pension Relief Act of 2010

In general, the relief strategies provided in the Pension Relief Act of 2010 consists of:

- Extending the amortization period during which the plan has to make up funding shortfalls;
- Extending the smoothing period for plan asset values so that drops in value will have less effect right away;
- Allowing plans to use a precrash lookback year for asset-to-liability ratios so that extra funding obligations or benefit limits may be delayed until asset values can recover; and
- Allowing charitable plans to use a delayed effective date for PPA requirements.

PPA funding. The temporary relief provisions of the Pension Relief Act of 2010 are best explored in the context of the PPA rules from which relief was deemed to be needed.

Funding relief for single-employer plans. To understand the relief given under the Pension Relief Act of 2010, the funding rules otherwise in force under PPA need to be examined. Under PPA, plan sponsors must make a "minimum required contribution" based on a comparison of the value of plan assets with the plan's "funding target" and "target normal cost."

Funding target under PPA rules. The *funding target* for a plan year is the present value of all benefits accrued or earned as of the beginning of the plan year (Code Sec. 430(d)(1) and ERISA Sec. 303(d)(1)). If the plan's assets do not exceed the funding target, the plan has a funding shortfall and the plan's minimum required contribution will be increased by the shortfall amortization charge (Code Sec. 430(c)(4), ERISA Sec. 303(c)(4), as added by PPA). The funding target functions as a benchmark for whether the plan is adequately funded as of the beginning of the plan year for benefits accruing in past plan years.

Target normal cost under PPA rules. The target normal cost is the present value as of the beginning of the plan year of benefits expected to accrue or to be earned during the plan year. A plan's target normal cost is increased by the amount of plan-related expenses expected to be paid from plan assets during the plan year and is decreased by the amount of mandatory employee contributions expected to be made to the plan during the plan year (Code Sec. 430(b)(1) and ERISA Sec. 303(b)(1)).

Minimum required contribution under PPA rules. If plan assets do not cover the funding target and target normal cost, the plan must make a minimum required contribution within eight and one-half months after the close of the plan year. If the plan has a funding shortfall for a plan year, the minimum required contribution is generally equal to the sum of the plan's target normal cost and the shortfall amortization charge for that year (Code Sec. 430(a)(1) and ERISA Sec. 303(a)(1)). If the value of the plan's assets equals or exceeds the plan's funding target for a plan year, then the minimum required contribution is generally equal to the plan's target normal cost for the year, reduced (but not below zero) by the amount by which the value of the plan's assets exceeds the plan's funding target (Code Sec. 430(a)(2) and ERISA Sec. 303(a)(2)).

STUDY QUESTION

> **7.** Under PPA rules, for the plan year the plan's target normal cost is _____ by the amount of expected plan-related expenses and _____ by the amount of expected mandatory employee contributions.
>
> **a.** Increased; decreased
> **b.** Increased; increased
> **c.** Decreased; decreased

Funding shortfalls amortization under PPA rules. The amount due for a plan year for purposes of a minimum required contribution with respect to a funding shortfall is an amortized payment of the amortization base. The amortization period is seven plan years, beginning with the current plan year. If the value of plan assets is equal to or greater than the funding target of the plan, then the shortfall amortization base for the plan year will be zero. By contrast, if the value of plan assets is less than the funding target for the plan year, a shortfall amortization base is established for the plan year (Code Sec. 430(c) and ERISA Sec. 303(c)).

> **EXAMPLE**
>
> Zeltac maintains a calendar year plan with a valuation date of January 1. The plan has a funding target of $2.5 million and assets totaling $1.8 million as of January 1, 2010. A $700,000 shortfall amortization base is established for 2010, which is equal to Zeltac's $2.5 million funding target less $1.8 million of assets. The $700,000 shortfall amortization base is amortized over a seven-year period beginning with the current plan year.

The Pension Relief Act of 2010: extended amortization for single-employer plans. Under the Pension Relief Act of 2010, a plan sponsor of a single-employer defined benefit pension plan may elect to determine shortfall amortization installments with respect to the shortfall amortization base under either of two alternative extended amortization schedules:

- The two plus seven amortization schedule; or
- A 15-year amortization schedule (Code Sec. 430(c)(2)(D) and ERISA Sec. 303(c)(2)(D), as added by the Pension Relief Act of 2010).

Two plus seven schedule. Under the two plus seven amortization schedule, the plan sponsor may elect to amortize the shortfall amortization base for the applicable plan year over a nine-year period beginning with that election year. The shortfall amortization installments for the first two plan years in the nine-year period are equal to the interest on the shortfall amortization base for the applicable plan year (i.e., election year), determined by using the effective interest rate for the plan for that year. The shortfall amortization installments for the last seven plan years in the nine-year period are equal to the amounts necessary to amortize the remaining balance of the shortfall amortization base for the applicable plan year in level annual installments over the seven-year period, determined by using the segment rates for the applicable plan year.

> **COMMENT**
>
> Under the two plus seven schedule, amortization is essentially postponed two years, though the plan must pay interest during those years. Cash flow is significantly improved for the first two years, and is adversely affected in the eighth and ninth years.

15-year schedule. Under the 15-year amortization schedule, the plan sponsor may elect to amortize the shortfall amortization base for an applicable plan year in level annual installments over a 15-year period beginning with the election year using the segment rates for the election year.

> **COMMENT**
>
> The 15-year schedule improves cash flow somewhat for the first 7 years, but adversely affects it for the following 8 years. Although the two plus seven schedule provides the employer with the maximum current breathing room, it might also prove to be a bit of a roller coaster ride if there is not a significant recovery in asset values in the near term. The 15-year schedule spreads out the payments and might make more sense if assets values stagnate, even if there is more of an upfront cost to the employer.

Eligibility for single-employer amortization relief. Plan years eligible for this relief include ones beginning in 2008, 2009, 2010, or 2011, but only if the due date for the payment of the minimum required contribution for the plan year occurs on or after June 25, 2010. An election to use an extended amortization schedule cannot be used for more than two eligible plan years with respect to a plan. A plan sponsor is not required to make an extended amortization schedule election for more than one eligible plan year or for consecutive eligible plan years. However, a plan sponsor who does make an election for two eligible plan years must elect the same extended schedule for each year (Code Sec. 430(c)(2)(D) and ERISA Sec. 303(c)(2)(D), as added by the 2010 Pension Relief Act).

> **COMMENT**
>
> A plan that elects either of these schedules must make additional contributions equal to the sum of aggregate excess employer compensation over $1 million and the aggregate amount of extraordinary dividends and redemptions. The idea is that the funding break employers get from this relief should be limited if the employer has enough money to pay big compensation to its executives.

Limits on future benefit accruals and prohibited payment freezes for single-employer plans under PPA. The financial health of a defined benefit plan depends in part on its *adjusted funding target attainment percentage* (AFTAP). A plan's AFTAP is basically the ratio of the plan's assets to its funding target for the year (Code Sec. 436(j) and ERISA Sec. 206(g)(9)). When a single-employer defined benefit plan's AFTAP falls below certain levels, special rules can limit its future benefit accruals and distribution of prohibited payments (Code Sec. 436 and ERISA Sec. 206(g)).

Benefit accruals. An endangered plan must cease future benefit accruals as of the valuation date for any plan year in which the plan's AFTAP is less than 60 percent (Code Sec. 436(e) and ERISA Sec. 206(g)(4)). Service during the freeze period continues to count for all purposes other than benefit accrual. The freeze is lifted as of the first day of the plan year when the plan sponsor makes a contribution (in addition to any minimum required contribution for the plan year) sufficient to bring the plan's AFTAP back to 60 percent.

Prohibited payments. Under the PPA, a plan must provide that if its AFTAP falls below 60 percent, it will freeze any prohibited payments after the valuation date for the plan year (Code Sec. 436(d)(1) and ERISA Sec.

206(g)(3)(A)). A prohibited payment is basically an acceleration of payments under a Social Security leveling feature. That feature allows a plan to pay higher benefits before and lower benefits after the participant's full Social Security retirement benefits commence, so that the participant receives a fairly consistent retirement income despite an early retirement (Reg. § 1.436-1(d)(3)(iii)(D)).

Temporary relief for benefit accrual freeze. The asset value crash in 2008 and subsequent recession did great harm to plan balance sheets, with resulting dire consequences for many plans' AFTAP. Left to their own devices, many plans would have had to cease benefit accruals under the PPA rules. The hope in Congress was that the downturn was temporary and that asset values (and hence AFTAPs) would soon recover. In the meantime, Congress provided temporary relief in the *Worker, Retiree, and Employer Recovery Act of 2008* (WRERA) (P.L. 110-458). For the first plan year beginning on or after October 1, 2008, and before October 1, 2009, a plan was to determine whether the benefit accrual freeze applies by using its AFTAP for the previous plan year (assuming it provide would provide a better result).

STUDY QUESTION

8. The adjusted target attainment percentage (AFTAP) of a defined benefit plan is the ratio of:
    a. The plan's assets to the year's funding target
    b. The distribution rate of scheduled benefit disbursements to the year's funding target
    c. The target normal cost to the benefits expected to accrue during the plan year

Lookback Funding Percentages

The temporary relief for benefit accrual freezes is extended, and plans can use a lookback AFTAP for prohibited payments freezes. In addition, plans of charitable organizations may use a lookback feature for determining whether a credit balance can be applied.

Temporary relief for benefit accrual freezes extended. The Pension Relief Act of 2010 extends the benefit accrual relief for another year (Code Sec. 436(j)(3)(A) and (C)(ii), and ERISA Sec. 206(g)(9)(D)(i) and (iii)(II), as added by the 2010 Pension Relief Act). Thus, if a plan's AFTAP for any plan year beginning after September 30, 2008, and before October 1, 2010, falls below 60 percent, the freeze on future benefit accruals applies only if the plan's AFTAP is also below 60 percent for the plan year beginning after October 1, 2007, and before October 1, 2008.

Lookback AFTAP for prohibited payments freeze. For any plan year beginning on or after October 1, 2008, and before October 1, 2010, an at-risk single-employer's defined benefit plan can determine whether it is allowed to make Social Security leveling payments by using its AFTAP for that plan year, or for its plan year beginning after October 1, 2007, and before October 1, 2008 (Code Sec. 436(j)(3)(A) and (C)(i), and ERISA Sec. 206(g)(9)(D)(i) and (iii)(I), as added by the 2010 Pension Relief Act). Thus, if a plan's AFTAP for any plan year beginning after September 30, 2008, and before October 1, 2010, falls below 60 percent, the freeze on payments made under Social Security leveling features applies only if the plan's AFTAP is also below 60 percent for the plan year beginning after October 1, 2007, and before October 1, 2008.

Charitable plans use of lookback year for credit balance. Under the Pension Relief Act of 2010, a plan's credit balances may be applied under PPA against a plan's minimum required contribution if the plan's funding ratio was at least 80 percent for the previous year. For plan years beginning after August 31, 2009, and before September 1, 2011, plans maintained by charitable organizations whose funded status for a certain lookback year was at least equal to 80 percent may offset their minimum required contributions by a credit balance, even if the plan would not otherwise be permitted to do so if it measured its funded status using the prior plan year (as is normally required). The lookback year is the plan year beginning after August 31, 2007, and before September 1, 2008,

Funding for Multiemployer (Union-negotiated) Plans Under PPA
Prior to the PPA changes, all plans subject to funding standards were required to have a funding standard account. Today, only delayed-PPA-effective-date plans and multiemployer union plans must maintain a funding standard account. The funding standard account is charged each year both for the plan's normal costs of future benefits allocated to the plan and for supplemental costs. A *supplemental cost* is the cost of future benefits that would not be met by future normal costs, future employee contributions, or plan assets. Experience losses are treated as supplemental costs. Supplemental costs (including experience losses) can generally be amortized over 15 years for multiemployer plans (Code Sec. 431(b)(2) and ERISA Sec. 304(b)(2)) with two 5-year extensions available.

> **COMMENT**
>
> All things being equal, a fall in the value of plan assets would result in an experience loss for the plan. The rules allowing such losses to be amortized helps spread out the cost of such losses over a period of years.

Funding relief for multiemployer plans under the Pension Relief Act of 2010: Extended amortization and asset smoothing. Under the Pension Relief Act of 2010, a plan sponsor of a multiemployer plan that meets a solvency test may use either one or both of two special funding relief rules for either or both of the first two plan years that end after August 31, 2008. The rules allow:

- Extended amortization of net investment losses; and/or
- Extended smoothing period for asset valuation.

Extended amortization. A multiemployer plan that passes a solvency test may treat the portion of any experience loss or gain attributable to net investment losses incurred in either or both of the first two plan years ending after August 31, 2008, as an item separate from other experience losses, to be amortized in equal annual installments (until fully amortized) over the period:

- Beginning with the plan year in which such portion is first recognized in the actuarial value of assets; and
- Ending with the last plan year in the 30-plan year period beginning with the plan year in which such net investment loss was incurred (Code Sec. 431(b)(8)(A)(i) and ERISA Sec. 304(b)(8)(A)(i), as added by *Preservation of Access to Care for Medicare Beneficiaries and Pension Relief Act of 2010* (P.L. 111-192)).

> **EXAMPLE**
>
> Multiemployer plan A incurs an net investment loss (NIL) in plan year 2008 that qualifies for extended amortization in the amount of $1 million. The amortization period for that amount begins in plan year 2009 (the plan year in which the NIL is first recognized in the actuarial value of assets). The period ends in plan year 2037 (the last plan year in the 30-plan year period beginning with plan year 2008, the plan year in which the NIL was incurred).

Asset smoothing rules for multiemployer plan. In determining the charges and credits to the funding standard account for a multiemployer plan, the value of plan assets may be determined on the basis of any reasonable actuarial method that takes into account fair market value and that is permitted under IRS regulations (Code Sec. 431(c)(2) and ERISA Sec. 304(c)(2)). A reasonable actuarial valuation method generally can include a smoothing method that takes into account reasonable expected investment returns and average values of the plan assets, as long as the smoothing or averaging period does not exceed the five most recent plan years (including the current plan year). In addition, there is a valuation corridor for any actuarial valuation method such that the value of plan assets must not be less than 80 percent and not more than 120 percent of their current fair market value (Reg. § 1.412(c)(2)-1(b); Rev. Proc. 2000-40, 2000-2 CB 357).

Expanded asset valuation smoothing period. A multiemployer plan that meets a solvency test may change its asset valuation method so that it:

- Spreads the difference between expected and actual returns for either or both of the first two plan years ending after August 31, 2008, over a period of not more than 10 years, or
- Provides that for either or both of the first two plan years beginning after August 31, 2008, the value of plan assets at any time shall not be less than 80 percent or greater than 130 percent of the fair market value of such assets at such time (Code Sec. 431(b)(8)(B)(i) and ERISA Sec. 304(b)(8)(B)(i), as added by 2010 Pension Relief Act).

Restrictions on benefit increases for multiemployer plans electing amortization or smoothing relief. If a multiemployer plan elects amortization or smoothing relief for any plan year, a plan amendment increasing benefits may not go into effect during either of the two plan years immediately following such plan year unless:

- The plan actuary certifies that any such increase is paid for out of additional contributions not allocated to the plan immediately before the application of this amendment to the plan, and the plan's funded percentage and projected credit balances for such plan years are reasonably expected to be at least as high as such percentage and balances would have been if the benefit increase had not been adopted; or
- The amendment is required as a condition of plan qualification or to comply with other applicable law (Code Sec. 431(b)(8)(D) and ERISA Sec. 304(b)(8)(D), as added by 2010 Pension Relief Act).

Eligibility for multiemployer relief. If a plan takes advantage of this special amortization relief for any plan year, no extension of the amortization period will be allowed. If an extension was granted for any plan year prior to the election, such election will not result in the amortization period exceeding 30 years (Code Sec. 431(b)(8)(A)(ii) and ERISA Sec. 304(b)(8)(A)(ii), as added by 2010 Pension Relief Act).

Funding relief under the Pension Relief Act of 2010 for delayed-PPA-effective-date plans. Most plans are subject to the PPA funding rules starting in the 2008 plan year, but several exceptions still operate under the old rules and have funding standard accounts. One of these exceptions is for multiple-employer plans (i.e., plans maintained by more than one employer, but not union negotiated) maintained by rural cooperatives that offer electrical, telephone, or certain agricultural services. For these plans, the PPA funding rules do not apply to plan years beginning before the earlier of:

- The first plan year for which the plan ceases to be an eligible cooperative plan; or
- January 1, 2017 (Act Sec. 104 of PPA).

Funding relief: Charity plans added to delayed PPA effective date for multiple-employer plans. The Pension Relief Act of 2010 allows charity plans maintained by more than one employer to use the delayed effective date rules for rural cooperatives (Act Sec. 104(d) of PPA, as added by the 2010 Pension Relief Act).

Funding relief: Extended amortization period for delayed-PPA-effective-date plans. The amortization period for experience losses (such as a drop in asset values) for delayed-PPA-effective-date plans is 5 years, with a possible extension of up to 10 years with permission from the Department of Labor (Code Sec. 412(b)(2)(C), prior to amendment by PPA). Under the Pension Relief Act of 2010, a plan sponsor of a delayed-PPA-effective-date plan may elect either a 15-year amortization period for any increased unfunded new liability of the plan, or a 2 year look back rule for the funded current liability percentage used to determine the deficit reduction contribution for the plan year. The 2-year lookback rule in effect allows the plan to postpone amortization of new experience losses for 2 years (Act Sec. 107 of PPA, as added by the 2010 Pension Relief Act).

> **COMMENT**
>
> In its effect, this relief is similar to the relief provided single-employer plans under the PPA rules, which gives PPA governed plans a choice of a two plus seven schedule or a straight 15-year schedule .

Eligibility for delayed PPA effective date relief. A plan sponsor may elect relief for no more than two eligible plan years (one year for plans of certain government contractors) (Act Sec. 107(d)(1) of PPA, as added by the 2010 Pension Relief Act). An *eligible plan year* means any plan year beginning in 2008, 2009, 2010, or 2011, except that a plan year beginning in 2008 will only be treated as an eligible plan year if the due date for the payment of the minimum required contribution for that plan year occurs on or after June 25, 2010, the date of enactment (Act Sec. 107(e)(1) of PPA, as added by the Pension Relief Act of 2010).

STUDY QUESTION

> **9.** The Pension Relief Act of 2010 enables charitable organizations to offset their minimum required contributions by a credit balance if their funded status for the target normal cost to the benefits expected to accrue during the plan year a certain lookback year was at least:
>
> **a.** 50 percent
> **b.** 75 percent
> **c.** 80 percent

THE IRS 401(K) QUESTIONNAIRE

The IRS is seeking information regarding 401(k) plans through its 401(k) Compliance Check Questionnaire Project. The questionnaire is administered by the Employee Plans Compliance Unit (EPCU). The IRS's goal is to take a comprehensive look at 401(k) plans to determine:

- Potential compliance issues;
- Any plan operational issues; and
- Additional education and outreach guidance that may be helpful for the IRS to provide to plan sponsors to improve compliance.

The IRS will issue a report describing the responses to its questionnaire and identifying those areas where additional efforts are needed. The report will also describe how the IRS can focus its enforcement efforts to address and avoid 401(k) plan noncompliance.

Procedure

The EPCU has sent a letter and instructions to 1,200 employers sponsoring 401(k) plans, asking them to complete the 401(k) Compliance Check Questionnaire. Plan sponsors have 90 days from the date of the letter to complete the questionnaire. Recipients are to limit their responses to the information requested and not submit any supplemental materials.

Employer selection process. The IRS chose the employers by taking a random sample of 1,200 401(k) plan sponsors that filed a Form 5500 for the 2007 plan year.

Filing out the online questionnaire. Responses are to be provided through a secure website. If the plan sponsor is physically unable to respond online or cannot access the questionnaire online, the plan sponsor should contact the person listed on the letter. Someone else can complete the questionnaire for the plan sponsor, but to have someone else discuss the questionnaire with the IRS the plan sponsor must submit Form 2848, *Power of Attorney and Declaration of Representative.*

> **COMMENT**
>
> To ease completion, the IRS recommends printing out a copy of the questionnaire and the glossary of terms provided with the online questionnaire. If multiple individuals are providing input on the plan's response, responses can be compiled on the *Guide to Completion of the 401(k) Compliance Check Questionnaire,* Form 14146, before entering the answers online. Form 14146 can be printed from the website (**http://www.irs.gov/pub/ irs-tege/epcu_401k_questionnaire.pdf**). The form should not be returned to the IRS.

Scope of Questionnaire

The 401(k) Compliance Check Questionnaire consists of multiple sections, not all of which will necessarily apply to every plan. The IRS designed the questionnaire so that questions that do not apply to a particular plan will not appear as the plan administrator completes the questionnaire.

- The questionnaire's categories are:
- Demographics;
- Participation;
- Employer and employee contributions;
- Top-heavy and nondiscrimination testing;
- Distributions and plan loans;
- Other plan operations;
- Automatic contribution arrangements;
- Designated Roth features;
- IRS voluntary compliance and correction programs; and
- Plan administration.

Problems accessing the questionnaire. If there is an error message when the responder tries to access the questionnaire, he or she should verify the accuracy of the PIN, password, and source ID that were entered. For example, it is possible the letter "I" was mistaken for the number "1." If this does not resolve the problem, he or she should notify the contact person listed on the letter received.

Information required. The recipient of a questionnaire cover letter must answer the questions for the specific plan referenced in the letter, not including controlled group or affiliated service group members. Unless otherwise indicated, responses should be based on information as of the end of the plan's 2008 plan year. If the plan was new in 2007 or 2008, the questionnaire should be completed using zeroes for periods prior to the inception of the plan. If the plan was not in existence in 2008, the administrator should notify the contact person whose name appears in the heading of the letter.

No books or records. The plan administrator should provide the most complete and accurate answers possible, but the IRS absolutely does not want the administrator to submit books or records with the completed questionnaire.

Rounding. When completing questions that ask for dollar amounts or percentages, the responder should round the amounts to the nearest dollar or percentage unless otherwise instructed.

Comments. The IRS is seeking comments through the questionnaire, especially with respect to areas in which the IRS can provide additional education, make improvements to programs and help ensure future compliance.

Questionnaire Is an IRS Compliance Check

The IRS is treating the questionnaire as a compliance check. A *compliance check* is an enforcement action to which the recipient of the letter must respond. A compliance check is not an audit or investigation, and it does not involve a review of an organization's books and records. However, failure to respond or provide complete information will result in further enforcement actions that may include an examination of the plan.

Qualification Failure Discovered While Filer Completes the Questionnaire

Plan sponsors may either self-correct or submit an application under the Voluntary Correction Program (Rev. Proc. 2008-50).

STUDY QUESTION

---

10. The goals of the IRS' 401(k) Compliance Check Questionnaire Project do *not* include:

a. Identifying issues in plan operations that require further guidance by the IRS

b. Specific examinations of large employers' funding procedures for plan year 2009

c. Identifying potential compliance issues

RESTRICTIONS ON PLAN TERMINATIONS

One of the options an employer has in reducing employment costs is termination of a costly retirement plan:

- Termination of defined benefit plans is complex and governed largely by Pension Benefit Guaranty Corporation (PBGC) rules that are designed to protect participants and beneficiaries who are owed accrued benefits; and
- Termination of defined contribution plans is handled outside of the PBGC regulatory framework.

However, in either case, a terminating plan must follow certain procedures in order to remain qualified under IRS rules.

COMMENT

Failure of the plan to remain qualified would result in the plan losing the tax advantages of qualification, which include:

- Tax free accumulation of plan income;
- Taxation of benefits only when they are paid to participants;
- The ability to roll over assets into another tax deferred arrangement (e.g., IRA); and
- Current deduction of contributions for the employer.

In the context of a termination, distributions from a plan that is no longer qualified might result in current taxation of all benefits.

Employers have fairly broad latitude in terminating retirement plans. Once a plan is terminated, however, plan participants become totally vested in their accrued benefits as of the date of termination to the extent the benefits are funded. In addition, ERISA imposes requirements on sponsors of terminating plans that are designed to further protect the benefits of plan participants and beneficiaries.

Voluntary Single-Employer Qualified Plan Terminations

Employers that want to terminate a single-employer retirement plan are subject to restrictions designed to protect plan participants. The nature of these restrictions depends on whether the plan is a defined benefit or defined contribution arrangement.

Voluntary termination of defined benefit plans. Single-employer defined benefit plans may be terminated voluntarily by the plan sponsor. ERISA Sec. 4041 provides two exclusive types of voluntary termination: standard and distress. A plan may be terminated in a *standard termination* only if plan assets are sufficient to cover liabilities. In the event plan assets are not sufficient, the sponsor may terminate the plan if specified conditions of financial *distress* (e.g., bankruptcy) are met.

Voluntary termination of defined contribution plan. An employer may terminate a defined contribution plan more easily than a defined benefit plan because ERISA's termination provisions do not apply to defined contribution plans (although such terminations are subject to IRS requirements). Typically, an employer merely adopts a resolution terminating the plan. ERISA's goal of protecting plan participants from employers that want to terminate a plan in order to recover excess assets does not apply to defined contribution plans because specific amounts are allocated to employees' accounts under these plans. Employees are entitled to all amounts in their respective accounts upon termination (IRS Reg. § 1.401-6(a)(1)).

Full vesting on plan termination. On the termination or partial termination of a plan, the rights of all participants to benefits accrued as of the date of the termination vest to the extent funded (Code Sec. 411(d)(3)). In the case of a plan that maintains individual accounts for participants (i.e., money purchase, profit-sharing, 401(k), and stock bonus plans), the amount credited to a participant's account must vest (IRS Reg. § 1.401-6(b)(2)).

> **COMMENT**
>
> Because participants in individual account plans must fully vest in amounts credited to their accounts upon the final or partial termination of the plan regardless of the participant's years of service or vesting status, there is no need for premium payments to provide for guaranteed benefits.

Partial plan termination. Under certain circumstances, a defined contribution plan or defined benefit plan will be considered partially terminated (IRS Reg. § 1.411(d)-2(b)(1)). The major difference between a partial termination and a full termination is that, in the case of partial termination, vesting is required only for the part of the plan that is terminated (IRS Reg. § 1.401-6(b)(2)).

Required allocation. A qualified plan must provide for the allocation of any previously unallocated funds to employees upon the termination or partial termination of the plan or, in the case of profit-sharing or stock bonus plans, upon the complete discontinuance of contributions (IRS Reg. § 1.411(d)-2(a)(2)(i). The allocation of assets to participants from a terminated plan may not be discriminatory in favor of officers, stockholders, and other highly compensated employees (IRS Reg. § 1.401(a)(4)-5(b)).

> **COMMENT**
>
> If the plan does not provide for such allocations when it is adopted, the plan will need to be amended prior to termination or discontinuance of contributions.

Plan qualification. Qualified plans still need to be qualified up to termination, and a plan will want to obtain an IRS determination letter to that effect. The plan files Form 5310, *Application for Determination Upon Termination,* with the IRS for this purpose. Plan participants and beneficiaries must be notified if the plan applies to the IRS for a determination letter regarding the qualification of the plan upon termination (ERISA Sec. 3001(a); IRS Reg. §§ 1.7476-1 and 1.7476-2).

Missing participants. If the plan has missing participants, it must file a Schedule MP with the PBGC (PBGC Reg. § Part 4050). An employer terminating a fully funded pension plan must distribute all plan benefits to participants and beneficiaries before completing the plan's termination. If a participant or beneficiary is missing after a diligent search, the plan must either purchase an annuity from a private insurer in that person's name and provide information on the missing person and insurer to PBGC, or transfer the value of the person's benefit to PBGC's Missing Participants Program.

> **COMMENT**
>
> This program is only available to terminating plans.

STUDY QUESTION

> **11.** In a partial termination of a defined contribution or defined benefit plan, vesting is required only for the portion of the plan being terminated. *True or False?*

Standard Terminations for Single-Employer Defined Benefit Plans

An employer maintaining a single-employer defined benefit plan may terminate a plan in a standard termination only if the assets in the plan are sufficient to satisfy all benefit liabilities as of the termination date. A single-employer plan will satisfy benefit liabilities if there are no unfunded benefit liabilities under the plan.

Limits on plan pending termination. The plan administrator must continue to carry out normal plan operations from the date the notice of intent to terminate (NOIT) is issued until the last day of the PBGC review period. Thus, plan administrators must continue to:
- Put participants into pay status;
- Collect contributions due the plan;
- Invest plan assets; and
- Make loans to qualified participants.

However, during the pendency of the termination proceedings, the plan administrator may not:
- Purchase irrevocable commitments to provide any plan benefits; or
- Pay benefits attributable to employer contributions, other than death benefits, in a form other than an annuity.

The plan administrator may pay benefits that are attributable to employer contributions through the purchase of irrevocable commitments or in a form other than an annuity. This option applies if the participant has separated from service and the arrangement is consistent with prior plan practice and not reasonably expected to jeopardize the plan's sufficiency for benefit liabilities (PBGC Reg. § 4041.22).

Overview of standard termination procedure. A single-employer plan may terminate under a standard termination only if:
The plan administrator timely
   — Provides an NOIT;
   — Files a standard termination notice with the PBGC,
   — Provides notices of plan benefits to plan participants and beneficiaries; and
- The PBGC does not issue a notice of noncompliance, distributes all plan assets in satisfaction of all benefit liabilities under the plan (ERISA Sec. 4041(b)).

> **COMMENT**
>
> The PBGC has provided a standard termination filing package with forms and instructions on its website.

Notice of intent to terminate. To begin either a standard or distress termination, the plan administrator must provide an NOIT to *affected parties,* which include:

- Participants;
- Beneficiaries of deceased participants;
- Qualified domestic relations orders' alternate payees; and
- Employee organizations representing participants.

The notice must be provided at least 60 days (and no more than 90 days) prior to the proposed termination date (ERISA Sec. 4041(a)(2); PBGC Reg. § 4041.23). The PBGC provides a model NOIT in its Standard Termination Filing instructions.

Notice of plan benefits. A plan administrator must provide plan participants, beneficiaries of deceased participants, and alternate payees with a notice of that individual's plan benefits by the date on which the plan administrator files the standard termination notice (i.e., on or before the 180th day after the proposed termination date). This notice must not be filed later than the date that the standard termination notice is filed. The notice must:

- Identify the plan and the contributing plan sponsor;
- Disclose the proposed termination date; and
- Provide the personal data used to calculate the benefits of an affected party (other than a party who has been in pay status for more than one year (PBGC Reg. § 4041.24).

Standard Termination Notice (PBGC Form 500). In a standard termination, the plan administrator must file PBGC Form 500, *Standard Termination Notice, Single-Employer Plan Termination.* along with Schedule EA-S, *Standard Termination Certification of Sufficiency,* with the PBGC within 180 days after the proposed termination date (PBGC Reg. § 4041.25). The forms certify to the PBGC that the plan will have sufficient assets to meet its benefit liabilities. *The PBGC has 60 days after receiving a complete Form 500 to review the termination for compliance with the law and regulations (PBGC Reg. § 4041.26).*

Annuity information. A Notice of Annuity Information must be provided to plan participants, beneficiaries of deceased participants, and alternate payees no later than 45 days before the distribution date if benefits may be distributed in an annuity form (PBGC Reg. §§ 4041.23 (b)(5) and 4041.27). In addition, a Notice of Annuity Contract must be provided to participants receiving their plan benefits in the form of an annuity no later than 30 days after the contract is available. (See 29 CFR 4041.28 (d).)

PBGC notice of noncompliance. If, after its review, the PBGC determines that plan assets as of the distribution date proposed in the standard termination notice will not be sufficient to satisfy all benefit liabilities, it issues a notice of noncompliance. A notice of noncompliance:

- Ends the standard termination proceeding;
- Nullifies all actions taken to terminate the plan; and
- Renders the plan an ongoing plan.

Once a notice is issued, the plan administrator must take no further action to terminate the plan, except by initiation of a new termination (PBGC Reg. § 4041.31).

Distribution of assets. Unless the PBGC issues a notice of noncompliance, the plan administrator must distribute all plan assets by the later of:

- 180 days following the end of the PBGC's 60-day review period or any extended period; or
- 120 days after receipt of a favorable determination letter from the IRS regarding the plan's qualified status upon termination (provided the request for a determination letter was made by the time the standard termination notice was filed) (PBGC Reg. § 4041.28).

The administrator must distribute assets to a participant by purchasing an irrevocable commitment from an insurer or in another permitted form that fully provides for benefit liabilities under the plan (PBGC Reg. § 4041.28(c), (d)).

Post-Distribution Certification (PBGC Form 501). PBGC Form 501 must be filed with the PBGC no later than 30 days after all plan benefits are distributed. The PBGC will assess a penalty for late filings only to the extent the certification is filed more than 90 days after the distribution deadline (PBGC Reg. § 4041.29).

Distress Terminations for Single-Employer Defined Benefit Plans

A single-employer defined benefit plan that does not qualify for a standard termination due to the plan sponsor's financial weakness may be voluntarily terminated through a distress termination. If the plan terminates in a distress termination without sufficient assets to pay all benefit liabilities, the contributing sponsor and each controlled group member are jointly and severally liable to the PBGC (ERISA Sec. 4062(b)).

Qualifying for distress termination. A plan can use the distress termination procedures if the contributing plan sponsor and each member of its controlled group satisfy one of the following criteria:

Liquidation in bankruptcy. The liquidation petition must have been filed by or against the employer as of the proposed termination date (PBGC Reg. § 4041.41(c)(1)).

Reorganization in bankruptcy or insolvency proceeding. The reorganization petition must have been filed by or against the employer as of the proposed date of termination. The employer must notify the PBGC of any request to the bankruptcy court (or other appropriate court) for approval of the plan termination by concurrently filing with the PBGC a copy of the motion requesting court approval. In addition, the court must determine that, unless the plan is terminated, the employer will be unable to pay all its debts pursuant to a reorganization plan and will be unable to continue in business outside the reorganization process. The court must also approve the plan termination (PBGC Reg. § 4041.41(c)(2)).

Inability to continue in business. An employer must demonstrate that, absent a distress termination, it will be unable to pay its debts when due and to continue in business (PBGC Reg. § 4041.41(c)(3)).

Unreasonably burdensome pension costs. An employer must establish that its costs of providing pension coverage have become unreasonably burdensome solely as a result of declining covered employment under all single-employer plans for which that employer is a contributing sponsor (PBGC Reg. § 4041.41(c)(4)).

Limits on plan pending termination. While the termination proceedings are pending, the plan administrator must continue to carry out normal operations of the plan, including:

- Placing participants in pay status;
- Collecting contributions due the plan; and
- Investing plan assets.

From the date that plan administrator first issues a NOIT, however, loans may not be made to plan participants. In addition, from the date the plan administrator first issues a NOIT until the plan administrator is authorized to distribute plan assets, the plan administrator may not:

- Distribute assets or take any other actions to carry out the proposed distress termination;
- Pay benefits attributable to employer contributions (except death benefits) in any form other than as an annuity; or
- Purchase irrevocable commitments to provide benefits from an insurer.

> **COMMENT**
>
> In contrast to the limits on plans in involuntary terminations, administrators in standard terminations may continue to make plan loans.

Beginning on the proposed termination date, the plan administrator must reduce benefit levels to no more than the accrued benefit payable at normal retirement age or the maximum guaranteeable benefit (PBGC Reg. § 4041.42).

Overview of distress termination procedure. A distress termination requires a plan administrator to provide a notice of intent to terminate (NOIT) to each affected party and the PBGC, and file a distress termination notice with the PBGC no later than 120 days after the proposed termination date.

> **COMMENT**
>
> The PBGC has posted a distress termination filing package with forms and instructions available on its website.

Notice of intent to terminate (PBGC Form 600). As with standard terminations, the plan must issue an NOIT to all affected parties:,

- Participants;
- Beneficiaries of deceased participants;
- Alternate payees under qualified domestic relations orders; and
- Employee organizations representing participants.

In addition, the plan must provide the NOIT to the PBGC. The NOIT must be provided at least 60 days but not more than 90 days before the proposed termination date.

> **COMMENT**
>
> Unlike in a standard termination, the PBGC must also receive the NOIT and the PBGC has a dedicated form (PBGC Form 600) for that purpose.

Distress termination notice (PBGC Form 601). The plan must file PBGC Form 601 *Distress Termination Notice, Single-Employer Plan Termination,* with Schedule EA-D, *Distress Termination Enrolled Actuary*

Certification, with the PBGC. Unless the enrolled actuary certifies that the plan is sufficient for guaranteed benefits or for benefit liabilities, the participant information and benefit information required by Form 601 must be filed with the PBGC by the later of the 120th day after the proposed termination date, or 30 days after receipt of the PBGC's determination that the distress termination requirements have been satisfied. The plan administrator's failure to provide the required information will allow the PBGC to void the distress termination (PBGC Reg. § 4041.45).

Participant benefit information. The plan must file participant and benefit information with the PBGC by the later of:

- 120 days after the proposed termination date; or
- 30 days after receipt of the PBGC's determination that the requirements for a distress termination have been satisfied.

PBGC determination of plan sufficiency. If the PBGC determines that the plan is sufficient for guaranteed benefits, but not for benefit liabilities, or is sufficient for benefit liabilities, it will issue a notice allowing the plan administrator to:

- Issue notices of benefit distribution;
- Close out the plan; and
- File a timely post-distribution certification with the PBGC.

If the PBGC is unable to determine that a plan's assets are sufficient to cover guaranteed benefits, it will issue a notice of inability to determine sufficiency and advise the plan administrator that the plan will continue to be administered under the restrictions imposed on plans terminating under a distress termination. The termination will be completed under the provisions permitting the PBGC to involuntarily terminate a plan (PBGC Reg. § 4041.47).

Notice of benefit distribution. After receiving a distribution notice from the PBGC, the plan administrator must issue a notice of benefit distribution to each participant, beneficiary of a deceased participant, and alternate payee within 60 days. Within 15 days after completion of the notice of benefit distribution, the plan administrator must file with the PBGC a certification that the notices were properly issued (PBGC Reg. § 4041.48).

Closing out the plan. If the plan administrator receives a distribution notice from the PBGC and neither the plan administrator nor the PBGC make a finding of insufficiency, the plan administrator must distribute the plan assets by the later of:

- The day on which the plan administrator completes the issuance of the notices of benefit distribution; or
- 120 days after receipt of a favorable determination letter from the IRS (PBGC Reg. § 4041.28).

Post-distribution certificate (PBGC Form 602). Within 30 days after the distribution of plan assets is completed, the plan administrator must file PBGC Form 602, *Post Distribution Certification for Distress Termination* (PBGC Reg. § 4041.29).

Involuntary Termination for Single-Employer Defined Benefit Plans

To protect the interests of plan participants, the PBGC under ERISA Sec. 4042 may take it upon itself to terminate a single-employer defined benefit plan under certain circumstances. The PBGC may institute termination proceedings in the United States District Court for the district in which the plan administrator resides or does business, or in which any of the plan's trust property is located.

The PBGC may bring an action to terminate if:

- The plan has not met the minimum funding standards;
- The plan sponsor is deficient in paying the tax for failure to meet the minimum funding standards;
- The plan will not be able to pay benefits when due;
- A distribution exceeding $10,000 that is a reportable event under ERISA is made to a substantial owner; or
- The loss to the PBGC will increase unreasonably if the plan is not terminated.

As soon as practicable, the PBGC is required to institute court proceedings to terminate a single-employer plan whenever it determines that the plan does not have assets available to pay benefits that are currently due under the plan.

COMMENT

The PBGC determines whether the plan will be able to pay benefits when due based on a review its records, including information supplied on the plan's Form 5500 actuarial schedules.

> **EXAMPLE**
>
> The PBGC learns that Acme, Inc., failed to meet minimum funding standards for its defined benefit plan for the most recently completed plan year. The PBGC reviews its records and the reporting provided on the Acme's annual Form 5500 actuarial schedule (currently, Schedule SB). The PBGC realizes that unfunded liabilities have been growing at an annual rate of 15 percent over the last five years. The PBGC may start taking steps to terminate the plan. The plan probably will not qualify as a standard termination, but by instituting a plan termination, the PBGC will at least be able to stop future benefit accruals and slow the 15 percent growth rate of unfunded liabilities, as well as reduce the plan's future liability.

STUDY QUESTIONS

12. A plan administrator who begins either a standard or distress termination of a single-employer plan provides affected parties (participants, beneficiaries, etc.) with:
    a. A Standard termination notice
    b. A Notice of intent to terminate
    c. Post-Distribution Certification

13. A PBGC notice of noncompliance for a single-employer plan seeking a standard termination does *not*:
    a. Render the plan an ongoing plan
    b. End the standard termination
    c. Require the plan administrator to distribute all plan assets within 180 days

Multiemployer Plan Terminations

Multiemployer plans may be voluntarily terminated under ERISA Sec. 4041A by either:

- The withdrawal of every employer from the plan (i.e., *mass withdrawal*); or
- Amendment of the plan that denies participants credit under the plan for any period of service with the employer after a specific date or that converts the plan into defined contribution plan.

Mass withdrawal from multiemployer plan. A plan from which every employer has withdrawn is terminated on the earlier of the date the last employer withdraws or the first day of the first plan year for which no employer contributions are required under the plan. A NOIT must be filed with the PBGC by a multiemployer plan that is terminated by mass withdrawal (or plan amendment). The notice is to be filed by the plan sponsor or a duly authorized representative of the sponsor.

Termination of multiemployer plans by plan amendment. Amendments of a multiemployer plan that either deny participants credit for any period for service with an employer after a date specified by the amendment or change the plan into a defined contribution arrangement will (as of the later of the date the amendment is adopted or effective) terminate the plan (ERISA Sec. 4041A(b)(1). A multiemployer plan that is terminated by plan amendment must file a NOIT with the PBGC (PBGC Reg. § 4041A.11(a)).

> **COMMENT**
>
> Unlike single-employer plans, multiemployer plans continue to pay all vested benefits out of existing plan assets and withdrawal liability payments. The PBGC's guarantee of the benefits in a terminated, multiemployer plan (payable as financial assistance to the plan) only starts if and when the plan is unable to make payments at the statutorily guaranteed level.

Involuntary terminations. A multiemployer plan may be terminated through proceedings instituted by the PBGC under ERISA Sec. 4042. The PBGC may initiate termination proceedings if the plan has not met the minimum funding standards or will not be able to pay benefits when due. In addition, a plan may be terminated in order to shield the PBGC from an unreasonably large loss. The PBGC may petition a federal court for the appointment of a trustee to administer the plan pending issuance of court decree terminating the plan.

STUDY QUESTIONS

> **14.** The PBGC may initiate court proceedings for involuntary terminations of single-employer or multiemployer plans if:
>
> **a.** The plan does not have assets available to pay benefits currently due
>
> **b.** The plan is voluntarily terminated
>
> **c.** The PBGC issues a notice of noncompliance and the plan administrator takes no further action

---

15. The following methods may be used to voluntarily terminate a multi-employer plan under ERISA *except*:

   a. Suspending distributions to current recipients

   b. Mass withdrawal

   c. Plan amendment that denies participants credit after a specific date

---

CONCLUSION

With the wilting of asset values and the downturn in business, defined benefit pension plans have been hit hard in recent years. Congress has provided funding relief that will allow employers to spread out the extra contributions required to maintain funding levels. For employers that want to terminate their plans completely, termination procedures are available.

Certain employers with 401(k) plans are required to answer an IRS questionnaire. These questionnaires are designed to identify compliance issues both with respect to the individual plan and with respect to problems common to 401(k) plans in general.

Recent changes in electronic filing of the Form 5500 series have resulted in updates to forms and schedules.

CPE NOTE: When you have completed your study and review of chapters 6-8, which comprise Module 3, you may wish to take the Quizzer for this Module.

For your convenience, you can also take this Quizzer online at **www.cchtestingcenter.com**.

TOP FEDERAL TAX ISSUES FOR 2011 CPE COURSE

Answers to Study Questions

MODULE 1 — CHAPTER 1

1. a. *Incorrect.* For tax years beginning in 2010 through 2013, 25 percent is the maximum Code Sec. 45R credit for qualified small *tax-exempt employers.*

b. *Correct.* For tax years beginning in 2010 through 2013, the maximum credit reaches 35 percent of qualified premium costs for qualified small for-profit employers.

c. *Incorrect.* The maximum Code 45R credit does not increase to 50 percent for qualified small for-profit employers until tax years beginning in 2014 through 2015.

2. a. *Incorrect.* The minimum number of days required to be worked by a seasonal worker for that worker to be taken into account for purposes of the Code Sec. 45R credit exceeds 100 during a one-year period.

b. *Incorrect.* The minimum number of days required to be worked by a seasonal worker for that worker to be taken into account for purposes of the Code Sec. 45R credit is not 110 days during a one-year period.

c. *Correct.* The minimum number of days required to be worked by a seasonal worker to be taken into account for purposes of the Code Sec. 45R credit is 120 days during a one-year period.

3. a. *Incorrect.* For purposes of Code Sec. 45R, a family member does not include a cousin of a qualified owner.

b. *Correct.* Sole proprietors are not taken into account as employees for purposes of the Code Sec. 45 credit.

c. *Incorrect.* Although a current father-in-law or mother-in-law of a qualified owner is not taken into account for purposes of the Code Sec. 45R credit, there is no similar limitation for a former in-law.

4. a. *Correct.* Hours of service by employees are not computed based using a monthly measurement.

b. *Incorrect.* Actual hours of service is a yardstick for determining hours of service.

c. *Incorrect.* Weeks-worked equivalency is a method for determining hours of service.

5. True. *Incorrect.* Qualified employers can claim the Code Sec. 45R credit even if they receive state credits for employees' insurance premiums.

False. *Correct.* State credits and payments do not reduce an employer's Code Sec. 45R credit.

6. a. *Correct.* The Code Sec. 45R credit is a general business credit, so an unused credit may be carried back 1 year and carried forward 20 years.
b. *Incorrect.* The Code Sec. 45R credit has a different carryover period.
c. *Incorrect.* The Code Sec. 45R credit may only be carried back for fewer than 20 years.

7. a. *Correct.* A full-time employee for purposes of the employer's shared responsibility penalty is considered a worker employed on average for at least 30 hours of service per week.
b. *Incorrect.* A different measure of hours applies under the employer's shared responsibility penalty terms for full-time employees.
c. *Incorrect.* A full-time employee has fewer required average hours of service per week.

8. a. *Incorrect.* The health care reform package regards a small employer with a greater number than 25 employees as qualified to access a state insurance exchange after 2014.
b. *Incorrect.* The health care reform package uses a different maximum number of employees to describe the qualified small employer with access to a state insurance exchange after 2014.
c. *Correct.* A qualified small employer with up to 100 employees may access a state insurance exchange starting in 2014.

9. True. *Correct.* The health care reform package allows young adults to remain on their parents' qualified health insurance plans until age 26. An employer plan need not cover adult children of employees but if the plan does offer this coverage, the plan must offer coverage to adult children until age 26.
False. *Incorrect.* The health care reform package extends coverage for young adults under their parents' qualified health insurance plans until age 26.

10. a. *Incorrect.* Employers claim a payroll tax credit quarterly on Form 941 for the portion of premiums they pay.
b. *Correct.* Assistance-eligible individuals pay 35 percent of COBRA premiums, and former employers or other coverage providers pay 65 percent, for which they receive a payroll tax credit.
c. *Incorrect.* The assistance is not claimed as a tax credit by former employees and does not apply if the separation from employment was voluntary.

MODULE 1 — CHAPTER 2

1. a. *Correct.* The NRP study is examining 2,000 Forms 941 filed by private and public sector employers, including tax-exempt organizations, for each tax year from 2008 through 2010.

b. *Incorrect.* The NRP study is not examining self-employment tax reporting by individuals for its compliance initiative.

c. *Incorrect.* An employer provides Form 1099-MISC to an independent contractor who is paid $600 or more by the employer during the tax year. The independent contractor generally reports total amounts from each client's Form 1099-MISC on Form 1040, Schedule SE, *Self-Employment Income.*

2. a. *Incorrect.* The HIRE Act's payroll forgiveness provisions offer relief from qualified employers' share of OASDI taxes for employees but not independent contractors.

b. *Incorrect.* The credit increases the employer's general business credit for each worker completing a minimum employment period.

c. *Correct.* The work opportunity tax credit was created prior to the 2010 HIRE Act.

3. a. *Incorrect.* Employers of common-law employees are required by the tax law to pay Railroad Retirement Tax Act taxes if applicable in the situation.

b. *Incorrect.* Employers must pay the entire share of FUTA (unemployment insurance) taxes from their own funds on behalf of employees.

c. *Correct.* Employers are required by the tax law to provide independent contractors, not employees, with Form 1099-MISC, to report the amount of payments made to the contractor during the tax year.

4. a. *Incorrect.* Employers must withhold and pay FICA taxes for statutory employees, and a real estate agent is a statutory nonemployee to whom payments made are not subject to employment tax.

b. *Correct.* Employers must withhold and pay FICA taxes for statutory employees, which include agent- or commission-drivers, full-time insurance sales representatives, homeworkers, and traveling or city salespersons. Thus, these workers do not pay self-employment tax.

c. *Incorrect.* A direct seller is a statutory nonemployee who must pay self-employment taxes.

5. a. *Correct.* A person who must perform services in an order or sequence established by the employer rather than simply producing a product shows that the worker is subject to the employer's control and generally indicates the worker is an employee.

b. *Incorrect.* Independent contractors generally may set their own work schedule. An employer–employee relationship is indicated when the employer controls the set hours of work.

c. *Incorrect.* Workers who are in a position to realize profit or risk loss as a result of providing services are generally deemed to be independent contractors. Workers paid a fixed rate based on time with the employer with no possibility of loss are more likely to be employees.

6. True. *Incorrect.* The IRS balances the 20 traditional factors with facts and circumstances of the specific situation.

False. *Correct.* The IRS considers the facts and circumstances of specific employment situations in determining worker status as well as the 20 traditional factors, which are not always determinative given changing employment arrangements such as telecommuting.

7. a. *Incorrect.* Reliance on long-standing industry practice is considered a reasonable basis for not treating a worker as an employee.

b. *Correct.* Withholding indicates the worker is an employee, even if the employer does not actually remit the tax.

c. *Incorrect.* Employers provide independent contractors with Forms 1099-MISC, and provide employees with Forms W-2 for withholding purposes.

8. a. *Correct.* Unless the IRS issues an NDWC or obtains a waiver of restrictions on assessment from the employer, an automatic abatement is granted.

b. *Incorrect.* The 90-day period may be suspended when the NDWC is mailed to an employer, but such a mailing does not extend the assessment period or affect taxes assessed.

c. *Incorrect.* The worker does not respond to this tax assessment, but he or she may request a determination of worker status using Form SS-8.

9. a. *Correct.* The administration's proposal would enable the IRS to require prospective reclassification, effective on the date of the reform's enactment.

b. *Incorrect.* The proposal retains the current reduced penalties for misclassification, but only for voluntary reclassifications employers make before contact by an enforcement agency.

c. *Incorrect.* The Section 530 safe harbor rules would increase funding to coordinate DOL and IRS enforcement actions.

10. a. *Incorrect.* The proposed legislation revising Section 530 rules would require the same treatment since 1977 for all workers holding substantially similar positions.

b. *Correct.* **The proposed legislation would not require employers to provide notices of classification status to all workers.**

c. *Incorrect.* The results of previous examinations would support classification of workers as independent contractors.

MODULE 1 — CHAPTER 3

1. a. *Correct.* **A C corporation is taxed at the entity level; shareholders are also taxed on dividends distributed.**

b. *Incorrect.* As a type of flow-through entity, the S corporation is not subject to entity-level taxation. However, when a C corporation converts to an S corporation, special taxes apply.

c. *Incorrect.* The LLC combined the features of limited liability and a single level of taxation.

2. a. *Incorrect.* A multimember LLC may elect tax treatment as an S corporation.

b. *Correct.* **Whereas a single-member LLC may elect to be a disregarded entity, which is taxed as a sole proprietorship, this option is unavailable when the LLC has more than one member.**

c. *Incorrect.* The multimember LLC may be taxed as a partnership.

3. a. *Incorrect.* Although shareholders are liable for unpaid employment taxes, sales and use taxes, and wages, they do not bear personal liability for the corporation's income tax.

b. *Correct.* **Shareholders who do not actively or materially participate in the business, however, may be held liable for employment taxes, sales and use taxes, and unpaid wages.**

c. *Incorrect.* Stock received in exchange for services to a corporation is compensation, and the taxpayer must recognize income on such assets.

4. True. *Correct.* **If an LLC or corporation serves as the general partner, the liability for the partnership's debts is limited to the investors' investment in the LLC or corporation. Also, noncorporate general partners may collect their shares of the debt from the LLC or corporation's assets.**

False. *Incorrect.* The general partner bears liability for the debts and obligations of the partnership. However, if the general partner is an LLC or a corporation, the LLC or corporation's investors' liability is limited to their investment in the LLC or corporation.

5. a. *Incorrect.* Boot received by a C corporation is taxable either as a divided or as a sale or exchange.

b. _Correct._ Boot is not taxable to the owner in a sole proprietorship.
c. _Incorrect._ The S corporation shareholders are taxed for the boot received.

6. a. _Incorrect._ The ESBT may elect to become an S corporation shareholder subject to the maximum noncorporate tax rate on its S corporation tax items.
b. _Correct._ Foreign trusts are not allowed to be S corporation shareholders.
c. _Incorrect._ Qualified pension plans, profit-sharing plans, and ESOPs are eligible to be S corporation shareholders, but Roth IRAS, SIMPLE plans, and SEPs are not.

7. a. _Incorrect._ The AMT exclusion allows a greater amount of average gross receipts.
b. _Correct._ Corporations that have gross receipts less than $5 million in their first tax year after December 31, 1996, and continue to average less than $7.5 million per year are not subject to the corporate AMT.
c. _Incorrect._ A lower maximum average gross receipts amount applies to C corporations excluded from paying AMT.

8. a. _Correct._ The AET does not help the C corporation to avoid double taxation but is applied at a 15-percent rate in addition to the regular corporate income tax.
b. _Incorrect._ The built-in gains tax, not the AET, may be applied when a C corporation converts to an S corporation.
c. _Incorrect._ The AET increases, not avoids, the C corporation's tax burden. The AET tax rate is 15 percent of the company's accumulated taxable income in addition to regular income tax.

9. a. _Correct._ The PIIT may not be imposed in a loss year.
b. _Incorrect._ The tax is imposed only when the S corporation has earnings and profits.
c. _Incorrect._ Under the _Small Business and Work Opportunity Tax Act of 2007,_ gains from such transactions are no longer considered passive investment income.

10. a. _Correct._ The Code Sec. 338 allocation rules do not apply to nontaxable asset acquisitions.
b. _Incorrect._ The transaction is an exchange of the seller's assets for receipt of stock by the buyer.
c. _Incorrect._ The seller's shareholders do not recognize gain or loss because the acquired assets that become owned by the buyer retain the inherent gain.

MODULE 2 — CHAPTER 4

1. a. *Incorrect.* Partnership income paid to partners is subject to the individual income tax rates.
b. *Incorrect.* Income paid to members of an S corporation is subject to the individual income tax rates.
c. *Correct.* C corporations distribute dividends, which are subject to the reduced tax rates also applied to long-term capital gains.

2. a. *Correct.* Given possible rate increases for wages, capital gains, and dividends beginning in tax year 2011, income recognition should be accelerated to 2010 to capitalize on the current rate structure.
b. *Incorrect.* Deferring deductions, rather than income, is advisable if EGTRRA provisions are allowed to expire.
c. *Incorrect.* This traditional approach to income and deductions is not advisable during the transitional period for rate changes.

3. a. *Incorrect.* EGTRRA did not repeal the Pease limitation permanently.
b. *Incorrect.* EGTRRA did not leave the Pease limitation unchanged; EGTRRA repealed it for the 2010 tax year.
c. *Correct.* For 2010 returns only, the Pease limitation repealed the limitation on itemized deductions for higher-income taxpayers.

4. a. *Incorrect.* Preference items are ineffective in avoiding the AMT. Many deductions allowed in the regular tax structure are not allowed in computing AMT liability.
b. *Correct.* Equalizing the amount of regular tax liability to close to that of AMT provides the optimal bunching of itemized deductions to avoid the AMT.
c. *Incorrect.* AMT liability is triggered, not avoided, when a taxpayer's tentative minimum tax exceeds regular tax liability.

5. True. *Incorrect.* Prepaying taxes that are not AMT preference items offers no offset to the tax liability for AMT.
False. *Correct.* Because such taxes are not AMT preference items, no tax benefit accrues from shifting payment of the taxes into a year in which the taxpayer is subject to AMT.

6. a. *Correct.* The shareholder must hold the common stock for at least 61 days during the 121-day period beginning 60 days before the ex-dividend date.
b. *Incorrect.* The holding period of 91 days applies to dividends attributable to preferred stock.

c. *Incorrect.* The 181-day period applies to preferred stock, during which the taxpayer must hold the stock for at least 91 days.

7. a. *Correct.* **The recapture amount is equal to either the total depreciation allowable on the asset or the total gain realized, whichever is less. For real estate used for home offices, only the depreciation accruing after May 6, 1997, counts.**
b. *Incorrect.* A different rate is used to tax recaptured depreciation on real estate. For real estate used for home offices, only the depreciation accruing after May 6, 1997, counts. For personal property, the recaptured amount is reported as ordinary income.
c. *Incorrect.* The maximum recaptured depreciation percentage is lower.

8. a. *Correct.* **The additional Medicare tax will be 0.9 percent, and a 3.8-percent Medicare contribution tax will apply to higher-income taxpayers as well.**
b. *Incorrect.* The 1.45 percent tax is the employee's portion of the Social Security portion of FICA deducted from employees' wages.
c. *Incorrect.* The employee's portion of Social Security tax is 6.2 percent. For Medicare, a different percentage of additional tax will be imposed on higher-income taxpayers, as well as a 3.8-percent contribution tax for the higher-bracket taxpayers.

9. a. *Incorrect.* In computing MAGI for the Medicare contribution tax, the taxpayer adds otherwise-excludable foreign earned income to the AGI.
b. *Correct.* **Under Code Sec. 911, such credits reduce foreign earned income and thus lower the taxpayer's adjusted gross income.**
c. *Incorrect.* Otherwise-excludable foreign housing costs under Code Sec. 911 are added to AGI in determining MAGI subject to the Medicare contribution tax.

10. a. *Incorrect.* Contributions to Roth accounts are not tax-free but subject to the taxpayer's ordinary income tax rate.
b. *Correct.* **Although contributions to the Roth IRAs are subject to the taxpayer's ordinary income tax rate, qualified distributions of both earlier contributions and earnings are not subject to federal income tax.**
c. *Incorrect.* Both traditional and Roth IRAs have the same annual maximum contributions: $5,000 for individuals younger than age 50, and $6,000 for those age 50 or above.

11. a. *Correct.* **Tax-free qualified distributions may begin when the owner turns age 59½ from an account that meets the five-year holding period.**

b. Incorrect. No required minimum distributions are required for Roth IRA owners. Thus, such accounts may be used to retain wealth without taxation to pass to heirs.

c. Incorrect. Qualified distributions from accounts meeting the five-year holding period may be taken tax- and penalty-free to fund a qualified first-time home purchase.

12. True. Correct. One person is named the eligible individual or beneficiary for the HSA, but funds from the account may be used to pay the health care costs of the beneficiary's spouse and dependents.

False. Incorrect. Although spouses cannot share an HSA, the account funds of the beneficiary can pay medical expenses for both and for their dependents.

13. a. Correct. HSA funds may be used to purchase OTC medications only if a health care professional prescribes them.

b. Incorrect. The additional tax is increased to 20 percent beginning in tax years after December 31, 2010.

c. Incorrect. The health care reform package narrows the definition to conform it with the medical expense deduction allowed by Code Sec. 213.

14. a. Incorrect. The adjustment date for the basis is not set as the end of calendar year 2010.

b. Correct. The basis of the recipient of the property is the lesser of the adjusted basis of the property in the decedent's hands or the fair market value on the date of death. No step-up or -down applies.

c. Incorrect. The alternate valuation date (six months after the decedent's date of death) is not automatically used as the measure for adjusting basis.

15. a. Incorrect. A longer period is used to exclude the basis increase provisions on carryover basis.

b. Correct. Property acquired by gift or transfer within the three-year period is generally not subject to the basis increase rules.

c. Incorrect. The prohibition on the basis increase provisions applies for a shorter period.

MODULE 2 — CHAPTER 5

1. a. Correct. Securities purchased for investment or the production of income are capital assets for individual taxpayers.

b. Incorrect. Supplies so used are not capital assets for businesses or individual taxpayers.

c. Incorrect. Copyrights and artistic compositions held by their creator are not that individual's capital asset.

2. a. *Incorrect.* The year of purchase is irrelevant to the deduction.

b. *Correct.* **The deduction is taken for the tax year in which the security becomes worthless, even if the taxpayer is unaware of the security's worthlessness.**

c. *Incorrect.* The security must be totally worthless; no deduction may be taken if the security merely declines in value.

3. a. *Incorrect.* Bad debt arising from a trade or business is treated as an ordinary loss, but nonbusiness bad debt is treated as a short-term capital loss.

b. *Correct.* **A bad debt from a secured loan is nondeductible until all related collateral has been sold.**

c. *Incorrect.* If the creditor has a reasonable expectation of collecting the amount owed, it is not a bad debt.

4. a. *Incorrect.* The carryover period for a small business casualty or theft is longer.

b. *Correct.* **The NOL rules allow a small business casualty or theft loss to be carried back 3 years and forward 20 years, although a loss discovered in 2008 by a small business is allowed to carry back such a loss for 4 or 5 years.**

c. *Incorrect.* A small business is allowed fewer years to carry back and carry forward a loss for casualty or theft.

5. a. *Incorrect.* Individuals may include rental property expenses in an NOL computation when the property is held for production of income.

b. *Correct.* **Deductions for net capital losses are excluded in computing the NOL.**

c. *Incorrect.* Income and expenses from separate businesses are aggregated to determine an individual's NOL for the tax year.

6. a. *Incorrect.* A higher threshold over more tax years is required to substantiate a profit motive.

b. *Correct.* **The activity's gross income must exceed its deductions for three or more years in the five-year period to prove a profit motive.**

c. *Incorrect.* An activity is not required to have its gross income exceed deductions for so many years.

7. a. *Incorrect.* Royalties are considered portfolio income

b. *Incorrect.* Tax refunds are not included in passive activity income

c. *Correct.* **Such gain is considered passive income unless the taxpayer disposes of the passive activity in a taxable transaction.**

8. a. *Correct.* This safe harbor grants the individual material participation status if he or she so participated for 5 or the 10 previous years.
b. *Incorrect.* A taxpayer has material participation if he or she provides professional services in any 3 preceding years.
c. *Incorrect.* Material participation must have occurred within 5 of the previous 10 years, or the individual must have fulfilled another of the safe harbor provisions, which required more recent participation.

9. a. *Incorrect.* If the seller finances the sale of the property and then reduces the debt, the transaction is treated as reducing the sales price, not as a discharge of the debt.
b. *Incorrect.* A discharge does not occur when the creditor has a reasonable expectation that the debt will be repaid; lengthening the payment period or reducing individual payments does not negate this expectation.
c. *Correct.* Because the creditor accepts less than the full amount of the debt as full payment, the transaction is a discharge of debt triggering COI income.

10. a. *Correct.* The disposition of this nonrecourse debt is treated as a sale applicable to the entire debt.
b. *Incorrect.* Because the loan is nonrecourse, there is no cancellation of indebtedness income.
c. *Incorrect.* Because there is no cancellation of indebtedness income, there is no ordinary income or loss.

MODULE 3 — CHAPTER 6

1. a. *Incorrect.* Tier I issues are so grouped because their issues are of the highest importance to the LB&I division.
b. *Correct.* Tier II issues in the Tiered Issue program reflect areas of potentially high importance to the LB&I and need require further development or clarification of the division's position.
c. *Incorrect.* Tier III issues are ones representing the highest compliance risk for an industry and thus require unique treatment only within that industry.

2. a. *Correct.* Such issues become reportable transactions that taxpayers must disclose by attaching Form 8886, *Reportable Transaction Disclosure Statement,* to their income tax return.
b. *Incorrect.* *Unlisted* is not the IRS designation for such compliance issues.
c. *Incorrect.* The IRS in fact requires disclosure of such transactions on a form attached to the taxpayer's income tax return.

3. a. *Incorrect.* Listed transactions appear in IRS published guidance and are not dependent on the involvement of a tax advisor.

b. *Incorrect.* Fees paid to advisors in confidential transactions are not contingent on the success of the tax position but are rendered for the advisor's provision of strategies and tax advice.

c. *Correct.* The advisor's promissory statement may be oral or written and may be for a fee refund or for contingency fees for tax benefits.

4. True. *Correct.* A contractually protected transaction must be made before the taxpayer enters it and reports its tax consequences.

False. *Incorrect.* The advisor's representations concerning the contractually protected transaction must be made before the taxpayer enters into the transaction and reports it on the tax return.

5. a. *Incorrect.* Code Secs. 6662A, 6707A, and 6011 are not inapplicable when a transaction becomes listed after the taxpayer's filing.

b. *Correct.* The disclosure must be included with the taxpayer's next tax return.

c. *Incorrect.* The statute of limitations period remains applicable for the tax year in which the taxpayer participated in the transaction.

6. a. *Correct.* The recent act encapsulates the doctrine and defines economic substance.

b. *Incorrect.* The doctrine was not defined in the 1986 major reform law, although the IRS and courts pursued cases of tax avoidance before the rules were codified.

c. *Incorrect.* Circular 230 concerns rules for practice before the IRS, not tax avoidance transactions.

7. a. *Incorrect.* The Code Sec. 6662 penalties are imposed for understatements of tax liabilities due to valuation misstatements.

b. *Incorrect.* Substantial understatements of tax trigger imposition of the Code Sec. 6662 accuracy-related penalties.

c. *Correct.* Understatements subject to the fraud penalty are not subject to the 40-percent penalty for failure to disclose a transaction lacking economic substance.

8. a. *Correct.* UTP reporting will be required for corporations and those insurance companies that file Form 1120 returns, but not for estates and trusts.

b. *Incorrect.* Corporations that file Form 1120 or 1120-F are required to file the schedule for the 2010 tax year.

c. *Incorrect.* Certain insurance companies are required to file Schedule UTP with Form 1120-L or 1120-PC for 2010.

9. True. *Correct.* To minimize duplicative disclosures, the IRS will treat taxpayers who file Schedule UTP as having filed Forms 8275 and 8275-R.

False. *Incorrect.* Announcement 2010-30 states that taxpayers that file Schedule UTP with their returns will be treated as having filed the other two forms.

10. a. *Correct.* These three requirements enabled taxpayers to avoid criminal charges by the IRS.

b. *Incorrect.* The compliance initiative offered those who reported the assets and offshore accounts a reduced penalty.

c. *Incorrect.* Taxpayer account holders were not responsible for reporting information about other customers.

11. a. *Correct.* The recent legislation added Code Sec. 6038D to require such taxpayers to disclose foreign assets on their income tax returns.

b. *Incorrect.* The American Jobs Act of 2004 imposed penalties for non-disclosure of foreign assets on the FBAR form.

c. *Incorrect.* Title 31 codified the Bank Secrecy Act and requires filing of Form TD F 90-22.1, or FBAR. More recent legislation requires disclosure of such assets on tax returns.

12. a. *Correct.* Only gratuitous transfers to a foreign trust are subject to reporting rules, including gift transfers. However, determination of whether the transfer is gratuitous is made independent of gift tax rules.

b. *Incorrect.* Gratuitous transfers to a foreign trust are those other than ones exchanged for fair market value or with respect to an interest that the trust holds.

c. *Incorrect.* Exchanges with respect to an interest held by the trust are not considered gratuitous.

13. a. *Correct.* To counter the presumption that the beneficiary is a U.S. person, the taxpayer must demonstrate that no portion of the assets will benefit a U.S. person.

b. *Incorrect.* The HIRE Act rules consider the foreign trust to be a grantor trust in such circumstances.

c. *Incorrect.* A foreign trust considered to be a grantor trust is subject to Code Sec. 6048 reporting requirements, and the transferor must report the transfer using Form 3520.

14. a. *Incorrect.* The 2008 law does not mandate the use of the FILO method.
b. *Incorrect.* The average basis method measures basis in stock acquired under a dividend reinvestment plan.
c. *Correct.* The FIFO method is required as of the 2011 tax year for computing basis in securities when the customer does not acquire the stock under a dividend reinvestment plan.

15. a. *Incorrect.* Scholarships and fellowship grants are exempt from the law's new reporting requirements.
b. *Correct.* Business payments such as compensation and annuity payments are subject to the act's new reporting requirements.
c. *Incorrect.* The reporting requirements do not apply to service fees listed but not charged to or canceled for recipients.

MODULE 3 — CHAPTER 7

1. True. *Correct.* Form 990-EZ is a four-page return used by filers having annual gross receipts of less than $200,000 and total assets of less than $500,000. Some Form 990-EZ filers may be required to complete one or more schedules from Form 990.
False. *Incorrect.* Short Form 990-EZ remained substantially unchanged during the 2008 and 2010 revisions of Form 990.

2. a. *Incorrect.* All charities are required to fully complete Schedule A, *Public Charity Status and Public Support,* and not to list donors as anonymous.
b. *Correct.* For Schedule B, *Schedule of Contributors,* the IRS instructs filers not to include personal information about contributors except that required for donors.
c. *Incorrect.* Schedule L requires filers to report individually excess benefit transactions, loans made to or from key officials and other interested persons, and grants or assistance to interested persons.

3. a. *Incorrect.* Filers must include the organization's EIN on the return.
b. *Correct.* Contributor information is not reported on Form 990-N.
c. *Incorrect.* The name and address of a principal officer are required to complete Form 990-N.

4. a. *Correct.* The VCP required returns for the three years of missed filings by organizations eligible to file Form 990-EZ.
b. *Incorrect.* A compliance fee of $100 to $500 was charged under the VCP, with the amount determined by the organization's gross receipts.
c. *Incorrect.* Midsize organizations could not use the VCP to avoid Form 990 requirements for past years.

5. True. *Correct.* Private foundations have fewer supporters than most public charities, so the IRS seeks to prevent abuse of foundations' tax-exempt status by imposing excise taxes and restrictions on the foundations.

False. *Incorrect.* Public charities have broader support and are not subject to the excise taxes and restrictions that apply to private foundations.

6. a. *Incorrect.* Since new requirements under the PPA were initiated, the supported organization appoints a member of the supporting organization's governing board and implements procedures to ensure that the supporting organization is responsive to it.

b. *Incorrect.* The integral part test of Type III supporting organizations requires significant involvement by the supporting organization in the supported organization's operations, or the distribution of 5 percent of specified assets.

c. *Correct.* The charitable trust test, by which a Type III organization could meet the responsiveness test, was eliminated by the PPA.

7. a. *Incorrect.* The PPACA requires nonprofit hospitals to adopt, implement, and widely publicize financial assistance policies.

b. *Correct.* Under the PPACA, nonprofit hospitals cannot charge patients who qualify for financial assistance more than insured patients, but the law does not require charges to be waived.

c. *Incorrect.* Under the PPACA, hospitals cannot conduct extraordinary collection procedures such as lawsuits or liens.

8. a. *Incorrect.* The 2005 regulations do not consider medical residents as a special category of employee for whom employers need not pay FICA taxes.

b. *Correct.* The 2005 amended IRS regulations require payment of the taxes, although payment of FICA refund claims for prior tax periods was allowed.

c. *Incorrect.* Although the IRS honors FICA refund claims made prior to the 2005 amended regulations, residents are career employees for whom health care employers must pay FICA taxes.

9. a. *Incorrect.* Although Form 990 requires inclusion of a statement of organizations' mission, other phases of overall operations are subject to IRS scrutiny.

b. *Correct.* The IRS continues to review governance practices of tax-exempt organizations from the time they apply for tax-exemption through annual return filings and any audits of governance functions.

c. Incorrect. The tax code does not require particular governance practices.

10. True. Incorrect. Because the IRS states that charities are managed on behalf of the general public, the recommendations urge them to maintain boards large enough to represent a broad public interest and to include independent members.
False. Correct. The IRS recommends that charities maintain boards large enough to reflect a broad public interest and include independent members not affiliated through family or business interests.

MODULE 3 — CHAPTER 8

1. a. Correct. The DOL forwards information about the returns to the IRS and PBGC.
b. Incorrect. Information pertaining to the form is forwarded to the IRS from a different government organization.
c. Incorrect. The PBGC receives information about the annual report from another agency.

2. True. Correct. One-participant plans must continue to file on paper using Form 5500-EZ, but other small plans may file Form 5500-SF through EFAST2.
False. Incorrect. Most small plans now file electronically using Form 5500-SF through EFAST2, but one-participant plans must continue to file on paper using the new Form 5500-SF.

3. a. Incorrect. Form 5500 must be filed using the EFAST2 processing system, and report information is subject to immediate publication on the Internet.
b. Correct. Form 5500-EZ must be filed on paper by one-participant plans. Thus, the information is not published on the Internet.
c. Incorrect. Because Form 5500-SF is submitted using the EFAST2 processing system, its information becomes available on the Internet.

4. a. Incorrect. The client's practitioner can sign on behalf of the plan's sponsor if given written authority to file through the EFAST2 system.
b. Correct. Obtaining a notary public's seal is not part of the authentication process for signer signature verification.
c. Incorrect. The filing should attach a .pdf copy of the form with the plan sponsor's actual signature.

5. a. *Correct.* Schedule A was revised as part of the move to an all-electronic filing system. It now requires that filers distinguish between allocated and unallocated contracts.
b. *Incorrect.* Schedule E was eliminated for Form 5500 files reporting employee stock option plans beginning with their 2009 returns.
c. *Incorrect.* Form SSA was eliminated as part of the move to the all-electronic filing systems for Form 5500 and its schedules.

6. a. *Incorrect.* Plans are required to submit information about participants separated from the service covered by the plan on an annual registration statement that cannot be supplied on Form 5500 SSA.
b. *Correct.* Such protected information is a security risk if published on the Internet. Practitioners should wait to file the information when Form 8955-SSA becomes available.
c. *Incorrect.* The schedule did contain pertinent information about participants with deferred vested benefits who had been separated from the service covered by the plan.

7. a. *Correct.* The target normal cost is the present value at the beginning of the plan year of benefits expected to accrue or to be earned during the plan year, increased by the amount of expected plan-related expenses to be paid from plan assets and decreased by the amount of expected mandatory employee contributions.
b. *Incorrect.* Both the expected accrued or earned benefits and the mandatory employee contributions are not increased in determining the plan's target normal cost.
c. *Incorrect.* To determine the plan's target normal cost, both expenses and expected contributions are not decreased.

8. a. *Correct.* When a plan's percentage falls below certain levels, the AFTAP rules limit the plan's future benefit accruals and distribution of prohibited payments.
b. *Incorrect.* The scheduled benefit disbursement totals are not part of the AFTAP ratio.
c. *Incorrect.* The target normal cost is the present value at the start of the plan year of the benefits expected to be earned or to accrue during the plan year.

9. a. *Incorrect.* A higher percentage of funded status is required to use the lookback year for offsetting the minimum required contributions.
b. *Incorrect.* The Pension Relief Act of 2010 created a different percentage requirement to offset minimum required contributions for charitable organizations' plans.

c. *Correct*. If the funded status for the lookback year was at least equal to 80 percent, the organizations may offset their minimum required contributions by a credit balance.

10. a. *Incorrect*. Identifying issues for which more education and outreach guidance would be helpful was a goal of the project.

b. *Correct*. The participants were selected randomly and not based on size of the employer. The sample was selected from sponsors filing for the 2007 plan year and is based on information as of the sponsor's 2007 plan year.

c. *Incorrect*. One IRS goal for the project was identifying potential compliance issues among the randomly selected plan sponsors selected to complete the questionnaire.

11. True. *Correct*. The major difference between a partial and full termination is in the level of vesting required. Upon partial termination, the qualified plan must allocate the portion of previously unallocated funds.

False. *Incorrect*. Upon partial termination, that portion of unallocated funds is vested.

12. a. *Incorrect*. PBGC Form 500, *Standard Termination Notice, Single-Employer Plan Termination,* or PBGC Form 601, *Distress Termination Notice, Single-Employer Plan Termination* (for distress terminations), with the PBGC, not participants.

b. *Correct*. Plan administrators provide the NOIT of PBGC Form 600 to affected parties in cases of standard or distressed termination of a plan.

c. *Incorrect*. PBGC Form 501, *Post-Distribution Certification,* is submitted to the PBGC, not participants, within 30 days after plan benefits are distributed. The form used for distress terminations is PBGC Form 602, *Post Distribution Certification for Distress Termination.*

13. a. *Incorrect*. The PBGC notice of noncompliance renders the plan ongoing.

b. *Incorrect*. The notice of noncompliance indicates that plan assets are insufficient to satisfy all benefit liabilities and thus ends the standard termination process.

c. *Correct*. The notice of noncompliance requires the plan administrator to take no further action to terminate the plan, including the distribution of plan assets.

14. a. *Correct.* Court proceedings may be initiated by PBGC for either a single-employer or multiemployer plan in cases when the plan does not have sufficient assets to pay benefits currently due.

b. *Incorrect.* Voluntary terminations typically do not involve court proceedings brought by the PBGC.

c. *Incorrect.* The PBGC issue a notice of noncompliance as a culmination of standard terminations. Once the notice is issued, the plan administrator must take no further action to terminate the plan.

15. a. *Correct.* A voluntary termination does not result from ceasing to make distributions.

b. *Incorrect.* A mass withdrawal, in which every employer has withdrawn, is a form of voluntary termination of a multiemployer plan.

c. *Incorrect.* Such a plan amendment voluntarily terminates a multiemployer plan when the amendment either denies participants credit for service after a specified date or converts the plan into a defined contribution plan.

TOP FEDERAL TAX ISSUES FOR 2011 CPE COURSE

Index

A

Abandonment of property ... 5.25

Accounting period (tax year), choice of ... 3.26

Accumulated earnings tax ... 3.7, 3.33

Adjusted funding target attainment percentage (AFTAP) ... 8.15–8.17

Adjusted minimum taxable income (AMTI)
AMT rate table use of ... 4.13
in calculating AMT liability ... 4.9, 4.11
exemption amount phaseout based on ... 4.14
miscellaneous itemized deductions as not reducing ... 4.10

Adult children, health care coverage for
age increased by health care reform package for ... 1.25–1.26, 1.27
income tax exclusion for employee-parent for ... 1.25, 1.26–1.27
with preexisting conditions ... 1.27

Advisor's fee
for confidential transactions ... 6.4
contingent ... 6.5, 6.6
for contractually protected transactions ... 6.5

Alternate tax year, three-month deferral election for ... 3.26

Alternative minimum tax (AMT) ... 3.3, 4.1–4.2, 4.8–4.14
adjustments and preferences for ... 4.11–4.12
computing ... 4.11
exemption amounts and phaseout for ... 4.13–4.14
nonrefundable personal credit allowable against ... 4.12
patch to ... 4.11, 4.12, 4.13, 4.14
planning to avoid ... 4.8–4.11
rate schedule for ... 4.13
timing strategies for ... 4.9–4.11

Amended return
to claim investment loss ... 5.10
disclosures included with ... 6.7
filed after IRS contact for examination ... 6.11
NOL refund claims on ... 5.12

American Health Benefit Exchange ... 1.5, 1.21. *See also* **State insurance exchanges**

American Jobs Act of 2004 ... 6.18

American Reinvestment and Recovery Act of 2009 ... 1.28, 5.11, 3.36

Annuity contracts, allocated and unallocated ... 8.9

Asset acquisitions, taxable and nontaxable ... 3.41–3.43

Assistance-eligible individual for COBRA premium assistance ... 1.28

At-risk rules ... 3.27, 3.35, 5.17–5.18

Attentiveness test of supporting organization ... 7.12

Audits
of college and university activities ... 7.21
of executive compensation ... 7.26
of hospital's practices ... 7.14
of nonprofit organizations' governance ... 7.24

Average basis method for securities reporting ... 6.24–6.25

B

Backup withholding ... 2.4

Bad debt ... 5.7

Bank Secrecy Act (BSA) ... 6.17

Bankruptcy
exclusions of COI income application in ... 5.23
liquidation petition in ... 8.30
reduction of tax attributes for taxpayer in ... 5.24
reorganization petition in ... 8.30

Basis defined ... 5.3–5.4

Basis in business
of corporation and shareholder ... 3.22
of partner ... 3.18–3.21
of sole proprietor ... 3.17

Basis of property
converted from personal to business use ... 3.28
at death, carryover ... 4.32–4.34

Behavioral control of worker's tasks ... 2.10, 2.11, 2.14

Bond investments ... 4.15

Broker basis reporting requirements
average basis method in ... 6.24–6.25
FIFO as default method for ... 6.24

Built-in gains tax ... 3.7, 3.36–3.37

Business entities ... 3.1–3.44
  choosing ... 3.10–3.44
  disposing of ... 3.38–3.43
  formation tax issues for new ... 3.15–3.27
  key factors in choice of, table of ... 3.9–3.10
  liability issues for new ... 3.11–3.12
  operating tax issues for ... 3.27–3.38
  organizational issues for ... 3.13–3.15
  table summarizing features of ... 3.8
  transfer of property and/or
      money to ... 3.15–3.17
  types of ... 3.1–3.8

Business expenses
  employee ... 2.12, 4.10, 5.12
  gambling losses as ... 5.16

Business income defined ... 4.4

**Business payments, reporting
    requirements for** ... 6.25–6.27

C

C corporations
  alternative minimum tax on ... 3.31
  closely held ... 5.19, 5.21
  comparison of other entity types to ... 3.8
  defined ... 3.6
  dividends of ... 3.31
  as double-tax entities ... 3.31
  as entity type ... 3.1
  operating tax issues of ... 3.31–3.34
  organizational issues for ... 3.14
  tax year types for ... 3.27
  taxation of S corporations versus ... 3.6

**Cancellation of indebtedness
    (COI)** ... 5.22–5.24

Capital asset defined ... 5.3

Capital gains
  of C corporation ... 3.31
  gifts to divert income from ... 4.6
  long- versus short-term ... 5.2–5.3
  as ordinary income ... 4.17
  postponing ... 4.15
  subject to Medicare contribution tax ... 4.23
  tax rates on ... 4.2, 4.15, 4.16–4.18, 5.3

Capital losses ... 5.2–5.6

Charitable contributions, timing ... 4.5–4.6

Charitable trust ... 7.12

Charity care by hospitals ... 7.14. *See
    also* Hospitals

COBRA premium assistance ... 1.27–1.29

**Code Sec. 45R small employer health
    insurance tax credit** ... 1.2–1.15
  average annual wages for ... 1.3, 1.4–1.5,
      1.7–1.8
  calculating, examples of ... 1.4, 1.12

  carry back and carry forward of ... 1.14–1.15
  full-time equivalent employees for ... 1.5–1.9
  increase beginning in 2014 of ... 1.5
  maximum ... 1.3
  phaseout of ... 1.3–1.5
  premiums counted in calculating ... 1.9–1.13
  reasons for creating ... 1.2
  as retroactive for 2010 ... 1.3
  state credits and subsidies in
      addition to ... 1.13
  for tax-exempt organizations ... 1.15
  transition relief for tax years beginning in
      2010 for ... 1.13–1.14

**Code Sec. 351 rules for tax-free
    property transfers** ... 3.21–3.22

**Code Sec. 754
    basis adjustments** ... 3.19–3.20

Colleges
  audits of ... 7.21
  compensation reported for ... 7.21
  congressional oversight of ... 7.22
  endowment funds of ... 7.20
  investment assets of ... 7.22
  IRS report of activities of ... 7.20, 7.21
  tax-exempt status of ... 7.19–7.22
  unrelated business activities of ... 7.20

Common-law employees
  common-law relationship of ... 2.7
  Section 530 safe harbor
      rule for ... 2.6, 2.7–2.8

**Community health needs assessment
    (CHNA)** ... 7.13, 7.16

Confidential transactions ... 6.3, 6.4

**Congress, U.S., oversight of higher
    education organizations by** ... 7.22

***Consolidated Omnibus Budget
    Reconciliation Act* (COBRA)** ... 1.27

Contingent tax liabilities ... 6.12–6.13

**Contractually protected
    transactions** ... 6.3, 6.5–6.6

Corporations. *See also* **C corporations,
    Professional corporations,** *and*
    S corporations
  formation issues of ... 3.21–3.25
  liability issues for ... 3.12
  LLC taxed as ... 3.5
  organizational issues for ... 3.14–3.15

Credit counseling organizations ... 7.27

D

Debt, forgiveness of ... 5.22–6.25

Deductions. *See also* **Itemized deductions**
  deferring ... 4.9
  maximizing ... 4.5–4.6

Defined benefit plans
blackout periods for ... 8.10
combined defined contribution and ... 8.4
deferred vested benefit from ... 8.9
effects of recession on ... 8.1, 8.11
employers' trend away from use of ... 8.1
funding relief for ... 8.11–8.21
large ... 8.2, 8.3, 8.10
multiemployer (union-negotiated) ... 8.11, 8.17–8.21, 8.34–8.35
multiple-employer ... 8.20
for nonresident aliens ... 8.8
short plan year for ... 8.5
single-employer ... 8.11, 8.12, 8.14–8.15, 8.24–8.34
small ... 8.2, 8.3
terminations of, restrictions on ... 8.24–8.35

Defined contribution plans, termination of ... 8.24
voluntary ... 8.25

Department of Labor (DOL), U.S., enforcement personnel of ... 2.20

Depreciation deduction, recapture of ... 4.17–4.18

Designated Roth accounts ... 4.27–4.28

Direct filing entities (DFEs) ... 8.2, 8.3
filing deadlines for ... 8.5
financial information reporting for ... 8.10

Discharge of debt ... 5.22–5.23

Disclosures ... 6.1–6.27
of business payments ... 6.25–6.27
duplicative ... 6.16
penalties for failing to make ... 6.8–6.9, 6.11–6.12, 6.18, 6.22–6.23, 6.26
required transaction ... 6.2–6.3
tax return, of foreign interests ... 6.18–6.20

Dividends, tax rates on capital ... 4.15, 4.16

Double taxation of employee-shareholders ... 3.32

E

e-Postcard. *See* Form 990-N, *Electronic Notice for Tax-Exempt Organizations Not Required to File Form 990 or 990-EZ*

Economic Growth and Tax Relief Reconciliation Act of 2001 (EGTRRA) ... 4.2, 4.7, 4.32

Economic substance doctrine ... 6.9–6.12
application of ... 6.10–6.11
development and codification of ... 6.9–6.11
penalties for underpayments under ... 6.11–6.12

EFAST2 electronic filing system for Form 5500 and 5500-SF ... 8.4
attachments for, .pdf ... 8.6
filing auditor's report with ... 8.7
signer credential for ... 8.6

Electing small business trusts (ESBTs) ... 3.23, 3.24, 3.25

Electronic filing system for pension and welfare benefits plans ... 8.2

Emergency Economic Stabilization Act of 2008 ... 6.24

Employee-shareholders, reasonable compensation of ... 3.33, 3.35

Employees
classification of workers as. *See* Worker classi8fication for employment taxes
common-law ... 2.7–2.8, 2.14
defined ... 1.2, 2.6
statutory ... 2.8
tax law incentives for hiring ... 2.4–2.5
withholding requirements for ... 2.1, 2.2, 2.5–2.7

Employment taxes
for partners ... 3.293.30
increased IRS enforcement in collecting ... 2.2
withholding of ... 2.1, 2.2, 2.4–2.7
worker classification issues for ... 2.1–2.23

Estate tax ... 4.32–4.34

Estates
Medicare contribution tax on ... 4.23
tax rates for ... 4.2

Executive compensation
at colleges and universities ... 7.21
in nonprofit organizations ... 7.26
NRP examination of ... 2.4

Exempt Organizations (EO) office of IRS
in NRP ... 2.2
oversight of tax-exempt organizations by ... 7.2
ROO and EOCAS compliance units of ... 7.26

F

Fair Labor Standards Act of 1938 ... 2.22

Federal employer identification number (FEIN)
entity types requiring ... 3.13, 3.14
obtaining ... 3.14

Federal Insurance Contribution Act (FICA) ... 2.1, 4.19

FICA tax
family member exception from, for minors in sole proprietorships ... 3.3

incorrectly paid employee
share of ... 2.6–2.7
of statutory employees ... 2.8
student exception from ... 7.17–7.19
wage base for ... 4.19
withholding requirements for ... 2.5, 2.6–2.7
worker misclassification affecting
employer's share of ... 2.1, 2.2

**15-year amortization schedule under
Pension Relief Act of 2010 ... 8.14–8.15**

**FIN 48, *Accounting for Uncertainty in
Income Taxes* ... 6.12–6.13, 6.15**
differences in requirements of
Schedule UTP and ... 6.17

**Financial assistance policy required for
nonprofit hospitals ... 7.16**

**Financial control of worker's activities ...
2.10, 2.11, 2.14**

**Financial statements of nonprofit
organizations, accounting
audit of ... 7.26**

**First-in, first-out (FIFO) method, basis of
securities under ... 6.24**

Foreclosures on loan ... 5.25

**Foreign asset/accounting
reporting ... 6.17–6.23**
penalties for failures of ... 6.18, 6.19–6.20
tax return disclosures for ... 6.18–6.20
for trusts ... 6.21–6.23

Foreign trusts
disclosures of transactions of ... 6.21
distributions from ... 6.21, 6.23
ownership of ... 6.22
penalties for nondisclosure of ... 6.22–6.23

**Form 500 (PBGC), *Standard Termination
Notice, Single-Employer Plan
Termination* ... 8.27, 8.28**

**Form 501 (PBGC), *Post-Distribution
Certification* ... 8.29**

**Form 600 (PBGC), *Notice of Intent
to Terminate* ... 8.31**

**Form 601 (PBGC), *Distress
Termination Notice, Single-Employer
Plan* ... 8.31–8.32**

**Form 602 (PBGC), *Post Distribution
Certification for Distress
Termination* ... 8.33**

**Form 941, *Employer's Quarterly
Employment Tax Return* ... 1.28, 2.2**

**Form 990, *Return of Organization Exempt
from Income Tax***
core form of ... 7.4, 7.5
filing deadlines for ... 7.4, 7.7
filing requirements for ... 7.7, 7.8

filing thresholds for ... 7.3–7.4
governing body uses of ... 7.26
public availability on Internet of
information on ... 7.2, 7.26
revisions of ... 7.4, 7.24
schedules for ... 7.4, 7.5–7.7
taxpayers not required to file ... 7.3–7.4
taxpayers required to file ... 7.2
voluntary compliance program
for filing ... 7.9

**Form 990-EZ, *Short Form Return (of
Exempt Organizations)***
filed by smaller
tax-exempt organizations ... 7.2
filing deadlines for ... 7.4, 7.7
filing thresholds for ... 7.3, 7.7
relief program for filing ... 7.8, 7.9
structure of ... 7.4

**Form 990-N, *Electronic Notice for
Tax-Exempt Organizations Not
Required to File Form 990 or 990-EZ***
filing deadlines for ... 7.4, 7.7
filing thresholds for ... 7.3, 7.7
information required on ... 7.8
relief program for filing ... 7.8, 7.9

**Form 990-PF, *Return of Private
Foundation or Section 4947(a)(1)
Nonexempt Charitable Trust Treated
as a Private Foundation* ... 7.7, 7.8**

**Form 990-T, *Unrelated Business
Income Tax* ... 7.26**

**Form 1023, *Application for Charitable
Exemption* ... 7.9, 7.26**

**Form 1024 application for
exempt status ... 7.9**

Form 1040-ES ... 3.28

**Form 1040-X, *Amended U.S. Individual
Income Tax Return* ... 5.12, 6.7, 6.11**

**Form 1045, *Application for
Tentative Refund* ... 5.12**

Form 1065 ... 3.3

**Form 1099-MISC, *Miscellaneous
Income* ... 2.4, 2.6, 2.9**

**Form 2553, *Election by a Small business
Corporation* ... 3.7, 3.14, 3.15**

**Form 3520, *Annual Return to Report
Transactions with Foreign Trusts and
Receipt of Certain Foreign Gifts* ... 6.21**

**Form 3520-A, *Annual Information Return of
Foreign Trust with a U.S. Owner* ... 6.21**

**Form 4797, *Sales of
Business Property* ... 3.39**

**Form 5310, *Application for Determination
Upon Termination* ... 8.26**

Form 5500, *Annual Return/Report of Employee Benefit Plan*
amended ... 8.6
extension of time for filing ... 8.4
filed with DOL's EBSA using EFAST2 ... 8.2, 8.4, 8.5–8.6
filing deadlines for ... 8.5
filing prior year delinquent ... 8.6
public availability on Internet of information on ... 8.6
revisions of ... 8.4–8.5
schedules for ... 8.3, 8.4, 8.9–8.10
signer credential for ... 8.6

Form 5500-EZ, *Annual Return of One-Participant (Owners and their Spouses) Retirement Plan* ... 8.2
filing deadlines for ... 8.5
filing options for ... 8.8
foreign plans required to use ... 8.8
for one-participant plans ... 8.4, 8.8
paper filing required for ... 8.4, 8.8

Form 5500-SF, *Short Form Annual Return/Report of Small Employee Benefit Plans* ... 8.2
filing deadlines for ... 8.5
plans eligible to use ... 8.7–8.8
schedules for ... 8.8

Form 5558, *Application for Extension of Time to File Certain Employee Plan Returns* ... 8.4, 8.5

Form 8082, *Notice of Inconsistent Treatment of Administrative Adjustment Request* ... 6.21

Form 8275, *Disclosure Statement* ... 6.16

Form 8275-R, *Regulation Disclosure Statement* ... 6.16

Form 8832, *Entity Classification Election* ... 3.14

Form 8869, election for Qsub using ... 3.24

Form 8886, *Reportable Transaction Disclosure Statement* ... 6.3, 6.7, 6.16

Form 8919, *Uncollected Social Security and Medicare Tax on Wages* ... 2.18

Form 8955-SSA, *Annual Registration Statement Identifying Separated Participants with Deferred Vested Benefits* ... 8.9

Form SS-8, *Determination of Worker Status for Purposes of Federal Employment Taxes and Income Tax Wi8thholding* ... 2.18–2.19

Form TD-F 90-221, *Report of Foreign Bank and Financial Accounts (FBAR)* ... 6.17

Form W-2, disclosure requirements for ... 1.24–1.25

401(k) Compliance Check Questionnaire Project by EPCU (IRS)
as compliance check ... 8.23
procedure used in ... 8.21–8.22
qualification failure discovered as filer completes questionnaire in ... 8.23
scope of ... 8.22–8.23

401(k) plans
annual reporting requirements for ... 8.2
trend toward use of ... 8.1

403(b) plans
annual reporting rules for ... 8.10
Form 5500 reporting required for most ... 8.4

Fraud, losses due to ... 5.9–5.10

Free choice vouchers under health care reform package ... 1.19–1.20

Fringe benefits
for S corporation shareholders ... 3.36
for shareholder-employees of C corporation ... 3.32
for sole proprietors ... 3.2, 3.28
for workers misclassified as independent contractors ... 2.4

Full-time equivalent (FTE) employees
calculating number of ... 1.5–1.6
hours of service counted for ... 1.2, 1.5, 1.6, 1.8–1.9
owners, partners, family members, and dependents not counted as ... 1.6, 1.8–1.9
phaseout of Code Sec. 45R credit based on number of ... 1.3–1.5
seasonal workers disregarded in computing ... 1.7

Funding standard account (FSA) ... 8.11

Funding target for defined benefit plan year ... 8.12–8.13

FUTA (unemployment) tax ... 2.1, 2.2
exclusion from, for employee family members younger than age 21 ... 3.3
of statutory employees ... 2.8
withholding requirements for ... 2.5, 2.7

G

Gambling losses ... 5.15–5.17

General basis increase ... 4.33

General partners ... 3.4, 3.11, 3.29–3.30

General partnership ... 3.3–3.4
co-ownership of real estate by ... 3.13
organizational issues for ... 3.13

Gifts to divert capital gain income ... 4.6

Governance of nonprofit
   organizations ... 7.21, 7.23–7.27
   check sheet for gathering data about ... 7.24
   compliance actions of IRS for ... 7.24
   compliance recommendations of
      IRS for ... 7.25–7.26
   future improvements for ... 7.26–7.27
   implicit tax code requirements for ... 7.23

Governing body of charity
   composition of ... 7.25
   review of Form 990 by ... 7.26

Grandfathered health insurance plans for
   enactment of PPACA ... 1.16–1.17

H

*Health Care and Education
   Reconciliation Act of 2010* ... 1.1, 2.4,
   4.19, 4.31, 6.10. *See also* Health care
   reform package

Health care reform package ... 1.1–1.29
   cost-sharing under ... 1.21
   coverage of adult children
      changed by ... 1.25–1.27
   employee under ... 1.2
   free choice vouchers
      mandated by ... 1.19–1.20
   household income under ... 1.20
   HSAs changed by ... 4.31
   large employer for ... 1.17
   Medicare contribution tax created by ... 4.19
   Medicare tax increased by ... 4.19
   minimum essential
      coverage under ... 1.1, 1.16, 1.19
   play or pay rules of ... 1.1, 1.2, 1.16
   premium assistance tax credit
      created by ... 1.20–1.21
   shared responsibility penalty for
      employers under ... 1.1, 1.16, 1.17–1.19
   small employer for ... 1.2, 2.4
   timeline for implementation of ... 1.29
   unaffordable plans under ... 1.1

Health insurance coverage for
   Code Sec. 45R credit
   coverage excluded for ... 1.10–1.11
   coverage included in ... 1.10

Health insurance premiums
   costs of, employer reporting of ... 1.24–1.25
   as deductible by employer ... 1.14–1.15
   free choice voucher amount
      indexed to ... 1.20
   table of, by state ... 1.11–1.12

Health savings accounts (HSAs) ... 4.28–4.31
   beneficiary of ... 4.29
   contributions to ... 4.30

health care reform impact on ... 4.31
high-deductible health plan (HDHP)
   required for ... 4.28, 4.30
   permitted coverage for ... 4.29

High-deductible health plan
   (HDHP) ... 4.28, 4.30

Highly compensated participant in simple
   cafeteria plans ... 1.22–1.23
   for small employers ... 1.23–1.24

*Hiring Incentives to Restore
   Employment Act* (HIRE Act) ... 6.19
   tax incentives for hiring under ... 2.4–2.5

Hobby loss limitations ... 5.2, 5.13–5.14

Homeworkers as statutory employees ... 2.8

Hospital Compliance Project ... 7.13

Hospitals, tax-exempt
   community benefit obligations of ... 7.12,
      7.13–7.15
   excise tax on ... 7.16
   PPACA requirements for ... 7.15–7.16
   reporting requirements
      expanded for ... 7.12–7.13, 7.15–7.17
   standards for reporting by ... 7.15
   state laws challenging ... 7.16–7.17
   studies of community benefit
      practices of ... 7.15

Hot assets ... 3.40

I

Inability to continue in business in
   distress termination of
   retirement plan ... 8.30

Income
   accelerating ... 4.9
   nonpassive ... 5.19–5.20
   passive ... 5.19
   recognized in conversions to
      Roth IRAs ... 4.26
   shifting ... 4.15–4.16

Income tax rates,
   individual marginal ... 4.2–4.4
   increases to, anticipated ... 4.13
   in IRA conversions ... 4.27
   tax planning affected by ... 4.4–4.7

Independent contractors
   hallmarks of ... 2.9
   proposals to modify standards for
      classifying ... 2.21–2.22
   reporting requirements for
      income of ... 2.6–2.7, 2.9–2.10

Independent contractors, employees
   misclassified as ... 2.2, 2.3
   fringe benefits paid to ... 2.4
   penalties for ... 2.20

Section 530 relief for ... 2.7–2.8, 2.15–2.18, 2.20–2.22

Individual retirement accounts. *See* Retirement plans *and* Roth IRA

Inside basis ... 3.19

Integral part test of Type III supporting organization ... 7.11, 7.12

Internet, availability of annual return information on
from Form 990 ... 7.2, 7.26
from Form 5500 and Form 5500-SF ... 8.6

Investments, maximizing returns and minimizing taxes on ... 4.15

Involuntary termination for COBRA premium assistance ... 1.28

Itemized deductions ... 4.6–4.7, 4.9–4.10

J

Jobs and Growth Tax Relief Reconciliation Act of 2003 (JGTRRA) ... 4.2, 4.16

Joint Committee on Taxation (JCT) ... 4.4, 7.13

K

Key employee
of nonprofit organization ... 7.5
for simple cafeteria plans ... 1.22–1.23

Kiddie tax ... 4.6, 4.16

L

Lack of control test of supporting organization ... 7.11

Large Business and International Division, IRS (LB&I) ... 6.1–6.2

Large employer
for health care reform package ... 1.17
for shared responsibility penalty ... 1.18–1.19

Liability issues in choice of entity ... 3.11–3.12

Life insurance contracts ... 8.9

LIFO recapture tax ... 3.38

Limited liability companies (LLCs)
comparison of other entity types to ... 3.8
defined ... 3.5
as entity type ... 3.1
liability issues for ... 3.12
manager-managed ... 3.5, 3.30
member-managed ... 3.5, 3.30
organizational issues for ... 3.14
passive activity losses of ... 3.31
service ... 3.30

single-member ... 3.5, 3.24

Limited liability limited partnerships (LLLPs) ... 3.4–3.5

Limited liability partnerships (LLPs) ... 3.4–3.5

Limited partners ... 3.4, 3.12, 5.21

Limited partnerships ... 3.4, 3.11, 3.30
deductions for ... 5.13
organizational issues for ... 3.13

Listed transactions ... 6.3–6.4

Loss transactions ... 6.3, 6.6

Losses ... 5.1–5.21. *See also* Net operating losses (NOLs) *and* Passive activity losses
bad debt ... 5.7
business ... 5.1, 5.2, 5.9
capital ... 5.2–5.6
casualty ... 5.7, 5.9
deductibility of ... 5.1, 5.8–5.9
disaster ... 5.8
gambling ... 5.15–5.17
hobby ... 5.2, 5.13–5.14
investment ... 5.9–5.10
ordinary ... 5.5, 5.7, 5.9
partnership ... 3.29
realized ... 5.5
recognition of ... 5.5
S corporation ... 3.34, 3.35
sole proprietorship ... 3.27
theft ... 5.9–5.10

M

Marriage penalty relief ... 4.3

Master trust investment account (MTIA) ... 8.3

Material participation in business ... 5.1, 5.20–5.21

Medical expenses
HAS distributions for ... 4.28–4.29, 4.31
as itemized deduction ... 4.6, 4.7, 4.9

Medical residents, FICA student exception issues for ... 7.17–7.19

Medicare taxes
employer's share of ... 2.1
health care reform package changes to ... 4.19–4.23
of sole proprietor ... 3.28

Minimum essential coverage under health care reform package ... 1.1, 1.16, 1.19

Minimum tax credit (MTC) ... 4.12

Mission of nonprofit organization ... 7.25

Modified adjusted gross income (MAGI) ... 1.20

Medicare contribution tax
  based on ... 4.21–4.22

**Mortgage interest, impact on AMT
  liability of ... 4.10**

N

National Research Project (NRP), IRS
  history of ... 2.2–2.3
  purpose of ... 2.3–2.4

Natural business year ... 3.26

**Negligence, underpayment of taxes
  because of ... 6.11**

Net investment income ... 4.21–4.23

**Net operating loss carryback and
  carryforward rules**
  for C corporation ... 3.31–3.32
  for sole proprietorship ... 3.27

Net operating losses (NOLs) ... 5.10–5.13
  carryback periods for ... 5.11
  claiming carrybacks of ... 5.12–5.13
  individuals' expenses includible in ... 5.12
  reduction of ... 5.24

Net passive investment income ... 3.37–3.38

New hire retention credit ... 2.4–2.5

**Nondisclosure of participation in reportable
  transaction, penalty for ... 6.8**

Nonprofit organizations ... 7.1–7.27
  assets of ... 7.1, 7.5, 7.25–7.26
  audits of ... 7.21
  governance of ... 7.21, 7.23–7.27
  growth of ... 7.1
  IRS maintenance of
    information about ... 7.8
  revocation and reinstatement of
    status as ... 7.9–7.10

Notice of Annuity Contract ... 8.28

Notice of Annuity Information ... 8.28

**Notice of benefit distribution for
  retirement plan ... 8.32**

**Notice of determination of
  worker classification by IRS
  (NDWC) ... 2.17–2.18**

**Notice of intent to terminate (NOIT) for
  retirement plan**
  for distress terminations ... 8.30
  for standard terminations ... 8.27, 8.28

**Notice of noncompliance issued
  by PBGC ... 8.27, 8.29**

**Notice of plan benefits in standard
  termination of retirement plan ... 8.28**

O

Obama Administration
  AMT exemption amount proposal of ... 4.14

fiscal year 2011 budget by ... 2.19–2.20, 2.21
initiative to address worker classification
  abuses by ... 2.19–2.21
modification of itemized deductions
  proposed by ... 4.7
tax bracket changes advocated by ... 4.3
tax rate changes for capital gains and
  dividends proposed by ... 4.17

**Offshore Voluntary
  Compliance Initiative ... 6.18–6.19**

**Organizational and operational test of
  supporting organization ... 7.10**

Organizational expenses ... 3.25–3.26

Outside basis ... 3.18–3.19

P

Partners
  allocation of tax items among ... 3.29
  debts of, assumed by partnership ... 3.19
  employment taxes for ... 3.29–3.30
  gains by, from nonliquidating
    distributions ... 3.41
  passive activity loss rules
    applicable to ... 5.19
  transfers of profits to ... 3.21
  types of ... 3.3

Partnership interest
  disposing of ... 3.39–3.40
  profits ... 3.20–3.21
  received for partner's services ... 3.20

Partnerships
  basis of ... 3.19
  comparison of other entity types to ... 3.8
  defined ... 3.3
  disclosures of reportable
    transactions of ... 6.4, 6.6, 6.7
  dispositions of property by ... 3.41
  as entity type ... 3.1, 3.3
  exempt from Form 5500 filing
    requirements ... 8.2
  formation issues of ... 3.18–3.21
  liability issues for ... 3.11–3.12
  LLCs taxed as ... 3.5
  operating tax issues of ... 3.29–3.30
  as pass-through entities ... 3.3
  S corporations compared with ... 3.8

**Pass-through entities,
  tax treatment of ... 3.3, 3.6, 3.7, 3.35**

Passive activity losses
  of LLC ... 3.31
  limitations on ... 5.1, 5.15–5.21
  for rental activities ... 5.20
  of sole proprietorship ... 3.27

**Passive investment income tax
  (PIIT) ... 3.37–3.38**

Patented tax advice or strategies ... 6.7

Patient Protection and Affordable Care Act (PPACA) ... 1.1, 2.4, 4.19, 4.31. See also Health care reform package
business payment disclosures under ... 6.25–6.26
date of enactment of ... 1.16
existing employer-provided plans grandfathered under ... 1.16–1.17
nonprofit hospital requirements of ... 7.15–7.16
shared responsibility penalty imposed by ... 1.1, 1.16, 1.17–1.18
small employer health insurance tax credit under ... 2.4
W-2 inclusion of health coverage costs required by ... 1.25

Payroll tax forgiveness ... 2.4

Payroll taxes. See Employment taxes

Peak business period ... 3.26

Pease limitation ... 4.7

Penalties
for failure to file Form 990 ... 7.8
for failure to provide minimum essential or affordable health care coverage ... 1.1, 1.16, 1.17–1.19
for failure to report business transactions ... 6.25
for failure to report foreign assets ... 6.18, 6.19–6.20
for reportable transactions ... 6.8–6.9
for transactions lacking economic substance ... 6.11–6.12
for worker misclassification ... 2.20

Pension Benefit Guaranty Corporation (PBGC)
determination of plan sufficiency by ... 8.32
filing distress termination notice with ... 8.31–8.32
filing Schedule EA-S for standard terminations with ... 8.28
filing Schedule MP for missing participants with ... 8.26
filing standard termination notice (NOIT) with ... 8.27, 8.28
liability to, in distress terminations ... 8.29
notice of noncompliance by ... 8.27, 8.29
review period of ... 8.27
rules of, for terminating defined benefit plans ... 8.24, 8.27
termination filing package of ... 8.27

Pension funding relief
need for ... 8.11
under Pension Relief Act of 2010 ... 8.12–8.16

Pension plans. See Defined benefit plans

Pension Protection Act of 2006 (PPA)
combined defined benefit and defined contribution plans authorized by ... 8.4
delayed-effective-date plans for ... 8.11, 8.20–8.21
funding for multiemployer (union-negotiated) plans under ... 8.17
funding relief from rules of ... 8.12–8.13
funding target under ... 8.12–8.13
information returns required under ... 7.7
limits on future benefit accruals under ... 8.15, 8.16–8.17
minimum required contribution under ... 8.13, 8.21
new requirements for Type III supporting organizations under ... 7.11
prohibited payment freezes under ... 8.15–8.16
purpose of ... 8.11
shortfall amortization base under ... 8.13
target normal cost under ... 8.12–8.13

Pension Relief Act of 2010 ... 8.2
eligible plan year under ... 8.20–8.21
expanded asset valuation smoothing period under ... 8.18, 8.19
extended amortization for multiemployer plans under ... 8.18–8.19
extended amortization for single-employer plans under ... 8.14–8.15
extended benefit accrual relief under ... 8.16–8.17
funding relief for multiemployer plans under ... 8.18–8.21
funding relief for single-employer plans under ... 8.12–8.17
lookback year for credit balance for charitable plans under ... 8.17
passage of ... 8.12

Personal holding company tax ... 3.34

Personal service corporations
material participation in ... 5.21
passive activity loss rules applicable to ... 5.19

Political organizations, information return requirements for ... 7.2

Ponzi schemes, losses from ... 5.9–5.10

Premium assistance tax credit ... 1.20–1.21

Preservation of Access to Care for Medicare Beneficiaries and Pension Relief Act of 2010. See Pension Relief Act of 2010

Private foundations, excise taxes and restrictions for ... 7.10

Professional corporations ... 3.6

Q

Qualified dividend income ... 4.16

Qualified employee for free choice

vouchers ... 1.19–1.20

Qualified individual for premium assistance tax credit ... 1.20

Qualified medical expenses for HSAs ... 4.31

Qualified nonresource financing ... 5.18

Qualified personal service corporations ... 3.32–3.33

Qualified S subsidiary (QSub) ... 3.24

Qualified small business stock ... 4.10–4.11

Qualified small employer for state insurance exchanges ... 1.22

Qualified Subchapter S trusts (QSSTs) ... 3.23, 3.24

Qualifying arrangement for Code Sec. 45R credit for health care coverage ... 1.9

Qualifying dividends, tax rates on ... 4.2

Questionable Employment Tax Practices (QETP) initiative of IRS ... 2.3

R

Real estate taxes, impact on AMT liability of ... 4.9–4.10

Relationship of parties for worker classification ... 2.10, 2.11, 2.14

Relationship test of supporting organization ... 7.11

Reportable transactions ... 6.2–6.6
categories of, list of ... 6.3
disclosures of, timing ... 6.7
penalties for ... 6.8–6.9

Repossessions of property ... 5.25

Responsiveness test of Type III supporting organization ... 7.11, 7.12

Retirement plans ... 8.1–8.36. *See also* **Defined benefit plans** *and* **Roth IRA**
annual report requirements for ... 8.2
distributions from, exception to Medicare contribution tax for ... 4.23
as S corporation shareholders ... 3.23
terminations of, restrictions on ... 8.24–8.35

Revenue Act of 1978 ... 2.4, 2.6, 2.8, 2.15–2.18, 2.20, 2.21. *See also* **Section 530 relief**

Revocation and reinstatement of exempt status of nonprofit organizations ... 7.9–7.10

Roth IRA
AGI limit for contributions removed for ... 4.24
contributions to ... 4.24–4.26
conversion of traditional IRA to ... 4.26–4.27
distributions from ... 4.25–4.26
features unique to ... 4.24–4.26

S

S corporations
C corporations' conversion to ... 3.36–3.37
comparison of other entity types to ... 3.8
disclosures of reportable transactions of ... 6.4, 6.6, 6.7
election of status as ... 3.7, 3.15, 3.22–3.23
as entity type ... 3.1
operating tax issues of ... 3.34–3.38
organizational issues for ... 3.14–3.15
partnerships compared with ... 3.8
as pass-through entity ... 3.3
single class of stock of ... 3.25
taxation of C corporations versus ... 3.6
voting and nonvoting shares of ... 3.25

Sales representatives considered statutory employees ... 2.8

Schedule A (Form 990), *Public Charity Status and Public Support* **... 7.4, 7.5, 7.7**

Schedule A (Form 1040) ... 5.14

Schedule B (Form 990), *Schedule of Contributors* **... 7.4, 7.5**

Schedule C (Form 990) ... 7.4

Schedule C (Form 1040) ... 3.2, 3.39

Schedule D (Form 990), *Supplemental Financial Statements* **... 7.6, 7.7**

Schedule D (Form 1040) ... 3.39

Schedule E (Form 990), *Schools* **... 7.4, 7.22**

Schedule E (Form 1040) ... 3.29

Schedule EA-D (PBGC), *Distress Termination Enrolled Actuary Certification* **... 8.31–8.32**

Schedule EA-S (PBGC), *Standard Termination Certification of Sufficiency* **... 8.28**

Schedule F (Form 990), *Statement of Activities Outside the United States* **... 7.6, 7.7**

Schedule G (Form 990) ... 7.4

Schedule H (Form 990), *Hospitals* **... 7.13, 7.14–7.15**

Schedule K-1, partner's share of partnership's tax items reported on ... 3.29

Schedule L (Form 990), *Transactions with Interested Persons* **... 7.4, 7.6, 7.7**

Schedule M-3 (Form 1120), *Net Income (Loss) Reconciliation for corporations with Total Assets of $10 Million or More* ... 6.16

Schedule N (Form 990), *Liquidation, Termination, Dissolution, or Significant Disposition of Assets* ... 7.4, 7.6

Schedule O (Form 990), *Supplemental Information* ... 7.5, 7.6

Schedule R (Form 990), *Related Organizations* ... 7.6, 7.7

Schedule SE (Form 1040), *Self-Employment Tax* ... 2.6, 3.2, 3.28

Schedule UTP, *Uncertain Tax Positions* ... 6.15–6.16, 6.17

Seasonal workers in determining Code Sec. 45R credit ... 1.7

Section 530 relief ... 2.7–2.8
consistent treatment of worker for ... 2.16–2.17
notice of availability of ... 2.17
notice of determination of status for ... 2.17–2.18
proposed reform of ... 2.20–2.22
reasonable basis for ... 2.15, 2.17, 2.21

Section 1231 property, gains and losses on ... 5.4–5.5

Self-employment tax ... 3.2, 3.28
components of ... 4.19
on self-employed taxpayer's income ... 4.21
tax rates of ... 4.20

Service partnership ... 3.30

Service provider information about compensation ... 8.9–8.10

Shareholders, S corporation
agreement for termination of S status by majority of ... 3.15
agreement to elect S corporation status by all ... 3.15
eligibility to be ... 3.7, 3.22–3.25
as employees, withholding tax for ... 3.8
family members aggregated as ... 3.7–3.8, 3.25
loans of ... 3.8
maximum of 100 ... 3.7, 3.25
more-than-2-percent ... 3.36
passive activity loss rules applicable to ... 5.19

Signer credential for using EFAST2 electronic filing system ... 8.6

Simple cafeteria plan ... 1.2, 1.22–1.24

Small Business Health Options Program (SHOP) Exchange ... 1.5, 1.21.
See also State insurance exchanges

Small Business Jobs Act of 2010 ... 3.36, 4.27, 6.9

Small businesses
reportable transactions of ... 6.9
state insurance exchanges used by ... 1.2

Small employer health insurance tax credit ... 2.4

Small employers for simple cafeteria plans ... 1.23–1.24

Small exempt organizations, e-Postcard filed by ... 7.3, 7.4, 7.7

Social Security taxes
employee's portion of ... 4.19
imposition of ... 4.19

Social Security taxes, employer's share of ... 2.1
payroll forgiveness for relief from ... 2.4

Sole proprietors
as exempt from Form 5500 filing requirements ... 8.2
fringe benefits for ... 3.2, 3.28
health insurance coverage for ... 3.2
self-employment tax paid by ... 3.2, 3.28

Sole proprietorship ... 3.1
business income from ... 4.4
comparison of other entity types to ... 3.8
defined ... 3.2
disposing of ... 3.39
family members employed in ... 3.2
formation tax issues of ... 3.17
liability issues for ... 3.11
operating tax issues of ... 3.27–3.28
organizational issues for ... 3.13
sale of ... 3.28
single-member LLCs taxed as ... 3.5

Spousal property basis increase ... 4.33

Start-up expenses ... 3.25–3.26

State and local taxes
impact on AMT liability of ... 4.9–4.10
as itemized deduction ... 4.6

State health insurance tax credits and premium subsidies ... 1.13

State insurance exchanges
deadline for creating ... 1.5
levels of coverage for ... 1.21–1.22
use by qualified small employer of ... 1.22
use by very small employers of ... 1.2

State law challenges of nonprofit hospitals ... 7.16–7.17

State mini-COBRA laws ... 1.27

Statutory employees ... 2.8

Statutory nonemployees ... 2.8

Stock
dividend-paying ... 4.15

nontaxable acquisitions of ... 3.43
sales of ... 3.41
taxable acquisitions of ... 3.42
transfers of corporate ... 3.21–3.22

**Student exception for
medical residents ... 7.17–7.19**

**Supporting organizations as public
charities ... 7.10–7.12**

T

**Tax attributes reduced to offset benefit of
excluding COI income ... 5.24**

Tax code, provisions of
affecting wealth-building
strategies ... 4.1, 4.17
disclosure ... 6.1
good governance ... 7.23

**Tax credits allowable against regular
income tax and AMT ... 4.12**

Tax-exempt status, loss of ... 7.8

Tax gap
components of ... 2.3
nonpayment and underpayment of
employment taxes in ... 2.1, 2.3

Tax gap, initiatives to reduce ... 6.23–6.27
for capital gains ... 6.24
IRS NRP project one of ... 2.2
TIGTA, GAO, and CRS ... 2.3

**Tax liability, statute of limitations for IRS
prosecution of ... 6.20**

Tax planning
to avoid AMT ... 4.8–4.11
for conversions to Roth IRAs ... 4.26–4.27
impact of marginal income tax
brackets on ... 4.4–4.7

Tax year, entity's choice of ... 3.26–3.27

**Temporary employment agencies,
classification of works from ... 2.14**

**Termination of employer
retirement plans ... 8.24–8.36**
for defined benefit plan ... 8.24–8.25,
8.26–8.29
for defined contribution plan ... 8.25
distress ... 8.25, 8.29–8.33
distribution of assets in,
deadline for ... 8.29
full vesting on ... 8.25
involuntary, for multiemployer plan ... 8.35
involuntary, for
single-employer plan ... 8.33–8.34
by mass withdrawal ... 8.34–8.35
missing participants during ... 8.26
partial ... 8.25
by PBGC ... 8.33–8.34

by plan amendment ... 8.34, 8.35
qualification of plan up to ... 8.26
required allocation in ... 8.25–8.26
standard ... 8.25, 8.26–8.29
voiding ... 8.32
voluntary, for
multiemployer plan ... 8.34–8.35
voluntary, for
single-employer plan ... 8.24–8.33

Tiered Issue program ... 6.1–6.2, 6.8

**Timing (accelerating or deferring)
income ... 4.4–4.7, 4.18**

Traditional IRA
conversion to Roth IRA of ... 4.26–4.27
features of ... 4.24

Transactions of interest ... 6.3, 6.6

Trust
charitable ... 7.2, 7.12
eligibility to be S corporation shareholder,
type of ... 3.23–3.24
Medicare contribution tax for ... 4.23
reportable transactions of ... 6.4, 6.6
tax rates for ... 4.2

**Two plus seven
amortization schedule ... 8.14–8.15**

U

**U.S. persons, reporting requirements of,
for foreign trust ... 6.22**

Uncertain tax positions (UTRs) ... 6.12–6.17
disclosures of ... 6.14–6.15
reporting of ... 6.13, 6.17

**Understatements of tax,
penalty for ... 6.8, 6.11, 6.20**

Unemployment (FUTA) taxes ... 2.1
worker misclassification affecting
employer's share of ... 2.2, 2.3

**Union-negotiated (multiemployer) defined
benefit plans ... 8.11, 8.17–8.21**
asset smoothing rules for ... 8.18–8.19
eligibility for relief of ... 8.19
extended amortization for ... 8.18, 8.19
funding relief for ... 8.18
supplemental costs of ... 8.17

Universities
audits of ... 7.21
compensation reported for ... 7.21
congressional oversight of ... 7.22
endowment funds of ... 7.20
investment assets of ... 7.22
IRS report of activities of ... 7.20, 7.21
tax-exempt status of ... 7.19–7.22
unrelated business activities of ... 7.20

Unreasonably burdensome pension coverage costs ... 8.30

Unrelated business income tax (UBIT)
of colleges and universities ... 7.21
of nonprofit organizations, public inspection of reports of ... 7.26

V

Valuation misstatements ... 6.11

Vesting for retirement plan being terminated ... 8.25

Voluntary compliance program (VCP) for filers of Form 990-EZ ... 7.9

Voluntary Correction Program (VCP) for 401(k) plans ... 8.23

W

Wagering transactions ... 5.15–5.17

Wash sale of stock ... 5.4

Wealth building, effects of tax law changes on ... 4.1–4.35

Worker classification for employment taxes ... 2.1–2.23
facts and circumstances for ... 2.13
IRS NRP focusing on ... 2.2
occupations using tests of ... 2.14
proposed reform of rules for ... 2.19–2.22
Section 530 safe harbor for ... 2.7–2.8, 2.15, 2.18
three aspects of control for ... 2.10
20 traditional factors for determining ... 2.11–2.13

Worker–employer relationship for directing and controlling worker's services ... 2.13

Worker, Homeownership, and Business Assistance Act of 2009 ... 5.11

Worker, Retiree, and Employer Recovery Act of 2008 (WRERA) ... 8.16

Workers' compensation ... 2.3

Workpapers, tax accrual, disclosure of ... 6.3, 6.13–6.14

Worthless securities ... 5.5–5.6

TOP FEDERAL TAX ISSUES FOR 2011 CPE COURSE

CPE Quizzer Instructions

The CPE Quizzer is divided into three Modules. There is a processing fee for each Quizzer Module submitted for grading. Successful completion of Module 1 is recommended for **6 CPE Credits.*** Successful completion of Module 2 is recommended for **5 CPE Credits.*** Successful completion of Module 3 is recommended for **8 CPE Credits.*** You can complete and submit one Module at a time or all Modules at once for a total of **19 CPE Credits.***

To obtain CPE credit, return your completed Answer Sheet for each Quizzer Module to **CCH Continuing Education Department, 4025 W. Peterson Ave., Chicago, IL 60646**, or fax it to (773) 866-3084. Each Quizzer Answer Sheet will be graded and a CPE Certificate of Completion awarded for achieving a grade of 70 percent or greater. The Quizzer Answer Sheets are located after the Quizzer questions for this Course.

Express Grading: Processing time for your Answer Sheet is generally 8-12 business days. If you are trying to meet a reporting deadline, our Express Grading Service is available for an additional $19 per Module. To use this service, please check the "Express Grading" box on your Answer Sheet and provide your CCH account or credit card number **and your fax number.** CCH will fax your results and a Certificate of Completion (upon achieving a passing grade) to you by 5:00 p.m. the business day following our receipt of your Answer Sheet. **If you mail your Answer Sheet for Express Grading, please write "ATTN: CPE OVERNIGHT" on the envelope.** NOTE: CCH will not Federal Express Quizzer results under any circumstances.

NEW ONLINE GRADING gives you immediate 24/7 grading with instant results and no Express Grading Fee.

The **CCH Testing Center** website gives you and others in your firm easy, free access to CCH print Courses and allows you to complete your CPE Quizzers online for immediate results. Plus, the **My Courses** feature provides convenient storage for your CPE Course Certificates and completed Quizzers.

Go to **www.cchtestingcenter.com** to complete your Quizzer online.

---

* Recommended CPE credit is based on a 50-minute hour. Participants earning credits for states that require self-study to be based on a 100-minute hour will receive ½ the CPE credits for successful completion of this course. Because CPE requirements vary from state to state and among different licensing agencies, please contact your CPE governing body for information on your CPE requirements and the applicability of a particular course for your requirements.

Date of Completion: The date of completion on your Certificate will be the date that you put on your Answer Sheet. However, you must submit your Answer Sheet to CCH for grading within two weeks of completing it.

Expiration Date: December 31, 2011

Evaluation: To help us provide you with the best possible products, please take a moment to fill out the Course Evaluation located at the back of this Course and return it with your Quizzer Answer Sheets.

CCH is registered with the National Association of State Boards of Accountancy (NASBA) as a sponsor of continuing professional education on the National Registry of CPE Sponsors. State boards of accountancy have final authority on the acceptance of individual courses for CPE credit. Complaints regarding registered sponsors may be addressed to the National Registry of CPE Sponsors, 150 Fourth Avenue North, Suite 700, Nashville, TN 37219-2417. Web site: www.nasba.org.

CCH is registered with the National Association of State Boards of Accountancy (NASBA) as a Quality Assurance Service (QAS) sponsor of continuing professional education. State boards of accountancy have final authority on the acceptance of individual courses for CPE credit. Complaints regarding registered sponsors may be addressed to NASBA, 150 Fourth Avenue North, Suite 700, Nashville, TN 37219-2417. Web site: www.nasba.org.

CCH has been approved by the California Tax Education Council to offer courses that provide federal and state credit towards the annual "continuing education" requirement imposed by the State of California. A listing of additional requirements to register as a tax preparer may be obtained by contacting CTEC at P.O. Box 2890, Sacramento, CA, 95812-2890, toll-free by phone at (877) 850-2832, or on the Internet at www.ctec.org.

Processing Fee:
$72.00 for Module 1
$60.00 for Module 2
$96.00 for Module 3
$228.00 for all Modules

CTEC Course Number:
1075-CE-9722 for Module 1
1075-CE-9723 for Module 2
1075-CE-9724 for Module 3

Recommended CPE:
6 hours for Module 1
5 hours for Module 2
8 hours for Module 3
19 hours for all Modules

CTEC Federal Hours:
3 hours for Module 1
2 hours for Module 2
4 hours for Module 3
9 hours for all Modules

CTEC California Hours:
N/A for Module 1
N/A for Module 2
N/A for Module 3
N/A for all Modules

One **complimentary copy** of this Course is provided with certain copies of CCH Federal Taxation publications. Additional copies of this Course may be ordered for $37.00 each by calling 1-800-248-3248 (ask for product 0-0971-200).

TOP FEDERAL TAX ISSUES FOR 2011 CPE COURSE

Quizzer Questions: Module 1

> Answer the True/False questions by marking a "T" or "F" on the Quizzer Answer Sheet. Answer Multiple Choice questions by indicating the appropriate letter on the Answer Sheet.

1. The maximum annual Code Sec. 45R small employer health insurance tax credit for a for-profit employer for tax years beginning in 2014 through 2015 is _____ percent.

   a. 25
   b. 50
   c. 100

2. The Code Sec. 45R credit uses _____ hours of service per year to calculate an employer's qualified full-time equivalent employees (FTEs).

   a. 2,080
   b. 2,200
   c. 2,500

3. Health insurance coverage for purposes of the Code Sec. 45R credit *excludes* premiums for:

   a. Workers' compensation
   b. Long-term care
   c. Vision insurance

4. A large employer for purposes of the shared responsibility penalty after 2013 is generally an employer that employed an average of at least _____ full-time employees on business days during the preceding calendar year with some limited exceptions, such as for seasonal workers.

   a. 20
   b. 50
   c. 100

5. Which of the following is *not* a new tax credit created by the health care reform package?

a. State insurance exchange credit
b. Code Sec. 45R credit
c. Premium assistance tax credit

6. The *Patient Protection and Affordable Care Act* (PPACA) expands the Form W-2 reporting requirement to applicable employer-sponsored health coverage starting with tax years beginning after:

a. December 31, 2010
b. December 31, 2013
c. December 31, 2017

7. Employer-provided health insurance coverage in effect on _____—the date of enactment of the *Patient Protection and Affordable Care Act* (PPACA)—is generally exempt from certain provisions in the PPACA under grandfather provisions.

a. December 31, 2009
b. March 23, 2010
c. January 1, 2014

8. For purposes of W-2 reporting under the *Patient Protection and Affordable Care Act* (PPACA), employers must report the _____cost of employer-sponsored health insurance coverage provided to the employee.

a. Projected
b. Net
c. Aggregate

9. The health care reform package requires employer health insurance plans that provide coverage to children of participants to make the coverage available to adult children until age____.

a. 24
b. 25
c. 26

10. Assistance-eligible individuals who were involuntarily terminated from employment between September 1, 2008, and May 31, 2010, may qualify for temporary COBRA premium assistance under the *American Recovery and Reinvestment Act of 2009* and subsequent legislation, which allow them to pay ___ percent of the cost of COBRA premiums and be treated as paying 100 percent.

    a. 25
    b. 35
    c. 40

11. During the IRS's National Research Program (NRP) examinations of employment tax compliance, the IRS will *not* examine issues related to:

    a. Fringe benefits and employee expense reimbursements
    b. Executive compensation
    c. Schedules SE, *Self-Employment Tax,* filed by independent contractors

12. When an employer hires employees, as opposed to independent contractors, the law imposes many tax requirements on the employer, including:

    a. Filing Form SS-8, *Determination of Worker Status for Purposes of Federal Employment Taxes and Income Tax Withholding*
    b. Paying the entire share of FUTA tax and half of FICA tax
    c. Filing Form 8919, *Uncollected Social Security and Medicare Taxes on Wages,* on the employee's behalf

13. Section 530 relief protects employers:

    a. Who have failed to properly withhold and remit payroll taxes on employees' wages
    b. Who have consistently treated workers as independent contractors that should in actuality be treated as employees for federal employment tax purposes
    c. Who have misclassified independent contractors as employees for federal employment tax purposes

14. Which of the following workers is classified as a statutory employee for whom an employer must pay FICA taxes, even though the worker may otherwise be classified as an independent contractor?

   a. Accountant
   b. Traveling salesperson
   c. Building trade worker

15. One hallmark of independent contractor status is that the worker:

   a. Stands to make a profit or loss from the work
   b. Does not render services in the employer's place of business
   c. Has an employment contract excluding other clients

16. The IRS issues a Notice of Determination of Worker Classification (NDWC):

   a. To resume the assessment period for taxes attributable to worker classification
   b. To offer an employer Section 530 relief for misclassified workers
   c. To inform an employer of the opportunity to seek review of employment taxes owed relating to worker misclassification

17. In order to receive a determination by the IRS in response to filing Form SS-8, *Determination of Worker Status for Purposes of Federal Employment Taxes and Income Tax Withholding*, a worker must:

   a. Be currently performing services or have already completed service for the employer
   b. Have first received a Notice of Determination of Worker Classification from the IRS
   c. Have filed Form 8919, *Uncollected Social Security and Medicare Tax on Wages*

18. Under the Obama Administration's proposed worker classification rules for independent contractors:

   a. Employers would be required to provide notice to workers classified as independent contractors explaining the tax consequences of their classification
   b. Different employer penalties would apply to new versus existing misclassified contractors
   c. Penalties would be waived for large employers of 100 or more independent contractors annually

19. Section 530 applies to workers who should otherwise be treated as common-law employees but does not apply to technical service workers. ***True or False?***

20. Longstanding industry practice is currently ***not*** considered to be a reasonable basis for an employer's failure to treat a worker as an employee for federal employment tax purposes. ***True or False?***

21. Which of the following is ***not*** a flow-through entity?

   a. Personal service corporation
   b. General partnership
   c. S corporation

22. Limited partners who are not involved in managing the partnership:

   a. Are nonetheless liable for the debts of the partnership
   b. Are subject to passive activity loss rules
   c. May not have capital investments in the partnership

23. Which of these owners is ***not*** subject to unlimited personal liability?

   a. LLC member who does not actively manage the company
   b. General partner in a partnership
   c. Sole proprietor

24. If a multiowner limited liability company fails to file Form 8832, *Entity Classification Election,* it is by default classified as a:

   a. Partnership
   b. C corporation
   c. S corporation

25. Once its S status election terminates, generally a company must wait for _____ before reapplying for S status, unless the IRS consents to an earlier reinstatement.

   a. Two years
   b. Three years
   c. Five years

26. An owner whose sole proprietorship is not subject to at-risk or passive activity loss rules:

    a. Pays no self-employment tax on net income
    b. May use a business loss to offset the owner's other income
    c. May set up a defined benefit retirement plan excluding the business's full-time employees

27. Shareholder-employees of a C corporation:

    a. Pay no self-employment tax on dividends received
    b. Pay no income tax on wages
    c. Have no employment tax withholding applied

28. A partner receiving a current nonliquidating distribution of gain must recognize the distribution as ordinary income if:

    a. The gain is attributable to a sale of hot assets
    b. The gain is received as part of a conversion of the partnership to an S corporation
    c. The distribution is not money

29. Expenses incurred after a business is formed are deductible, whereas organizational expenses usually must be amortized. *True or False?*

30. A partnership's interest in its assets is inside basis, whereas the partners' basis in their partnership interest is outside basis. *True or False?*

Quizzer Questions: Module 2

Answer the True/False questions by marking a "T" or "F" on the Quizzer Answer Sheet. Answer Multiple Choice questions by indicating the appropriate letter on the Answer Sheet.

31. The *Jobs and Growth Tax Relief Reconciliation Act of 2003* (JGTRRA) and subsequent legislation reduced the maximum tax rate on qualified capital gains from _____ percent to _____ percent for taxpayers in tax brackets above 15 percent.

   a. 30; 20
   b. 20; 15
   c. 15; 10

32. Individuals age 50 and older by the end of the year can make an additional catch-up contribution to a Roth IRA of:

   a. $1,000
   b. $2,500
   c. $500

33. Itemized medical expenses are only deductible for AMT purposes to the extent they exceed ___ percent of adjusted gross income (AGI).

   a. 10
   b. 7.5
   c. Medical expenses are not deductible for AMT purposes

34. Under the JGTRRA and subsequent legislation, the zero-percent capital gains/dividends tax rate for taxpayers in the 10 and 15 percent income tax brackets sunsets after:

   a. December 31, 2009
   b. December 31, 2010
   c. The tax rate for those brackets is permanent

35. For 2010, the wage base for the Social Security portion of the FICA tax is:

   a. $106,800
   b. $200,000
   c. Abolished for 2010

36. Under the sunset provisions of EGTRRA, the top individual income tax rate will revert to ___ percent after December 31, 2010

   a. 36
   b. 39.6
   c. 45

37. Under the sunset provisions in JGTRRA and subsequent legislation, qualified dividend income after 2010 is taxed at:

   a. 10 percent
   b. 25 percent
   c. The taxpayer's ordinary income tax rate

38. The health care reform package enacted a Medicare contribution tax of ___ percent on qualified unearned income of certain higher-income individuals effective for tax years beginning after_____

   a. 0.9; 2010
   b. 2.0; 2011
   c. 3.8; 2012

39. Taxpayers making a Roth IRA conversion in 2010:

   a. May recognize the conversion amount ratably in their taxable income on 2011 and 2012 returns, unless the taxpayer elects to recognize the amount all on a 2010 return
   b. Pay no federal income tax on the amount being converted
   c. Defer any income tax payable until after 2015

40. For 2010, an individual (self-only) plan is a high-deductible health plan for purposes of the health savings account (HSA) rules if it has at least a _____ annual deductible.

   a. $1,200
   b. $5,950
   c. $7,500

41. After December 31, 2010, nonqualified distributions from a health savings account (HSA) are subject to an additional _____ tax.

    a. 20 percent
    b. 25 percent
    c. 50 percent

42. EGTRRA's repeal of the federal estate tax sunsets after:

    a. December 31, 2010
    b. January 1, 2012
    c. December 31, 2015

43. The marriage penalty relief applicable to joint filers is not part of the EGTRRA provisions due to expire after 2010. *True or False?*

44. Qualified contributions to a health savings account (HSA) are tax deductible. *True or False?*

45. After 2012, the additional 0.9-percent Medicare tax is imposed on the combined wages of a married couple if they file a joint return. *True or False?*

46. After offsetting capital gains, individuals can deduct_____ of capital losses against ordinary income.

    a. $1,000
    b. $2,000
    c. $3,000

47. If a creditor has a bad debt that is not from a trade or business, the loss is treated as a(n):

    a. Short-term capital loss
    b. Ordinary loss
    c. Nondeductible loss

48. Gains from an involuntary conversion of Section 1231 property are treated as:

    a. Capital gains
    b. Ordinary gains
    c. Exempt gains

49. To claim an NOL carryback, all of the following filing limitations apply **except:**

    a. Filing a request for tentative refund within one year of the end of the tax year generating the NOL

    b. Filing an amended return within five years of the return due date for the year in which the NOL arose

    c. Filing an amended return within two years from the time the tax was paid

50. Gambling losses may **not:**

    a. Be combined by spouses filing jointly to offset their combined winnings

    b. Be carried forward or back to offset gambling winnings from a different tax year

    c. Offset winnings from raffles or lotteries

51. Which of these is **not** an at-risk amount for figuring loss deductions?

    a. Adjusted basis of property contributed to the activity

    b. Value of personal services for the activity

    c. Money loaned by the taxpayer to conduct the activity

52. Passive activity loss rules apply to:

    a. Partners in a limited partnership

    b. S corporations

    c. Widely held C corporation shareholders

53. On a forgiveness of debt, the debtor:

    a. Recognizes capital gain income

    b. Recognizes ordinary income unless an exclusion applies

    c. Recognizes income and reduces tax attributes

54. Unlike corporations, which may carry back capital losses, an individual taxpayer may not carry back excess capital losses to a prior tax year. **True or False?**

55. A home demolished as a result of a presidentially declared disaster qualifies as a disaster loss. **True or False?**

Quizzer Questions: Module 3

> Answer the True/False questions by marking a "T" or "F" on the Quizzer Answer Sheet. Answer Multiple Choice questions by indicating the appropriate letter on the Answer Sheet.

56. The IRS program that addresses risk levels of noncompliance is the:

   a. Field Examination and Audit program
   b. Tiered Issue program
   c. Preassessment and Penalty Imposition program

57. A reportable transaction in which an unrelated advisor charges the taxpayer a minimum $50,000 fee to participate and about which the taxpayer cannot tell others is most likely a:

   a. Listed transaction
   b. Confidential transaction
   c. Loss transaction

58. A transaction in which an S corporation with _____ or more of Code Sec. 165 losses in a single tax year is considered to rise to the level of a reportable transaction regardless of other factors.

   a. $10 million
   b. $500,000
   c. $2 million

59. To avoid penalties for participating in a reportable transaction that resulted in understated taxes, the taxpayer must prove all of the following *except:*

   a. Reasonable belief that the position was more likely than not the proper treatment
   b. Contractual protection for the position
   c. Substantial authority for the position

60. Which of the following is **not** a factor in directly determining whether a taxpayer can survive IRS scrutiny of a transaction under the economic substance doctrine?

a. Step doctrine standard
b. Objective standard
c. Subjective standard

61. Under FIN 48 reporting standards for uncertain tax positions, taxpayers generally provide an independent auditor with:

a. Previously audited financial statements
b. Tax accrual workpaper information
c. Copies of federal tax returns for the previous five tax years

62. The U.S. Supreme Court ruled in **Arthur Young** that there is no:

a. Client–auditor privilege
b. Attorney–client privilege
c. Workpaper restraint policy

63. Reporting of uncertain tax positions using Schedule UTP will begin for the _____ tax year.

a. 2010
b. 2011
c. 2012

64. The statute of limitations for IRS prosecution of a taxpayer failing to disclose a foreign account or asset is:

a. Three years
b. Six years
c. Eight years

65. The HIRE Act requires Code Sec. 6048 reporting of foreign grantor trusts by:

a. Nonresident aliens
b. U.S. persons
c. Foreign grantors

66. If a foreign jurisdiction does not impose penalties for undisclosed transfers involving a foreign trust:

    a. The taxpayer is not exempt from the Code Sec. 6677 penalty for nondisclosure
    b. The rules of that jurisdiction preempt U.S. regulations that would otherwise apply to the transfers
    c. The taxpayer is not subject to the Code Sec. 6677 penalty for nondisclosure of the transfer

67. The *Patient Protection and Affordable Care Act* requires disclosure of total annual payments made to a corporation of _____.

    a. $600 or more
    b. A minimum of $10,000
    c. $1,000 per quarter

68. The economic substance doctrine applies to individuals insofar as they have estate or gift tax transactions during the tax period. *True or False?*

69. Taxpayers report their tax reserve amounts and an analysis of the merits of their uncertain tax position to the IRS on Schedule UTP. *True or False?*

70. Reporting requirements of Schedule UTP and FIN 48 differ: Schedule UTP requires reporting maximum possible tax liabilities on tax returns, whereas FIN 48 limits tax benefits reported on financial statements. *True or False?*

71. A tax-exempt organization must file a Form 990-T for any year in which it has a gross income from an unrelated trade or business of _____ or more.

    a. $1,000
    b. $5,000
    c. $10,000

72. For the 2010 tax year, a small tax-exempt organization may file Form 990-N (the e-Postcard) if its gross receipts normally are no more than _____.

    a. $50,000
    b. $200,000
    c. $500,000

73. Which of the following types of relief did *not* apply to filers of Form 990-N (the e-Postcard) during 2010?

   a. Extension of the filing deadline to October 15 for calendar year filers

   b. Extending the compliance fee for nonfilers until January 31, 2010

   c. Publication of a list of "at–risk organizations" for filers needing to determine their status

74. In the relationship test of supporting organizations, a Type II relationship exists when the same people exercise common control of supporting and supported organizations in a:

   a. Parent–subsidiary relationship

   b. Brother–sister relationship

   c. Functionally integrated relationship

75. Under the *Patient Protection and Affordable Care Act* (PPACA) enacted in 2010, starting in tax years beginning after March 23, _____, each hospital must conduct and develop implementation strategies on a community health needs assessment (CHNA) at least every three years to avoid a $50,000 excise tax.

   a. 2011

   b. 2012

   c. 2013

76. IRS follow-up audits of tax-exempt education institutions will focus on all of the following tax areas *except:*

   a. Executive compensation

   b. Unrelated business income tax

   c. Donors to endowment funds

77. The primary reporting mechanism that all charities filing Form 990 must complete to detail their governance practices to the IRS is:

   a. Form 990 Schedule L, *Transactions with Interested Persons*

   b. Form 990 core form, Part VI

   c. Form 990 Schedule O, *Supplemental Information*

78. An organization that fails to file Form 990 for three consecutive years:

    a. Must pay unrelated business income taxes
    b. Loses its tax-exempt status
    c. Becomes a private foundation

79. If it provides support to a public charity, a private foundation is itself considered a public charity and avoids excise taxes and antiabuse restrictions applicable to private foundations. *True or False?*

80. Form 990 Schedule E, *Schools,* focuses on compensation of college presidents and institutional policies involving endowments. *True or False?*

81. A pension or welfare benefit plan that covers fewer than _____ participants at the beginning of the plan year follows the small plan rules for Form 5500 reporting.

    a. 10
    b. 25
    c. 100

82. The plan reporting form that must be used for one-participant plans and must be filed on paper is the:

    a. Form 5500-EZ
    b. Form 5500-SF
    c. Revised Form 5500(R)

83. An employer does **not** need any EFAST2 credentials for Form 5500 if:

    a. The plan administrator has not requested an extension for filing
    b. The plan sponsor grants a tax practitioner written authority to file on its behalf
    c. No distributions were made during the tax period being reported

84. For the 2009 plan year, a one-participant retirement plan may **not** file an annual return on:

    a. Form 5500
    b. Form 5500-EZ
    c. Form 5500-SF

85. A pension benefit plan maintained outside the United States for nonresident aliens and not subject to Title I of ERISA must file:

    a. Form 5500
    b. Form 5500-EZ
    c. Form 5500-SF

86. Under the *Pension Protection Act of 2006,* the present value of all benefits accrued or earned as of the beginning of the plan year is the:

    a. Target normal cost
    b. Funding target
    c. Value of all plan assets

87. Extended amortization for single-employer defined benefit plans under the Pension Relief Act of 2010 does **not** include:

    a. The deferred recognition schedule
    b. The two plus seven schedule
    c. The 15-year schedule

88. An endangered plan is one in which the plan's adjusted funding target attainment percentage (AFTAP) or ratio of assets to funding target for the year is less than:

    a. 50 percent
    b. 60 percent
    c. 80 percent

89. Except for plans of certain government contractors, a delayed-PPA-effective-date plan sponsor may elect relief for no more than _____ plan years.

    a. Two
    b. Three
    c. Five

90. In completing the IRS 401(k) Compliance Check Questionnaire, the plan administrator:

   a. Must submit books and records that substantiate the answers for the plan
   b. Must not supplement answers with comments or suggestions for revising the program
   c. Should complete only questions in sections that apply to the particular plan

91. Which of the following is *not* a type of voluntary termination for defined benefit plans?

   a. Standard
   b. Conversion
   c. Distress

92. In a distress termination of a single-employer plan, a contributing sponsor and each controlled group member of the defined benefit plan:

   a. Are released from all liability for the guaranteed benefits
   b. Are jointly and severally liable to the PBGC
   c. Are eligible to resume operation of the plan as a defined contribution plan

93. One-participant pension plans can include a partnership's partners and their spouses. *True or False?*

94. Reporting rules for ERISA-covered retirement plans do *not* apply to 403(b) plans. *True or False?*

95. The 15-year amortization schedule adversely affects a plan's cash flow for the first 7 years but improves cash flow somewhat for the later 8 years. *True or False?*

TOP FEDERAL TAX ISSUES FOR 2011 CPE COURSE   (0770-3)

Module 1: Answer Sheet

NAME _____

COMPANY NAME _____

STREET _____

CITY, STATE, & ZIP CODE _____

BUSINESS PHONE NUMBER _____

E-MAIL ADDRESS _____

DATE OF COMPLETION _____

CFP REGISTRANT ID (for Certified Financial Planners) _____

CRTP ID (for CTEC Credit only) _____(CTEC Course # 1075-CE-9722)

On the next page, please answer the Multiple Choice questions by indicating the appropriate letter next to the corresponding number. Please answer the True/False questions by marking "T" or "F" next to the corresponding number.

A $72.00 processing fee wil be charged for each user submitting Module 1 for grading.

Please remove both pages of the Answer Sheet from this book and return them with your completed Evaluation Form to CCH at the address below. You may also fax your Answer Sheet to CCH at 773-866-3084.

You may also go to **www.cchtestingcenter.com** to complete your Quizzer online.

METHOD OF PAYMENT:

☐ Check Enclosed   ☐ Visa   ☐ Master Card   ☐ AmEx

☐ Discover   ☐ CCH Account* _____

Card No. _____ Exp. Date _____

Signature _____

* Must provide CCH account number for this payment option

EXPRESS GRADING: Please fax my Course results to me by 5:00 p.m. the business day following your receipt of this Answer Sheet. By checking this box I authorize CCH to charge $19.00 for this service.

☐ Express Grading $19.00   Fax No. _____

Mail or fax to:
CCH Continuing Education Department
4025 W. Peterson Ave.
Chicago, IL 60646-6085
1-800-248-3248
Fax: 773-866-3084

TOP FEDERAL TAX ISSUES FOR 2011 CPE COURSE　　　(0770-3)

Module 1: Answer Sheet

Please answer the Multiple Choice questions by indicating the appropriate letter next to the corresponding number. Please answer the True/False questions by marking "T" or "F" next to the corresponding number.

1. ___	9. ___	17. ___	24. ___
2. ___	10. ___	18. ___	25. ___
3. ___	11. ___	19. ___	26. ___
4. ___	12. ___	20. ___	27. ___
5. ___	13. ___	21. ___	28. ___
6. ___	14. ___	22. ___	29. ___
7. ___	15. ___	23. ___	30. ___
8. ___	16. ___		

Please complete the Evaluation Form (located after the Module 3 Answer Sheet) and return it with this Quizzer Answer Sheet to CCH at the address on the previous page. Thank you.

TOP FEDERAL TAX ISSUES FOR 2011 CPE COURSE   (0771-3)

Module 2: Answer Sheet

NAME _____

COMPANY NAME _____

STREET _____

CITY, STATE, & ZIP CODE _____

BUSINESS PHONE NUMBER _____

E-MAIL ADDRESS _____

DATE OF COMPLETION _____

CFP REGISTRANT ID (for Certified Financial Planners) _____

CRTP ID (for CTEC Credit only) _____ (CTEC Course # 1075-CE-9723)

On the next page, please answer the Multiple Choice questions by indicating the appropriate letter next to the corresponding number. Please answer the True/False questions by marking "T" or "F" next to the corresponding number.

A $60.00 processing fee wil be charged for each user submitting Module 2 for grading.

Please remove both pages of the Answer Sheet from this book and return them with your completed Evaluation Form to CCH at the address below. You may also fax your Answer Sheet to CCH at 773-866-3084.

You may also go to **www.cchtestingcenter.com** to complete your Quizzer online.

METHOD OF PAYMENT:

☐ Check Enclosed   ☐ Visa   ☐ Master Card   ☐ AmEx

☐ Discover   ☐ CCH Account* _____

Card No. _____ Exp. Date _____

Signature _____

* Must provide CCH account number for this payment option

EXPRESS GRADING: Please fax my Course results to me by 5:00 p.m. the business day following your receipt of this Answer Sheet. By checking this box I authorize CCH to charge $19.00 for this service.

☐ Express Grading $19.00   Fax No. _____

CCH
a Wolters Kluwer business

Mail or fax to:
CCH Continuing Education Department
4025 W. Peterson Ave.
Chicago, IL 60646-6085
1-800-248-3248
Fax: 773-866-3084

TOP FEDERAL TAX ISSUES FOR 2011 CPE COURSE   (0771-3)

Module 2: Answer Sheet

Please answer the Multiple Choice questions by indicating the appropriate letter next to the corresponding number. Please answer the True/False questions by marking "T" or "F" next to the corresponding number.

31. ___	38. ___	44. ___	50. ___
32. ___	39. ___	45. ___	51. ___
33. ___	40. ___	46. ___	52. ___
34. ___	41. ___	47. ___	53. ___
35. ___	42. ___	48. ___	54. ___
36. ___	43. ___	49. ___	55. ___
37. ___			

Please complete the Evaluation Form (located after the Module 3 Answer Sheet) and return it with this Quizzer Answer Sheet to CCH at the address on the previous page. Thank you.

TOP FEDERAL TAX ISSUES FOR 2011 CPE COURSE (0772-3)

Module 3: Answer Sheet

NAME _____

COMPANY NAME _____

STREET _____

CITY, STATE, & ZIP CODE _____

BUSINESS PHONE NUMBER _____

E-MAIL ADDRESS _____

DATE OF COMPLETION _____

CFP REGISTRANT ID (for Certified Financial Planners) _____

CRTP ID (for CTEC Credit only) _____ (CTEC Course # 1075-CE-9724)

On the next page, please answer the Multiple Choice questions by indicating the appropriate letter next to the corresponding number. Please answer the True/False questions by marking "T" or "F" next to the corresponding number.

A $96.00 processing fee wil be charged for each user submitting Module 3 for grading.

Please remove both pages of the Answer Sheet from this book and return them with your completed Evaluation Form to CCH at the address below. You may also fax your Answer Sheet to CCH at 773-866-3084.

You may also go to **www.cchtestingcenter.com** to complete your Quizzer online.

METHOD OF PAYMENT:

☐ Check Enclosed   ☐ Visa   ☐ Master Card   ☐ AmEx

☐ Discover   ☐ CCH Account* _____

Card No. _____ Exp. Date _____

Signature _____

* Must provide CCH account number for this payment option

EXPRESS GRADING: Please fax my Course results to me by 5:00 p.m. the business day following your receipt of this Answer Sheet. By checking this box I authorize CCH to charge $19.00 for this service.

☐ Express Grading $19.00   Fax No. _____

Mail or fax to:
CCH Continuing Education Department
4025 W. Peterson Ave.
Chicago, IL 60646-6085
1-800-248-3248
Fax: 773-866-3084

TOP FEDERAL TAX ISSUES FOR 2011 CPE COURSE   (0772-3)

Module 3: Answer Sheet

Please answer the Multiple Choice questions by indicating the appropriate letter next to the corresponding number. Please answer the True/False questions by marking "T" or "F" next to the corresponding number.

56. ___	66. ___	76. ___	86. ___
57. ___	67. ___	77. ___	87. ___
58. ___	68. ___	78. ___	88. ___
59. ___	69. ___	79. ___	89. ___
60. ___	70. ___	80. ___	90. ___
61. ___	71. ___	81. ___	91. ___
62. ___	72. ___	82. ___	92. ___
63. ___	73. ___	83. ___	93. ___
64. ___	74. ___	84. ___	94. ___
65. ___	75. ___	85. ___	95. ___

Please complete the Evaluation Form (located after the Module 3 Answer Sheet) and return it with this Quizzer Answer Sheet to CCH at the address on the previous page. Thank you.

TOP FEDERAL TAX ISSUES FOR 2011 CPE COURSE   (0971-2)

Evaluation Form

Please take a few moments to fill out and mail or fax this evaluation to CCH so that we can better provide you with the type of self-study programs you want and need. Thank you.

About This Program

1. Please circle the number that best reflects the extent of your agreement with the following statements:

	Strongly Agree				Strongly Disagree
a. The Course objectives were met.	5	4	3	2	1
b. This Course was comprehensive and organized.	5	4	3	2	1
c. The content was current and technically accurate.	5	4	3	2	1
d. This Course was timely and relevant.	5	4	3	2	1
e. The prerequisite requirements were appropriate.	5	4	3	2	1
f. This Course was a valuable learning experience.	5	4	3	2	1
g. The Course completion time was appropriate.	5	4	3	2	1

2. This Course was most valuable to me because of:

_____ Continuing Education credit   _____ Convenience of format

_____ Relevance to my practice/   _____ Timeliness of subject matter
employment   _____ Reputation of author

_____ Price

_____ Other (please specify) _____

3. How long did it take to complete this Course? (Please include the total time spent reading or studying reference materials and completing CPE Quizzer).

Module 1 _____   Module 2 _____   Module 3 _____

4. What do you consider to be the strong points of this Course?

5. What improvements can we make to this Course?

TOP FEDERAL TAX ISSUES FOR 2011 CPE COURSE   (0971-2)

Evaluation Form *cont'd*

General Interests

1. Preferred method of self-study instruction:
   ____ Text ____ Audio ____ Computer-based/Multimedia ____Video

2. What specific topics would you like CCH to develop as self-study CPE programs? ____
   _____
   _____
   _____

3. Please list other topics of interest to you _____
   _____
   _____

About You

1. Your profession:

   ____ CPA   ____ Enrolled Agent
   ____ Attorney   ____ Tax Preparer
   ____ Financial Planner   ____ Other (please specify)
   _____

2. Your employment:

   ____ Self-employed   ____ Public Accounting Firm
   ____ Service Industry   ____ Non-Service Industry
   ____ Banking/Finance   ____ Government
   ____ Education   ____ Other _____

3. Size of firm/corporation:
   ____ 1 ____ 2-5 ____ 6-10 ____ 11-20 ____ 21-50 ____ 51+

4. Your Name _____
   _Firm/Company Name _____
   Address _____
   City, State, Zip Code _____
   E-mail Address _____

THANK YOU FOR TAKING THE TIME TO COMPLETE THIS SURVEY!

NOTES

NOTES

NOTES

NOTES